Living with Mount St.Helens

Living with Mount St.Helens

Human Adjustment to Volcano Hazards

Ronald W. Perry and Michael K. Lindell

Washington State University Press
Pullman, Washington
1990

Washington State University Press, Pullman, Washington, 99164-5910

Copyright 1990 by the Board of Regents of Washington State University

All Rights Reserved

Printed and Bound in the United States of America

00 99 98 97 96 95 94 93 92 91   1 2 3 4 5 6 7 8 9 10

Library of Congress Cataloging-in-Publication Data

Perry, Ronald W.
    Living with Mt. St. Helens : human adjustment to volcano hazards /
    Ronald W. Perry and Michael Lindell K.
    p.   cm
    Bibliography : p.
    ISBN 0-87422-059-9 (alk. paper)

I. Lindell, Michael K. II. Title

Cover Design by Melissa Rockwood

ISBN 0-87422-053-X

For the people on the front line:

Ben Bena and the Cowlitz County
Department of Emergency Services

C O N T E N T S

ACKNOWLEDGMENTS

This book draws on a variety of research projects between 1980 and 1986 that were funded by the National Science Foundation (Grants: CEE-8311868, CEE-8120426, PRA-8312800, and PFR-8019297). The conclusions and opinions herein are those of the authors and do not necessarily reflect the views of the National Science Foundation.

We are particularly indebted to Dr. William A. Anderson who has served for nearly a decade as our NSF technical monitor on a number of projects. In addition to his expertise as project monitor, Bill contributed valuable criticism and guidance based on his own extensive research experience. In terms of our research projects and professional growth, we are beneficiaries of Bill's experience and wisdom.

We also wish to acknowledge our long-time colleague and friend, Marjorie R. Greene, with whom we have shared many research adventures. Somehow we three survived the early Mt. St. Helens hazard perception study and the hectic research on citizen response to the cataclysmic eruption of 1980. Indeed, through many years of collaboration we have developed a great respect for Marge's skills.

It is in the nature of a long-term project that one develops debts to many people and organizations. While it is impossible to thank everyone who has contributed to this study, we would like to mention several in particular. First among these is the Cowlitz County Department of Emergency Services, and especially Director Ben Bena. Without the encouragement, access, and help granted to us over a period of years by these emergency management professionals, our studies simply could not have been done. We are indebted to Jack Kartez for many long discussions of our mutual research around Mt. St. Helens; Jack helped us crystalize our conceptual thinking and provided many insights into regional hazard management. Thomas Drabek, Enrico Quarantelli, Gary Kreps, Dennis Wenger, and John Sorensen also provided helpful commentary and criticism of the research design and data analysis. Don Nichols, Jim Kerr, Forest Wilcox, and Patrick LaValla provided much-appreciated technical critiques in their roles as state and federal emergency managers. While we are grateful for the generous guidance and help from our colleagues, we accept total responsibility for the contents of this book.

Ronald W. Perry

Michael K. Lindell

Volcanism at Mt. St. Helens

Captain George Vancouver, the British explorer, sighted and named Mt. St. Helens in 1792 as his vessel sailed past the mouth of the Columbia River. The name he assigned to the volcano honored the British ambassador to Spain, but said little about the mountain itself. Local Indian lore, having grown from generations of closer observation, characterizes the mountain more precisely in terms of its moods. Klickitat tribal legends refer to St. Helens either as *Loo-Wit*, a mountain given special beauty by the Great Spirit, or as *Tah-one-lat-clak*, the fire mountain. These legends reflect the dualism of Mt. St. Helens: sometimes a place of snow-covered beauty, rich with fish and wildlife, and sometimes a "smoking" inferno dealing destruction to the entire region.

Of course, the eruptive phases of Mt. St. Helens were established long before humans were present to label geologic structures and phenomena. Eruptions and associated hazards constitute a human danger largely in proportion to our encroachment upon volcanoes. Interestingly, it is probably equally accurate to characterize people as lured or attracted to volcanoes as to portray them as invasive. Fertile volcanic soil yields lush natural or cultivated vegetation that contributes to an ecosystem rich with animal life. During noneruptive periods, such environments serve as a magnet to human settlement. Indeed, the high potential for sustenance coupled with the cycle of long dormancy interspersed with relatively short eruptive periods captures both the allure of volcanoes and their special danger to humans.

Volcanoes are typically characterized as a low probability/high consequence natural hazard. That is, in general the chance of an eruption at any given time is relatively low. Although periodicity may not be a wholly appropriate concept for volcanoes, geological evidence suggests that time between eruptions may be as much as one thousand to ten thousand years in some cases. When an explosive eruption does occur, however, the destructive potential is very great. The human toll of cataclysmic eruptions has been chronicled throughout recorded history, from Pliny the Younger's descriptions of Vesuvius in AD 79, through Krakatau in 1883 to the recent eruptions of Mt. St. Helens, Mt. Usu

(Japan), El Chichon (Mexico), and Nevado del Ruiz (Columbia). Furthermore, human life and structures are almost as vulnerable to the by-products of eruptions, such as lava flows at Kilauea and Mauna Loa (Hawaii), mudflows from Ruapehu Volcano (New Zealand), ash fall at Paricutin (Mexico) and Mt. Pelee's glowing avalanche (Martinique). Whether the form is a "big bang" or something less spectacular, the variety of volcanic threats and their relative insusceptibility to human influence make active volcanoes one of the most potentially destructive geophysical threats to man.

The danger posed by volcanoes is also heightened by special characteristics that set them apart from other natural hazards. One of the most important of these characteristics lies in the relationship of time to local residents' beliefs about environmental risks. Historically, people are drawn to volcanoes during dormant periods, becoming established over many years or sometimes many generations. Those who have spent their lives on the slopes of peaceful volcanoes tend to conceptualize the mountain as part of a nurturing and supportive, rather than threatening, environment. Based on such experience, residents are often reticent to heed natural warnings (earthquakes, steam, etc.) that may signal the onset of an eruption. For example, an octogenarian fishing lodge operator named Harry Truman repeatedly proclaimed that he had lived on Mt. St. Helens for decades and had personally seen all of the "moods" of the mountain. He was sufficiently convinced that the steam eruptions "meant him no harm"; he ignored official warnings and later died in the May 18, 1980 eruption. Thus, the tendency to judge volcanic hazards in terms of human time, rather than understanding their place in geologic time—where a human life span is an insignificant unit—contributes to complacency which exposes people to dangers that might otherwise be escaped.

Another feature of volcanic eruptions which sets them apart from other natural hazards lies in the idea of multiple or repeated impacts. During any active period a volcano may erupt dozens of times, and the magnitude and nature of each eruption may vary widely. Consequently, unlike floods, hurricanes or tornadoes, a volcanic event is not clearly circumscribed by a single pre-impact period of threat, a short impact period, and a postimpact quiet time. Instead, the entire volcanic sequence, which may last for several years, is a time of continual threat during which the likelihood of an eruptive event is uncertain. Thus, multiple eruptions constitute multiple impacts, a condition that places different coping demands upon both the population-at-risk and emergency managers. Citizens must develop an understanding of volcanic and associated dangers while remaining vigilant against eruptive threats for extended periods of time. This vigilance involves both attention to warning and preparedness measures devised by authorities, and the adoption of personal protective measures that may alter daily living patterns. Emergency managers must educate and motivate the population-at-risk on a continuing basis and maintain a long-term close coordination with a variety of hazard-management agencies, in addition to capturing and retaining administrative and fiscal resources for such sustained operations.

The primary focus of this book is upon the processes through which local residents adapt to the dangers associated with living with an active volcano. Much research attention has been given to the warning and response phase, particularly in connection with cataclysmic eruptions. During this period of acute threat, with volcanoes and other natural disaster agents as well, the attention of the public and governmental officials is directed toward the shared danger. Resources are often made available on an emergency basis, administrative roadblocks are temporarily cleared, esprit de corps is high among emergency response personnel, and the public is predisposed toward cooperation with emergency measures (cf. Kartez 1982; Perry 1985). Researchers have documented, however, that these positive conditions are quite transitory and can decline rapidly over time. There are few cases in which single impact disasters have had long-term positive effects upon emergency preparedness and hazard mitigation efforts. Less is known about the situation when multiple impact disasters are involved, especially volcanoes. Certainly after a cataclysmic eruption, continued smaller eruptions serve to keep emergency management issues salient longer. Significant questions remain, however, about *how much longer*, and about the extent to which salience is translated into motivation for citizens to adopt and maintain protective measures.

The first step in understanding citizen adaptation to the volcano hazard involves describing the history of eruptive activity at Mt. St. Helens. This history can be divided into three periods: the time before volcanicity began in this century, the period between the first eruptions of March 1980 through the cataclysmic eruption of May 18, 1980, and the most recent period following that major eruption. The research reported here focuses upon the last period and explores the ways in which citizens have come to view the volcano hazard over the long-term, and the actions they have undertaken to protect themselves since the catastrophic eruption of May 18, 1980. The analyses are structured around four basic issues: hazard awareness, perceived vulnerability, the adoption of protective measures, and volcano-induced community change. The examination of hazard awareness reviews the ability of individuals to identify specific volcanic threats and to describe their consequences for human health and property. Considerable attention is given to identifying variables which correlate with or explain citizens' accumulated knowledge of the volcano threat. Sources of volcano-related information are studied to provide a view of the system through which hazard intelligence is obtained by local residents. These analyses involve both the identification of channels and specification of content received through different channels. The analyses also assess perceptions of the credibility of different information sources and citizen knowledge of official emergency management plans.

Citizen adoption of measures designed to minimize the dangers from Mt. St. Helens is examined in two stages. First, attention is given to documenting the range and types of adjustments that have been undertaken in local households. This inventory is subsequently examined in terms of the origin of ideas for adjustments, specific characteristics of people who undertake different adjustments, and citizen perceptions of the protective efficacy of those adjustments. The second stage of analysis involves the development of a model of variables important in individuals' decisions to undertake protective measures.

Finally, the closing chapter discusses citizens' outlooks for the future; particularly conceptions of how the community has changed and will change as a consequence of the continuing volcanic activity. This chapter also reviews the major findings of the study and details their implications for the conduct of emergency management for volcano hazards. This review is undertaken in the larger context of attempting to order the findings and place them within a preliminary theoretical framework. We are acutely aware that this study is largely exploratory in nature. As we point out in Chapter 2, there is simply no coherent general theory of human adjustment to volcanic hazards. Knowing this at the outset, however, we structured our study to focus upon what we believed to be the central concept—hazard adjustment—and its two logical antecedents—hazard awareness and perceived vulnerability. In the final chapter we develop a model of the interrelationships between these three concepts and the network of correlates identified for each. While this effort is certainly best characterized as a prolegomenon to a theory of volcano hazard adjustment, it does represent a compilation of empirical findings currently unavailable in disaster recovery literature.

Mt. St. Helens Volcano

Mt. St. Helens is a composite volcano located in southwest Washington State with a long history of explosive eruptions. Until 1980, its symmetrical cone rose to 9,677 feet. Mt. St. Helens is surrounded by other large volcanoes in the Cascade chain; Mt. Adams to the east, Mt. Hood to the south and Mt. Rainier to the north. Interestingly, most of Mt. St. Helens' eruptive activity has taken place before recorded history (Crandell and Mullineaux 1978, C3). The part of the cone visible today is young, probably created in the past one thousand years; its symmetrical shape caused St. Helens to be called the Mt. Fujiyama of America (Harris 1980, 168).

Because the northwestern United States was settled relatively recently, there are few descriptions and fewer still records of the eruptions of Mt. St. Helens. Indeed, almost all of our knowledge of the volcano's eruptive history comes from geologic analyses. Early human accounts of eruptive activities can be found in legends and the creation myths of numerous Northwest Indian tribes. Although it seems likely that these legends evolved as retrospective attempts to explain eruptions occurring between 1500 and 1700, it is difficult to trace and date their origins. The most often cited legend is probably a variant of an early Puyallup-Nisqually Indian tale, preserved in the oral tradition of the Klickitat Tribe (Clark 1953, 21). This legend explained periodic eruptions as fighting between two brothers who lived in the mountains and competed for the affection of a beautiful woman.

The theme of volcanic eruptions runs through many legends describing many events significant to Northwest Indian life. Mt. St. Helens plays an important role in legends associated with the "Bridge of the Gods" (Bunnell 1933), a fabled rock bridge presumed to have spanned the Columbia River. Mt. St. Helens, called Loo-Wit by the Klickitats, was appointed by the Great Spirit to serve as guardian of the bridge. The bridge was created as a monument to the end of a war between Mt. Adams (Patoe) and Mt. Hood (Yi-East), brothers who fought for the favors of a woman. In time the war between the brothers restarted. Loo-Wit tried to intervene for peace, but she was burned by the "fire and hot rocks" thrown by the brothers. Eventually, both Loo-Wit and the "Bridge of the Gods" collapsed. Upon discovering this tragedy and learning of Loo-Wit's faithfulness to her mission, the Great Spirit rewarded her with a gift of eternal youth and beauty. Loo-Wit then moved far to the west, away from the combative brothers, and acquired a new physical appearance, including a permanent white cloak.

The legend covers an indeterminate period of time, but is consistent with conditions of Mt. St. Helens that may be inferred from geological research. Upon first being appointed guardian of the bridge, Loo-Wit was characterized as an ugly, bent old woman. This may be descriptive of a young St. Helens still building its cone. The references to the blackening of Loo-Wit also reflect what the volcano probably looked like during much of the time between 1300 and 1600. This was a period of sporadic subsummit eruptions characterized by pyroclastic flows, lava flows and airborne tephra. The result would have been a relatively shorter blackened and pockmarked appearance for Mt. St. Helens. The restoration of beauty by the Great Spirit is consistent with the volcano's appearance during the nineteenth and twentieth centuries, when the cone reached sufficient height to maintain a year-round snow cover. These legends provide an image and social record—albeit distorted and stylized—of some recent (geologic time) eruptions of Mt. St. Helens. Sporadic references in the legends to Indians hiding among "more friendly mountains" during apparent eruptive periods suggests that for the most part sparse population density minimized the social impacts of the volcanic activity, but that periodic temporary migrations occurred.

Mt. St. Helens has experienced three eruptive periods since 1800. The first of these took place about 1800, before Caucasian settlers appeared in the area, and involved at least one large-scale pyroclastic eruption (Harris 1980, 173). Wilkes (1845, 439-440) reports a discussion with a Spokane Indian who recalled being awakened as a young man by "a great noise of thunder" and experiencing ash fall which accumulated to a depth of six inches. The Spokane tribe was much alarmed by the eruption, believed it heralded the end of the world and apparently left the area.

The second recent eruptive sequence took place after the area had become more populated following the establishment of Fort Vancouver, a trading outpost approximately forty miles south and west of the volcano. It is possible to date this eruptive period as beginning in 1831 and ending in 1857. Due to the scattered and sometimes difficult to interpret reports, however, it may be misleading to assume continuous eruptive activity between these dates. Evidence does suggest that there were major eruptions between 1831 and 1835, 1842 and 1843, and between the late 1840s and middle 1850s.

Meredith Gairdner, a physician for Hudson's Bay Company stationed at Fort Vancouver, described eruptions which occurred in 1831 and 1835. Gairdner (1836, 266) published a brief letter in the *Edinburgh New Philosophical Journal* recounting periods of heavy ash fall. Private correspondence between other physicians of the time are consistent with Gairdner's reports, and add the claim that travelers reported sighting lava flows at Mt. St. Helens (Harvey 1945). The next major documented eruption was observed in the winter of 1845. A missionary named John Frost reported sighting a steam and ash plume in November from his vantage point near Portland, Oregon (Pipes 1934, 373), where light ash fall was documented. Another missionary, Father Bolduc, reported additional eruptions and lava flows in December (Holmes 1955). Subsequent eruptions were documented in 1843 (Plummer 1893), 1844 (Burnett 1902), 1847 (Kane 1925, 136), 1848 (Holmes 1955, 207), 1854 (Semple 1888), and 1857 (Holmes 1955, 209). Geologic evidence indicates that these eruptions included heavy ash fall, laval flows, dome-building (effusive) eruptions and mudflows. The social consequences of these eruptions were minimal, however, due to the sparse population of the area and the location of settlements some distance from the cone.

The Early Eruptive Activity

Mt. St. Helens remained quiet from 1857 until March 20, 1980 when seismologists detected earthquakes under the volcano. A summit crater opened on March 27, and several steam and ash eruptions were witnessed during the first weeks of April. After this first activity the volcano was quiet until the calm was broken by a cataclysmic eruption on the morning of May 18. The enormous devastation of this eruption was followed by large eruptions on May 25, June 12, July 22, August 7, and October 16, 1980 (Decker and Decker 1981, 78-79). Eruptions, though considerably less violent and frequent, continue through the present time, marking more than seven years in the present eruptive sequence.

The initial volcanic activity of March 1980, particularly the steam and ash eruptions, generated substantial interest from the news media and the public. In general, residents near the volcano responded with excitement and curiosity. Tourist traffic in the area increased considerably. A souvenir industry grew rapidly as entrepreneurial local residents recognized a new market.

In the 123 years since the 1857 eruptions, the number of people living and working near Mt. St. Helens has increased significantly. This growth in the risk area population was accompanied by an increase in the number of homes, businesses, roads and bridges, as well as other public and private structures. These developments demanded that local authorities examine the severity of threats to citizen safety. There are three nearby areas subject to serious impacts from an eruption at Mt. St. Helens. The communities along the Lewis River south of the volcano, the Toutle River communities on the north, and towns along the Cowlitz River to the west were all potentially subject to mudflows, flooding and ash fall.

In response to the March 27 eruption, emergency managers moved eighty residents of the Lewis River Valley from their homes because of the possibility of flooding if reservoirs on the river were affected by mudflows. The Weyerhaeuser Company responded by evacuating 300 loggers from its Camp Baker operations on the north side of the volcano. Approximately 100 residents were evacuated from the north and south forks of the Toutle River, as were 20 Washington State personnel from a salmon hatchery on the Toutle River (Sweeney 1980). Minor activity on March 30 produced ash falls that were detected 90 miles from the volcano. On April 1, strong earthquakes were reported, and ash and steam plumes rose to heights of 20,000 feet. Mudflows descended a short distance down the south flank of the volcano and a blue flame was reported at the crater, possibly signifying the presence of magma within the volcano. U.S. Geological Survey scientists reported on April 2 that the chances of a serious eruption were increasing (Connelly 1980). Harmonic tremors began April 3, indicating subsurface movement of magma (Sweeney and Perkins 1980). Ash and steam eruptions were reported to be accompanied by ejection of blocks of ice 10 to 12 feet in diameter from the volcanic crater (Broom 1980).

Washington Governor Dixie Lee Ray formed a Mt. St. Helens Watch Group, composed of the heads of various state agencies. By April 4, the Governor had declared a state of emergency, roadblocks were strengthened (and in some cases extended farther from the mountain), and sightseers were urged to stay away. The U.S. Geological Survey distributed a pamphlet to the mass media and public officials describing what to do in the case of a major eruption. The U.S. Forest Service also distributed warning flyers to recreationists visiting the Gifford Pinchot National Forest. There was no further volcanic activity through April 7 and some loggers began to pressure the Forest Service to permit reopening of timber operations (Dardarian 1980). Businessmen whose operations were located behind the roadblocks also began lobbying state officials to remove the roadblocks which kept tourists away from towns nearest the volcano (Perkins 1980).

The public maintained a high level of interest throughout this sixweek period from initial activity to the cataclysmic eruption of May 18, fostered in part by mass media attention to the volcano. There is some evidence that citizens in the vicinity of the mountain were concerned that specific contingency plans be developed and that officials prepare for a major eruption (Perkins 1980). There is also evidence that the public believed officials were too restrictive in their policies concerning access to the volcano. On the south side of Mt. St. Helens, for example, Cougar residents were reported to be angered by the roadblocks which cut their town off from a "booming" volcano business (*The Columbian* 1980, 20).

The Major Eruptions

The cataclysmic eruption began after an earthquake of approximately magnitude 4.9 was recorded at 8:32 a.m. on May 18 (Rosenfeld 1980, 498). This earthquake triggered a tremendous landslide on the north face of the volcano which was immediately followed by an explosion (Geophysics Program 1980, 530). A member of the U.S. Geological Survey volcano team described the eruption in detail, writing that the avalanche was within seconds overtaken by a larger, laterally directed blast that exploded outward with hurricane force winds felling trees more than 20 kilometers from the volcano's summit:

> Then the displaced water of Spirit Lake, the melting blocks of ice from the former glaciers of the volcano's north flank, water displaced from the river bed, and melting snow and ice on the volcano's remaining slopes produced mudflows that . . . generated floods (Christiansen 1980, 532).

These mudflows and floods destroyed bridges, roads and homes and partially filled the channel of the Columbia River, temporarily stranding oceangoing ships upstream in the Port of Portland.

Immediately after the initial blast, a plume of ash, steam and gas rose to 63,000 feet and began to drift eastward, blackening the sky and turning day into night for towns in a wide swath. Heavy ash fall was recorded in parts of eastern Washington, Idaho and Montana, and the cloud deposited measurable amounts at points even further east.

The effects of the eruption were catastrophic. The once symmetrical 9,671 foot peak now has a rim that reaches a reported 8,400 feet at its highest point. The north flank opening to the crater is now at about a 4,400 feet above sea level (Korosec et al. 1980, 16). Nearly a cubic mile of the mountain was ejected into the atmosphere or carried off in mudflows. The blast destroyed 150 square miles of forest, killing both vegetation and wildlife. Sixty-eight people have been listed as killed or missing. Three billion board feet of timber valued at approximately $400 million were damaged or destroyed (U.S. Senate Hearings 1980, 151), 169 lakes were either moderately damaged or destroyed, and over 3,000 miles of streams are either marginally damaged or destroyed (U.S. Senate Hearings 1980, 139). In total, after the first two major eruptions (May 18 and May 25) it was estimated that damages totalled more than $1.8 billion in property and crops; this included damages in the vicinity of the volcano as well as those areas exposed to the ash fall (U.S. Senate Hearings 1980, 18). Washington State officials estimate that short-term losses to the economy following the May eruptions exceeded $860 million (Hunt and MacCready 1980).

The Communities Studied

Toutle and Lexington, by virtue of their differing proximity to the volcano, have been exposed to slightly differing dangers throughout the volcanic sequence since 1980 (see Map 1). Toutle is an unincorporated town in Cowlitz County approximately twenty-five miles northwest of Mt. St. Helens, situated along the Spirit Lake Highway. Year-round area residents are for the most part involved in some aspect of the logging industry. The other mainstay of the local economy is tourism. Toutle is located just north of the point at which the north and south forks of the Toutle River join. The area's population is relatively small, approximately 1,500.

Few people in Toutle reported hearing any noise from the initial eruption on May 18. For most citizens, the first evidence of the eruption was the huge mushroom-shaped ash cloud which filled the horizon to the south. Residents reported feeling a dramatic increase in temperature; with it came the sounds of trees and automobile windshields cracking

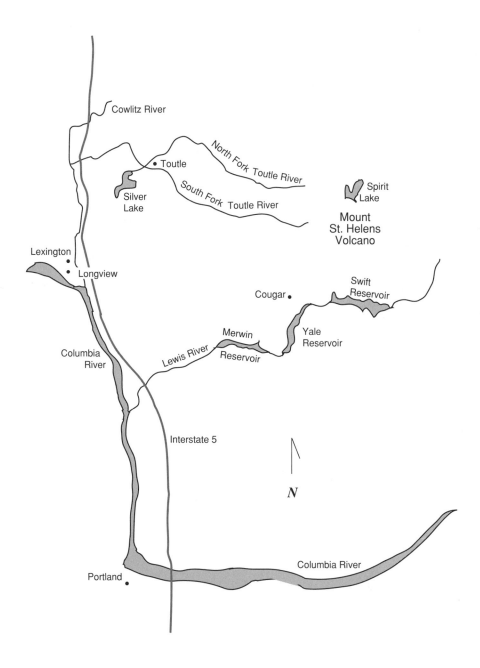

River systems and communities surrounding Mt. St. Helens.

from the heat. The area also experienced a light ash fall about one and a half hours after the eruption (Korosec et al. 1980, 14). The most serious threat, however, was associated with mudflows and flooding.

After the blast, the water temperature in the Toutle River rose above 80 degrees Fahrenheit. These temperatures and the subsequent mudflows contributed to the destruction of most of the anadromous fish in the river. The mudflows and floods destroyed seven state highway bridges and numerous country and private bridges over the Toutle, as well as almost 300 homes in low-lying areas.

Official concern about flood danger along the Toutle remained high for several days. The eruption had raised and reshaped Spirit Lake which fed into the north fork of the Toutle River. Down the valley from Spirit Lake, a large debris flow raised the valley floor near the South Fork Toutle River by several hundred feet for a distance of about fourteen miles. At first the massive debris flow was thought to be only marginally stable, but a study of the deposit by soils engineers concluded that remobilization and movement of the flow as unlikely.

Cowlitz County Sheriff's deputies issued warnings to endangered residents at the time of the initial eruption. The deputies drove predesignated routes, using their high-low sirens and public address systems to disseminate an evacuation notice. A telephone ring-down system was also implemented in predesignated areas that had a high probability of flooding. Although the Toutle Fire Department did not receive official notification of the eruption from the County Sheriff's Office, once there was physical evidence of the eruption, Fire Department volunteers assisted in the warning process and also helped staff roadblocks. A large proportion of the residents evacuated; a process that was facilitated by unfounded rumors that a cloud of poison gas was moving toward Toutle (Perry and Greene 1982).

The situation in Lexington, about thirty-five miles southwest of Mt. St. Helens, was somewhat different. A community of slightly more than 2,000, Lexington lies along the Cowlitz River. Prior to the May 18 eruption, official concerns about the likely impact of Mt. St. Helens centered on the risks of flooding in the low-lying parts of the community. This concern stemmed from the fact that the Cowlitz River could be filled to overflowing by debris and ash moving down the Toutle River. Beyond the threat from flooding, the risks—at least as they were described in the media and by officials—were not thought to be great. To prepare for the possibility of flooding, however, the Cowlitz County Sheriff's Office did develop contingency plans and distribute a pamphlet on their warning system to residents.

The May 18 eruption produced significant flows of mud, ash and debris down the north fork of the Toutle River. When this flow reached the Cowlitz River some downstream flooding resulted, but the Lexington area was, for the most part, spared severe flooding. This area, like Toutle, did receive a light dusting of volcanic ash. Thus, the destructive impact of the May 18 eruption was less for Lexington than for Toutle.

Current Volcanic Dangers

Since 1980, Mt. St. Helens has engaged in a process of dome building. Effusive eruptions have extruded thick, "doughy" lava into the crater. By May 1985 the dome had grown to 800 feet in height and 2,700 feet at its base, with the sides of the dome nearly touching the walls of the crater. Currently, the dome is growing at a rate of approximately 35 million cubic meters of material each year (Gillins 1985). Over a long period of time such lava extrusions could refill the crater, replacing the portion of the cone blasted away on May 18, 1980.

The dome building eruptions have been punctuated by smaller, but more explosive, steam and ash eruptions. At times these explosive eruptions have been violent enough to destroy portions of the dome (Decker and Decker 1980, 76). Ash and other light ejecta (e.g., pumice) continue to fall periodically on communities within a fifty-mile radius of the volcano. While the possibility of future large-scale explosive eruptions is slight, it does seem likely that the preponderance of eruptions in the near future will be of the effusive, dome-building type (Findley 1981).

The eruptive activity at Mt. St. Helens should not be characterized as having reached a peak of violence in the summer of 1980 and since then fallen into an active—but unviolent—state. Although dome building is marked by relatively "gentle" effusive eruptions, the chance that its expansions will be accompanied by renewed violent eruptions increases with the size of the dome. Dr. Donal Mullineaux of the U.S. Geological Survey succinctly describes the threat:

> The larger it grows, the larger its potential for collapse with mudflows down its flanks. . . . The mountain's history is one of moderate to major eruptions . . . periods when activity is less strong, followed by another significantly voluminous eruption. (quoted in Connelly 1985, E4)

Consequently, one cannot realistically eliminate the prospect that Mt. St. Helens will again pose an eruptive threat to nearby communities.

One of the most significant noneruptive threats from Mt. St. Helens is associated with a debris dam on Spirit Lake. The lake is located five miles north of the volcano, and once served as a reflecting pond for the symmetrical cone. After the May 18 eruption, ash, boulders, timber and other debris completely blocked Spirit Lake's outlet channel causing the size of the reservoir to increase from 123,000 acre feet to 275,000 acre feet in less than two years (Swift and Kresch 1983, 2). By the summer of 1982 it was determined that the debris dam was considerably less stable than previously thought; unexpected erosion suggested the possibility of a breach. Depending upon the severity of the breach, such an event could produce serious flooding in communities along the Toutle, Cowlitz and Columbia Rivers. It was also acknowledged that an explosive eruption, an earthquake, or a mud or debris flow into Spirit Lake could produce an overtopping or complete collapse of the dam.

In the face of the danger, Washington Governor John Spellman declared a state of emergency on August 2, 1982. Potential flooding from Spirit Lake endangered more than 40,000 citizens as well as commercial and industrial facilities, a nuclear power plant, a major interstate highway and shipping lanes at the Port of Portland. On August 19, 1982, following a request from the Governor, President Ronald Reagan issued a Presidential Emergency Declaration for the State of Washington (Comptroller General of the United States 1982, 51). This declaration directed the Federal Emergency Management Agency, in coordination with the Forest Service, Geological Survey and Army Corps of Engineers, to develop and implement a plan to reduce the flood danger associated with possible failure of the debris dam. The threat mitigation plan involved creating an outlet channel from the debris dam to the north fork of the Toutle River and, in the short run, pumping water from Spirit Lake into the outlet. The Army Corps supervised construction of 3,800 feet of five-foot diameter pipes connecting the lake with the Toutle River in October, 1982 (Comptroller General of the United States 1982, 53). Beginning in November of that year, a pumping barge was used to siphon water out of Spirit Lake. This pumping operation was aimed at stabilizing the lake at a volume of 275,000 acre feet (Swift and Kresch 1983, 2). More permanent measures for creating drainage were proceeding concomitant with the pumping. After considering several alternative solutions, the Army Corps adopted a plan to create a tunnel through rock to

South Coldwater Creek which empties into the North Fork Toutle River (U.S. Forest Service 1984). Work began in the summer of 1984 by a private contractor to recreate a permanent outlet for Spirit Lake. The temporary pumping operation continued until the new tunnel was completed in the spring of 1985.

A final resolution of the debris dam threat, however, did not end concern with noneruptive flood threats. There remains a danger to the Toutle, Cowlitz and Columbia rivers from long-term sedimentation, as ash and soil from Mt. St. Helens' slopes are introduced into the river systems. As the beds rise, the flood threat increases; in the Columbia River, there is the added concern that sedimentation could again close the Port of Portland to deep-draft oceangoing vessels. Initially, the problem with sediments was combatted by dredging the Toutle River and thereby capturing deposits before they could move into the Cowlitz and Columbia. In late spring of 1984, a plan to handle long-term sedimentation via a series of dams was adopted. The strategy is to construct several dams to trap sediments; the dams are to be built sequentially, as needed, to reduce the costs in any single fiscal year. In 1985, the Army Corps of Engineers announced intentions of placing the first dam on the Toutle River. Toutle residents near a section of the Spirit Lake Highway, who would lose their homes after the construction expressed vehement opposition to the dam (Connelly 1985). It is too soon to estimate the effects of citizen opposition on the completion of this or other sedimentation projects. The danger is real and inevitable. What remains to be determined is how the projects may be completed so that the maximum number of potential victims are protected, and to determine if those who suffer from construction should and can be adequately compensated.

Emergency management of the flood and eruption threats associated with Mt. St. Helens is handled within Cowlitz County by the Department of Emergency Services (DES), a division of the Sheriff's Office. The DES coordinates the efforts of all federal, state and local agencies that pertain to threatened residents of the county. In general, two strategies dominate plans to preserve public safety: development of an elaborate warning and evacuation system, and enforcement of a policy of restricted access to danger areas around the volcano.

Mt. St. Helens is carefully monitored for seismic activity, changes in volcanic gas emissions, and changes in the surface of the volcano (e.g., fissures, swelling). These systems, as well as hydrologic systems (supplemented by observation) for assessing potential flood threats, constitute the instrumentation for hazard monitoring. At Mt. St. Helens, hazard monitoring is aimed at detecting dangers sufficiently in advance to make citizen warning systems feasible. Since before the May 18 eruption, Cowlitz County Emergency Managers have maintained a capacity to warn, evacuate and shelter citizens in the event of an eruption (Perry and Greene 1983, 34-39). The preparedness system involves multiple channels for warning dissemination (Emergency Broadcasting System, sirens, telephone ring-down, and in-person warnings), and a vigorous public information program to disseminate evacuation route and shelter data, tips on damage prevention, guidelines for coping with an emergency in progress, and precautions to be followed after a flood or major eruption. In the winter of 1982-1983, when informed of the possible failure of the debris dam, Cowlitz County authorities codified the warning-and-response plan in the form of an eight-page "flood preparation guide" with maps (Nelson 1983). The guide was distributed to county residents through the major area newspaper and from all county offices. A survey conducted in spring 1983 showed an estimated 90 percent coverage of citizens in the Toutle and Lexington areas (Perry 1983). The warning system has been used effectively in numerous areas in response to flood and eruption threats (cf. Barber 1984). Surveys indicate that area residents are familiar with official emergency plans and view the Cowlitz County DES as a credible and authoritative agency (Perry et al. 1980; Perry and Greene 1983).

Providing warnings about the volcano to sightseers and short-term visitors to Mt. St. Helens is a complicated task that has also been vigorously tackled by county and state authorities. Tourism is important to the local economy. To maintain the tourist business, visitors must be protected, but they also must still have the greatest feasible access to the recreation sites near the volcano. In order to inform tourists about the warning system, pamphlets and flyers have been placed at all visitor centers and many places of business near access points to the volcano. Signs have been posted along all primary roads leading to the volcano that identify:

1) the meaning of warning sirens,

2) radio stations broadcasting information

3) evacuation routes.

These measures allow visitors to recognize and comply with warnings to evacuate danger areas in which they are permitted access. The visibility of volcano hazard information and the actual implementation of some evacuations initially caused some concern on the part of those charged with promoting tourism. It was argued that such visible reminders of the volcano's dangers might discourage visitors and lead to a recurrence of the tourist "drought" of 1981-1983. Those concerns were met by authorities' serious restatement of the safety hazards associated with Mt. St. Helens. Since the protective measures were unquestionably justified, local authorities decided to focus on the "positive" side. Thus, public announcements acknowledged that St. Helens was an active volcano, but stressed that the danger was mediated by a strong emergency plan. In this way, the signs marking evacuation routes and other measures became reinforcements for the view that authorities maintained some degree of control over the situation.

Another means of protecting both residents and tourists involves forbidding admission to places deemed too dangerous. Since April 1980, access controls of some type have been continuously enforced around the volcano. These restrictions continue to constitute one of the most controversial hazard management strategies used by authorities. In the fall of 1985, a three-mile radius access control zone still existed around the crater itself. Prior to May 18, access restrictions were enforced to keep tourists and sightseers from wandering dangerously close to the volcano. After the cataclysmic eruption, the restricted zone was extended to cover a twenty-mile radius around the volcano and was strictly enforced. For a time, National Guard soldiers staffed roadblocks and even residents who had evacuated were not allowed to return. Subsequently, a permit system opened much of the area to residents and others with "urgent needs" for access (Washington Department of Emergency Services 1980). These restrictions virtually closed the towns of Cougar, Toutle, Silverlake, Maple Flats, and St. Helens to all except residents.

Mt. St. Helens' continued activity served as a reminder to officials that the volcano remained a threat to human health and safety. In spite of the efforts of area businessmen to convince state authorities to alter the access controls, the tight restrictions remained in effect through 1980 and into 1981. At this point, considerable controversy arose regarding the restricted zone. Cougar and parts of the Toutle Valley had continued to lose permanent population, businesses had begun to fail, and prospects were not good for those businesses that remained. Behind the barricades, the service-oriented section of the economy was almost completely stagnant. Thus, the business community, supported by the Weyerhaeuser

Company, vehemently argued that the access controls should be liberalized.

The opposite point of view—that restrictions must remain—was argued with equal ardor by emergency management and law enforcement personnel. These authorities saw themselves as responsible for the safety of both tourists and area residents. Emergency decision-makers were frustrated because of scientists' limited success in predicting the timing or magnitude of eruptions. Emergency managers who had grown accustomed to obtaining highly accurate information on other natural hazards—floods, for example—found that volcanologists could not provide precise estimates of eruption times or even imprecise estimates of magnitude. Emergency authorities therefore faced a difficult problem: how does one protect the public from a threat that can arise at any moment with little or no warning? To these authorities, the most acceptable option seemed to be maintaining access controls. If the public was simply kept away, then certainly no harm would befall them. To understand the plight of emergency managers, it is important to remember that bodies of persons killed in the May 18 eruptions were still being discovered—some distance from the volcano—as late as September and October, 1980. Holding the public an acceptable distance from the volcano seemed to be the only strategy that offered complete protection.

Over time, numerous compromises on restricted zones were attempted. A red zone/blue zone system was implemented such that the red zone was a small area with limited access, while entrance into the blue zone was less difficult. Subsequently, the blue zone was abolished altogether and the size of the red zone continues to be reduced. At present, general access has been restored to all of the communities near the volcano. A primary function of existing access restrictions is to keep recreationists and campers from venturing too close to the volcanic cone itself and outside the area covered by warning systems.

While the reopening of the towns did not at once produce the results businessmen hoped for, it did result in at least some basis for the survival of the local economy. With access permitted, the close proximity of the towns to Mt. St. Helens served as an attraction to tourists. In 1982 and 1983, the general area had begun to see increases in tourists, although by no means did either the number of visitors or the volume of business approach predisaster levels.

In part, business volume changes during this period were related to changes undergone by the local economy. To take advantage of the partial lifting of access controls, the business economy had to undergo a change in functional orientation. Before the imposition of strict access restrictions, local businesses were geared to the needs of recreationists, hunters and fishermen, who tended to be in the area for two or more nights; some of these visitors required overnight lodging, some groceries, and some sought the entertainment of a tavern. After the access restrictions were lifted, tourism developed a more short-term character. Visitors tended to be families making a day trip to see the volcano. Consequently, the demand for overnight lodging declined, while the market for souvenirs, snack foods, and prepared meals increased. Surviving businesses have adapted to this change in the market which reflects a change in the public use pattern of the area. Interestingly, the progressively greater lifting of access restrictions has introduced a need for a functional change *back* to the pre-cataclysmic eruption tourist orientation.

Nearly five years after the cataclysmic eruption, the towns around Mt. St. Helens still occupy somewhat precarious positions demographically and economically. The population of the area has declined very slightly. Moreover, although tourism was growing as the 1984 season began, the record stream of visitors which were expected in 1981 never materialized. In part, the small number of visitors was probably related to the generally poor economic conditions. Unemployment in the Northwest has been slightly higher than the national average as a whole, and Northwest residents have been more conservative about expenditures, particularly for vacations. Finally, the eruption of Mt. St. Helens produced some death and much destruction, all of which was widely publicized and sometimes exaggerated. This apparently produced reticence among potential tourists, who felt that some risk remained and the area might still be dangerous. The State of Washington subsequently embarked on an aggressive tourism campaign to attract visitors from the western United States and Canada.

During the 1985 season, the area around Mt. St. Helens began to experience the surge in tourism that had been predicted, but had not materialized, in previous years. The principal attraction was the 110,000 acre Volcanic National Park at Mt. St. Helens established by the U.S. Congress. By 1985, the U.S. Forest Service had established several visitor centers, information centers and viewpoints for the volcano, the closest just little farther than three miles from the crater. Seven hundred thousand tourists visited the centers in 1984 and larger numbers are projected for the future: three million annually by the year 2,000 (Connelly 1985). A multimillion dollar visitors complex, with more than 15,000 square feet of exhibition space is scheduled for completion by the 1986 season. Development of the National Park is founded upon a visitor interpretive center concept involving participatory exhibits, a motion picture theatre, book stores, portal facilities (viewpoints and camp-grounds) and roads and trails. Independent of the federal effort, nearby towns and Chambers of Commerce are also developing tourism plans. It is believed that the increase in tourism resulting from such developments would go far toward restoring economic viability. In addition, further reduction of the restricted zone would again open up recreational facilities and hunting and fishing areas. Together, these stimuli would create an even stronger local economy than that which prevailed before the eruptions.

The flora and fauna of the ecosystem surrounding Mt. St. Helens are in the process of reestablishing themselves. Soon after the cataclysmic eruption, scientists noticed small bracken ferns peeking through the deep layers of volcanic ash. Subsequently, fireweed, vine maple, moss, lupine and horsetail greens began to appear. Douglas fir and alder trees, with some help from reforestation efforts, are in the process of reclaiming their positions in the landscape. Some of the plant growth stems from the return of the burrowing insects and mammals, as well as birds. Pocket gophers are well established and deer and elk are returning in ever-larger numbers (Barnes and Haupt 1985, 23).

In summary, while the threat of an explosive eruption persists, some of the noneruptive threats have been mitigated, and local authorities have developed effective systems for alerting residents and visitors to vol-canic dangers. The local economy is not only being restored, but shows signs of significant growth in the future. Thus far, we have focused upon the experiences and recovery of the region around Mt. St. Helens as a whole. The remainder of the book is devoted to a closer examination of ways in which local residents have adapted to the challenge of living near an active volcano.

Data Collection Techniques

In the classic case study tradition, the data reported in this book come from a variety of sources (cf. Yin, 1984). These sources include govern-ment records and documents, social surveys, autobiographical writings and diaries, interviews with victims and key actors, and even Indian legends. The majority of the data reported here, however, come from personal interviews conducted with probability samples of residents of Toutle and Lexington, Washington.

The general survey design used to obtain the primary data base was developed on a "pre-letter follow-up" strategy frequently used when trained interviewers administer questionnaires to inhabitants of an area exposed to natural hazards (cf. Perry, Greene and Lindell 1980). Identical research designs and procedures were used in each community. The data gathering procedure was based upon a series of attempted contacts with potential survey respondents. A pre-letter was mailed to all sampled households which described the purpose and sponsorship of the study. Three weeks later, project staff began the first wave of personal interviews. The pattern of interview call-backs involved one initial attempt to locate and interview, followed by a maximum of three repeat calls on respondents not contacted the first time. After the first wave of interviews, all potential respondents who had not been reached were sent a followup letter describing the importance of their participation and announcing a second wave of interviews to commence in three weeks. The second wave of interviews followed the same contact and call-back procedure as the first.

The return or completion rates generated by this field procedure are high enough to permit statistically meaningful analyses of the data (cf. Perry and Lindell 1986, 21). Table 1 summarizes survey completion

TABLE 1

Survey Completion Rates   Survey Completion Rates
Survey Completion Rates

Description	Lexington	Toutle
1. Total households in sample	120	122
2. Moved, could not trace, or house not standing	5	9
3. Could not locate	7	6
4. Refused interview	9	4
5. Complete or partial interview	99	103
6. Percent of total households interviewed	82.5	84.4
7. Percent of persons contacted interviewed	86.1	91.2

information for each study site. Line six shows that 82.5 percent of the total households sampled were interviewed successfully in Lexington, while 84.4 percent of the Toutle sample completed interviews.

The sampling design was aimed at obtaining probability samples of residents in each community. Because both communities are in semi-rural areas, community boundaries were established by a mapping procedure. That is, area maps were used to delineate the geographical boundaries of each community. It should be noted that what is referred to here as the geographical boundaries do not necessarily coincide with the political boundaries of the community. The Toutle sample, for instance, includes the "Tower Road" area, an area adjacent to the town of Toutle but not served by its post office. Using a Polk's Directory, Cowlitz County Department of Emergency Services maps, and a "reverse" telephone directory, a full listing of addresses lying within each community area was constructed. A systematic sample from a random start was drawn from each list, using a sample fraction designed to yield approximately 120 households.

The information gathered from these households form the data on hazard awareness, perceived vulnerability, hazard adjustment and perceived community change that shape the analyses which follow. The subsequent chapters address each of these topics in turn, beginning with the problem of hazard awareness. As we pointed out earlier in this chapter, we believe that ultimately these four concepts are interrelated and in Chapter 5 we develop a formal logic for a more comprehensive model of factors that explain citizen hazard adjustment. As support for more comprehensive modeling, however, it is important to develop theoretically meaningful definitions of each concept as well as an understanding of what other factors related to each target concept. Thus, we begin this exploration process in Chapter 2, focusing upon hazard awareness.

CHAPTER TWO

Understanding the Volcano Threat

Both research scientists and emergency managers have decried what they perceive as a persistent ignorance of the hazardous nature of the environment on the part of the general public. Perhaps even more vexing to these scholars and professionals than public misunderstanding, however, is apparent public indifference. Particularly in peaceful times, citizens seem not especially interested in seeking for themselves or accepting from authorities information about environmental hazards. Research indicates that identifying and trying to understand potential dangers associated with natural hazards are not activities which often capture the public mind. Social psychologists have offered a range of reasons for this state of affairs, but Thomas E. Drabek (1984, 4) succinctly summarized the issue by pointing out that this behavior represents "... reflections of people being busy and occupied with their own life priorities—day-to-day issues of living. . . . They simply don't have the luxury of leisure to become absorbed in such matters." Among the constellation of concerns about social and personal matters that constitute demands upon the individual's time, environmental hazards do not usually merit a high priority. This situation changes only when some person or event intervenes to increase the salience of hazards relative to other demands upon the individual.

It is generally argued that citizen hazard awareness—the understanding of a threat coupled with some subjective appreciation of its likely consequences—is a positive state of affairs. Certainly it makes intuitive sense that someone who understands a given threat is more likely to be successful in coping with it. This idea, coupled with the knowledge that it usually requires some intervention to cause a reordering of individual priorities to focus on hazards, may be seen as the stimulus for two types of emergency management practice. The first of these is the tendency for authorities to disseminate materials aimed at "risk education" to communities soon after a disaster occurs. The objective is to take advantage of the awareness produced by the event itself in the education process. The second emergency management tactic centers upon the conduct of hazard awareness campaigns, which may or may not coincide with any given disaster impact. The latter approach is based on the idea that authorities can make the hazard salient by establishing reasons that citizens should attend to it, thereby increasing the chance that the affected population will be receptive to risk information.

Whether or not the hazard awareness program is initiated after a disaster event, emergency services personnel must select the appropriate content and evaluation procedures for the awareness program. It is essential to determine what information about a hazard should be disseminated and what factors contribute to citizens' understanding of the information. The purpose of this chapter is to explore these issues in the context of the current eruptive sequence at Mt. St. Helens. In particular, we will assess citizen knowledge of the potential consequences of volcanic activity and identify variables that correlate with accurate knowledge. As a preface to these discussions, however, we will examine more broadly the question of hazard awareness, its conceptualization in hazards research, what empirical literature tells us about it, and how it may be understood in the case of multiple impact disaster events.

Hazard Awareness

The theoretical underpinnings of our concern with hazard awareness are primarily social psychological. As it is generally defined, the concept embodies both an informational dimension and an evaluative dimension. One accumulates accurate knowledge of the characteristics and consequences of a given threat, and based upon this knowledge assesses the threat as potentially harmful. In this sense, hazard awareness is an abstraction or a state of mind, similar to an attitude. The informational component of awareness may be measured on some metric varying from low to high that represents an individual's understanding or knowledge of the environmental threat.

From an emergency manager's standpoint, hazard awareness requires an educational activity that has an implicit meaning for citizen behavior. It interweaves social psychological reasoning with an applied orientation, the development of hazard awareness may be viewed as a process in which an individual's initial belief is that the natural environment is "nurturing" or, at least, neutral. This is consistent with the view that people tend to focus upon day-to-day short-term demands, and in most cases the hazardous nature of the natural environment is not psychologically central (cf. Slovic et al. 1980b; Nigg 1982). Emergency managers deal intensively with threatening aspects of the environment. From their perspective, the development of hazard awareness involves both education and persuasion. It is education in the sense that it requires that emergency managers share their specialized knowledge of hazards with citizens. It is persuasion to the extent that emergency managers hope that by giving citizens shared information about a threat, citizens will also come to share the same orientation toward the threat—namely vigilance. If having accurate threat information makes citizens more vigilant, they are likely to be more supportive of official efforts to minimize the negative consequences of the hazard.

Another reason emergency managers attempt to raise the public's level of hazard awareness goes beyond mere knowledge of the threat and passive acceptance of mitigation measures. This is the expectation that knowledge will somehow be translated into action. Not just any action, but fairly specific actions related to threat reduction. Many hazards researchers and emergency managers have made the inference that a change in the level of hazard awareness will result in a corresponding change in the behavior of citizens at risk. This assumption follows on intellectual tradition in social psychology wherein it is assumed that the concept of attitude incorporates an action orientation toward the attitude object, and that one should be able to anticipate or predict some degree of consistency between one's attitude and one's behavior relative to the attitude object. Given the similarity of the assumptions of the hazard awareness-adjustment and attitude-behavior literatures, it is not surprising that the awareness literature reflects the mixed empirical results that were observed in the attitude-behavior literature of decades past (Perry et al. 1976).

Studies of hazard awareness have typically shown that citizens are generally uninformed about environmental hazards and that being aware of hazards is not closely connected with either undertaking preparedness behaviors or a propensity to comply with emergency measures (such as evacuation warnings). This is indeed a fairly discouraging pronouncement if taken at face value. The lack of public awareness of many hazards implies that information dissemination is needed. However, if awareness is not in some way related to positive action, the purpose for creating awareness is seriously called into question.

The concept of hazard awareness is unquestionably important. It gives scientists and practitioners a common way of conceptualizing or representing the extent to which citizens understand the hazardousness of the natural environment. In so doing, it allows us to explore the role of such understanding in the ways people adjust to living with hazards. In assessing the "connectedness" of awareness with concrete behaviors, however, one needs to consider some relevant methodological issues. The purpose here is to critically examine the question of whether hazard awareness should be eliminated from our lexicon because its apparent lack of interconnectedness with concrete behavioral dimensions renders it useless.

Only small proportions of the populations tested to date could be classified as having "high" levels of awareness of specific hazards affecting their communities. This tells us something about variation on the awareness dimension—that people are apparently clustered at the low end—but by no means renders the concept unusable. Furthermore, it raises a statistical question about research on hazard awareness and its connection to other variables (behaviors, for example). When there is little variance on a "predictor" variable, meaning that most subjects have the same or a similar "value" (in this case, low), it is statistically not possible to assess the covariation between the predictor variable and some criterion variable. This is particularly true of data obtained via sample surveys where lack of variability simply means that you do not have subjects to examine who represent the full range on the predictor of interest. In essence, the "predictor variable" becomes a constant value and by definition can't be assessed as a way of explaining variance in the criterion or dependent variable.

What this tells us about hazard awareness is that much of the data available to date examines the relationship between having a low level of hazard awareness and the frequency and style of individual adjustments to hazards. Comparatively little is known about the adjustment styles of people showing high levels of hazard awareness. It may be that in studies which show a wider range of hazard awareness values, connections may exist between awareness and many other variables. Of course it may be that added variance on the awareness dimension may not produce findings different from those to date; the important point is that this remains an empirical question. Consequently, this argument reveals one reason to not eliminate hazard awareness from practical or research consideration based upon existing studies.

Two additional methodological points may be raised that tend to support the argument that hazard awareness may indeed be an important concept in hazards research. Both of these points derive from the deliberations of social psychologists who were attempting to sort out apparently contradictory empirical studies of the correlation between attitudes and behaviors. The first deals with developing congruence between measurement and prediction practices, while the second addresses the theoretical context of the prediction paradigm.

Saarinen (1976) has suggested that hazard awareness is best thought of as an attitude—a collection of knowledge, beliefs and feelings about a hazard and its relevance for the individual. More recently he has noted that awareness has been measured in so many different ways that it is difficult to determine the comparability of findings among various studies of awareness and its consequences (Saarinen 1982, 2). Saarinen's reasoning allows one to draw a parallel between the literature on attitudes and behaviors and the question of hazard awareness and hazard adjustment. The attitude literature was wrought with apparently contradictory and inconclusive findings about the connection between attitudes and behavior. This is also true of hazard awareness; most studies report weak correlation, if any, between awareness and adjustment behaviors, while a few have found moderate correlations (cf. Sorenson 1983).

When faced with sorting out such apparently ambiguous findings, social psychologists initially looked to questions of measurement. Upon examination of these measurement issues, it was recognized that there was little agreement on how attitudes should be operationalized (measured) and upon what kinds of behaviors should be checked as criteria. In large part, the contradictory and inconclusive nature of empirical studies in the area (Perry 1976; Wicker 1969; Fishbein 1967) could be attributed to these two problems. To some extent the same problems exist with hazard awareness. Awareness has been measured in a variety of ways, including: a) general assessment of knowledge about hazards; b) equally general questions about a single hazard; and c) specific questions about the physical characteristics or about the environmental and social consequences of a single hazard. Hazard adjustment has also been operationalized in a variety of ways as a means of checking on behaviors in response to hazards. Adjustments have been measured as lists of general preparedness measures undertaken, general emergency planning activity, lists of specific mitigation or preparedness measures undertaken, participation in hazard insurance programs, or possession of specific knowledge of community emergency plans.

It is significant that for each concept—hazard awareness and hazard adjustment—the above lists give a variety of possible measurement schemas ranging from fairly general to fairly specific. The attitude-behavior literature indicates, however, that measuring hazard awareness in terms of a person's general information about environmental hazards should be expected to differ from measuring awareness in terms of specific lists of the consequences of a specific hazard. Although the two measures tap similar (or related) concepts, it is not necessarily the *same* concept. An equivalent argument may also be made for measures of hazard adjustment.

In a research setting then, it is possible for investigators to "mix" their indicators; matching a general measure of awareness with a specific measure of adjustment or vice versa. The psychological literature on scaling (Perry 1976) and the causal modeling literature on rules of correspondence and epistemic correlation (Costner 1971) show that such mixing of measures creates interpretive ambiguities in data analysis. In particular, for conceptual and measurement reasons, one should not expect general attitudinal measures to correlate highly with specific behavioral measures, or specific attitudinal measures to correlate highly with general behavior measures (cf. Fishbein 1967; Crespi 1971; Poppleton and Pilkington 1964).

In summary, the apparent lack of correspondence between awareness and adjustment, may be partially attributed to inappropriate mixing of measures reflecting different levels of generality. To obtain a more appropriate assessment of the awareness-adjustment correlation requires that the measure of awareness be matched in terms of specificity of referent to the adjustment measure.

Finally, one may raise a theoretical question regarding the question of the correlation between hazard awareness and adjustment actions. Namely, is it reasonable to expect that any *single* predictor would explain all or even most of the variance in a dependent variable? Since the act of undertaking an adjustment (no matter how general or specific) to one or more natural hazards is a complex process, many variables other than hazard awareness would also bear upon this process. It would seem that the salience of the threat, perceived risk, knowledge of the threat, and knowledge of protective measures, and availability of resources for protection would all be related to the propensity to engage in hazard adjustment. The point here is that hazard awareness is only one of many variables that would be expected to come into play in any given adjustment decision. Consequently, it is not reasonable to expect that, taken alone, hazard awareness would be highly predictive of hazard adjustment. Instead, this logic suggests that researchers should be engaged in the theoretical process of constructing models that specify the linkages among a variety of variables, all of which contribute to explaining why individuals undertake hazard adjustments. We will explore this concept of a network of explanatory variables for adopting mitigation and preparedness measures more thoroughly in Chapter four.

The primary purpose of the preceding discussion is to suggest that hazard awareness, in spite of the mixed empirical results, remains a viable concept in the study of human response to environmental hazards. It has been pointed out that conceptually hazard awareness constitutes a way of representing individual knowledge about hazards in a meaningful way. We have also suggested that studies which report that hazard awareness does not appear to be correlated with other important hazard behaviors need *not* be interpreted as indicating that awareness is not a useful concept. The scarcity of studies showing high awareness-adjustment correlations was approached from three perspectives. The first two were primarily methodological: restricted range on the predictor variable (awareness), and a tendency to mix general predictor measures with specific adjustment behaviors. The third was theoretical: it is known that many variables impinge upon the decision to adopt a hazard adjustment, and there is no reason to believe that any single variable would correlate particularly highly with the behavioral criterion.

Given this reasoning, it is appropriate to begin to more carefully examine the concept of hazard awareness in the context of volcanic eruptions. The remainder of this chapter will focus upon further delineating the antecedents or "causes" of hazard awareness.

Threats at Mt. St. Helens

Among natural hazards, volcanos are distinguished by a variety of characteristics. Eruptions, or impacts, tend to be low probability events. With a few notable exceptions, such as the Hawaiian volcanos, eruptive events are spaced far apart in time. Although technology is developing and improving, scientists' ability to predict initial eruptions in a volcanic sequence remains highly limited (Decker and Decker 1981). Volcanic activity involves a wide range of primary and secondary threats to humans: explosive eruptions, pyroclastic flows, ash fall, lava flows, mud-flows, flooding, gases and acid rains, earthquakes, tsunami, and ballistic projectiles. Finally, while the intervals between eruptive periods may be extended, an eruptive sequence may itself extend for many years and be characterized by repeated impacts of any of the specific threats just mentioned.

These characteristics, particularly eruption periodicity and the extended nature of eruptive sequences, demand careful treatment of the issue of volcanic hazard awareness. In particular, awareness should be considered in two contexts: the time period between eruptive sequences and the time period during an eruptive sequence.

Volcanos in the Cascade Range, of which St. Helens is one, appear to have extended eruption cycles. Except for Mt. St. Helens, only one—Mt. Baker—has been active this century. Indeed, for most of the time human settlements have existed in the Pacific Northwest, the Cascade volcanos have been silent. The absence of activity has encouraged human encroachment into potential volcano impact areas. Historically, the desire to capitalize on volcanic resources had drawn people near this environmental hazard. Rich volcanic soils promote forest industries and farming. The ecosystems that surround volcanos are often characterized by abundant wildlife, fowl and fish, inviting commercial exploitation and creating recreational opportunities.

During long periods of geologic quiet, then, people have little impetus to view volcanos as hazardous. Indeed, local residents often define volcanos in positive terms, as a source of jobs, a site for recreation, and an important aesthetic contribution to the quality of life. Warrick (1979, 164-165) notes that around Mt. Rainier, to the north of Mt. St. Helens, ". . . it is very likely that most inhabitants are blissfully unaware of the violent potential . . . and . . . unlikely that the risk and uncertainty of volcanic events, as rare as they are, have entered into individual and collective decisions about location, livelihood, or land use." Still further to the north lies Mt. Baker, whose activity since the spring of 1975 provided visible cues of its status as a potentially threatening volcano. Case studies of residents and recreationists, however, showed that while people acknowledged the existence of a volcanic hazard, the likelihood of a volcanic event that would endanger humans was judged to be quite low (Hodge, et al. 1979, 228).

Research on Mt. St. Helens tends to support Warrick's speculation about local residents' lack of awareness during the time between eruptive sequences. Prior to the initial volcanicity of March 1980, surveys indicated that about two-thirds of the citizens in nearby towns—Cougar, Woodland and Longview—were aware that Mt. St. Helens was a potentially active volcano (Greene et al. 1981, 52). The same surveys showed, however, that about 85 percent of the respondents in each community believed it was *unlikely* that volcanic activity would *ever* threaten their property or personal safety. Even after the earthquakes and steam and ash eruptions of March and April 1980, residents' evaluations of Mt. St. Helens as largely unthreatening persisted. Newspaper reports indicated that local inhabitants were "excited" and viewed the volcano as "more an object of curiosity than danger" (Broom 1980; Connelly 1980; Sweeny and Perkins 1980). Thus, during this phase, residents' beliefs about the dangers of Mt. St. Helens could be described by saying that many people knew of the mountain's status as a volcano, but few linked this knowledge with any likely danger.

On the morning of May 18, 1980, Mt. St. Helens erupted with tremendous force, collapsing the north face of the cone. Hurricane force winds, pyroclastic flows, lava flows, mud-flows, ash fall, and intense heat which melted glaciers all followed (cf. Rosenfeld 1980; Geophysics Program 1980; Christiansen 1980). Virtually all of the communities north of the cone and those along river systems associated with the volcano experienced some negative impacts. And the nature of the negative consequences taxed the human imagination. Nearly one cubic mile of the cone itself disappeared; at its highest point, the peak's elevation had dropped more than one thousand feet (Korosec et al. 1980, 16). The blast destroyed 150 square miles of forest, killing both vegetation and wildlife and leaving 68 people dead or missing (Perry and Greene 1983, 3). Three billion board feet of timber were damaged or destroyed, 169 lakes were damaged—some simply evaporated—and more than 3,000 miles of streams and rivers were negatively affected either through heat, which killed fish, or clogging with mud, ash, or other debris (U.S. Senate Hearings 1980). Estimates by Washington State officials for short-term losses to the economy (before reimbursement by federal disaster relief programs) exceeded $860 million (Hunt and MacCready 1980).

The incredible force of the May 18 eruption radically changed the context in which the public viewed Mt. St. Helens. From the standpoint of hazard awareness, this eruption—as well as several large eruptions in the following months and years—created and sustained *salience*. It made local inhabitants not just aware that St. Helens was a volcano, but sensitive to the idea that it was a hazard; something that could periodically impose almost unfathomable harm on people and the environment.

Although Mt. St. Helens had not seen sustained activity for 123 years, people were now forced to entertain the notion that the volcano posed a variety of threats, which were potentially very destructive, somewhat unpredictable and likely to persist for an extended period of time.

In August 1980, Perry, Greene and Lindell (1980) surveyed the community most damaged by the eruptions—Toutle—and restudied the community of Woodland on the Cowlitz River. Three months following the catastrophic eruption, hazard awareness in Toutle was high. Residents were able to describe accurately a wide range of volcanic threats in general, and they were also able to correctly identify the specific threats—ash fall, mud-flow and floods—which emergency managers believed most likely to affect their community. Furthermore, Toutle residents were sensitive to the question of *vulnerability*, which forms an aspect of hazard awareness more personally relevant than knowledge of the physical characteristics of the hazard event. When asked about risk or danger associated with St. Helens' eruptions, more than half of the Toutle respondents described it as "high," reporting the belief that eruptions were likely to create moderate or severe damage.

Two interesting patterns of attitudinal change were identified in the community of Woodland. The first deals with the extent to which citizens felt "certain" that the information or knowledge they had accumulated about Mt. St. Helens would allow them to adequately protect themselves from the negative effects of eruptions. In April 1980, more than half of the Woodland residents questioned claimed to be "very certain" that they knew enough about the volcano to protect themselves; only about 18 percent admitted they were "uncertain" (Perry et al. 1980, 110-116). In August, following the series of large eruptions of May, June and July, only about one-fourth of the Woodland respondents were "very certain" about their ability to protect themselves, while more than forty percent now reported that they were uncertain. The second attitudinal change dealt with peoples' beliefs about the likelihood that volcanic activity at St. Helens would constitute a future threat to safety. In April, about forty-five percent of those questioned responded that future safety threats were "unlikely"—this proportion dramatically dropped to twenty-five percent in August of the same year.

The August data reflect a "different era" in hazard awareness than the April data. By August, citizens were sensitized to the potential magnitude of the consequences of volcanic events, although their attention no doubt centered on the May 18 event, which represented the extremely negative anchor point of the possible range. People had become less confident about their ability to protect themselves. Residents had just begun accumulating specific knowledge regarding eruption threats. Finally, citizen views of the volcano had radically changed from the pre- -May measures, now acknowledging danger and human vulnerability.

The eruptions have continued, most intensely in 1980 and early 1981, but steadily decreasing in explosive magnitude through time into the present. Gradually, eruptive activity became less explosive and more effusive as the volcano began a "dome building" phase, ultimately destined to rebuild the destroyed cone by filling the crater with lava. This has not been uneventful, however. On several occasions, explosive eruptions have intervened to pulverize all or part of the accumulating dome, causing the process to begin anew. Such events have served as reminders to residents over time of the unpredictability of eruption magnitudes and to reinforce the idea that risks are ongoing by nature. Also as time passed, more of the secondary noneruptive threats were identified. These include persistent earthquakes and flood dangers from sedimentation and the debris dam at Spirit Lake.

A distinguishing feature of the risk environment just described is the concept of volcanic sequence. This is the idea that people must face multiple threats from natural forces concentrated during an extended period of time. Such a situation raises the issue of how citizens will adjust to "living with" the volcano. For our concerns in this chapter, an important component of the coexistence issue is: what happens to hazard awareness? More specifically, in 1983—more than three years into St. Helens' eruptive sequence—what do local residents know about the threat? What sorts of knowledge have been accumulated and retained? A common pattern in single impact disasters, even those of a seasonal nature such as floods, hurricanes and tornadoes, is that people gather knowledge in connection with some particular event and subsequently forget the information. Unlike single impact events, a volcanic sequence involves repeated impacts which intuitively suggests that retention would be extended, both because people have more opportunities to acquire information and more frequent opportunities to utilize information. In the two sections which follow, we will explore both the salience of different volcanic threats and the breadth of citizen knowledge of these threats.

Threat Perception

As a means of identifying the volcanic threats which most occupied the minds of local residents, we asked respondents to name the single most important danger posed by Mt. St. Helens. In Toutle, 83.5 percent (86 people) of our sample named flooding, which was followed in frequency of mention by mud-flows (10.7%), explosive eruptions (4.9%), and earthquakes (1.0%). Most Lexington residents also cited flooding as a prime concern (96.0% or 95 people), followed by mud-flows (2.0%), earthquakes (1.0%) and explosive eruptions (1.0%). The identification of flooding as the most important danger in Toutle and Lexington is consistent with threat assessments by authorities. Because flooding can be precipitated by a variety of volcanic events, it is indeed the most likely form of danger. Respondents in Toutle who reported that they worried most about mud-flows and explosive eruptions cited threats that technical experts also identified, although these events are statistically less likely to affect that community than flooding. It is probable that these respondents were remembering the catastrophic damage perpetrated by mud and the blast and heat waves associated with the May 18, 1980 eruption. The fact that in Lexington only four people named threats other than flooding also reflects correct technical information, since distance from the volcano makes it almost impossible—except under the most extreme conditions—that earthquakes, explosive eruptions or true volcanic mud-flows would reach that area.

The above data were generated using an open-ended question format. That is, respondents were asked to name a threat and given no prompting by the interviewer. This procedure allows us to identify the "most important dangers" from the *citizen's* point of reference. It is also useful to understand residents' views of the relative importance of threats that are of concern to scientists and emergency managers. This type of information gives cues regarding the extent to which local residents' threat definition overlaps or is consistent with that of authorities. It has already been pointed out that congruence between citizens' and authorities' beliefs about an environmental danger promotes citizen compliance with official preparedness and emergency response measures (cf. Perry 1985). To obtain such comparative threat data, respondents were given a list of seven volcanic threats and asked to rank them in order of their importance as a significant risk. Table 2 shows the frequency that each of the seven threats was ranked as number one (most dangerous) for each community.

The largest proportion of Toutle respondents (45.6%) cited flooding as the threat of greatest concern among the seven. Mud-flows—which created significant damage during the May 1980 eruptions—were ranked as the number one danger by 35.9 percent of those questioned. Together, these two threats account for the number one rankings of most of the Toutle respondents. Emergency managers would agree that Toutle is subject to mud-flows and floods, though they would emphasize flooding as considerably more likely (in a statistical sense) than mud-flows. It is probable, however, that our respondents do not clearly distinguish between mud-flows and floods; at least they may not make the technical distinction drawn by experts. Volcanic mud-flows tend to produce floods in river systems originating on the cone, but our respondents appear to equate (incorrectly) mud-flows with debris and ash-filled rivers which overflow their banks. If one assumes that those who cited mud-flows as the most significant threat were probably thinking of flooding associated with mud-flows, there is substantial agreement between Toutle residents and technical authorities regarding significant threats.

Table 2

Frequency of Ranking as Number One Threat
(among 7) by Community Residents

	Toutle		Lexington	
Threat	N	%	N	%
Ash fall	11	10.7	2	2.0
Mud-flows	37	35.9	27	27.3
Flooding	47	45.6	67	67.7
Explosive eruptions	6	5.8	3	3.0
Forest fires	1	1.0	0	0.0
Pyroclastic flows	1	1.0	0	0.0
Earthquakes	0	0.0	0	0.0

Ash fall was labelled the most significant volcanic threat by 10.7 percent of Toutle residents. Ash has certainly been a persistent problem for the community since the beginning of the volcanic sequence. However, aside from the eruptions of May and June 1980, ash fall in Toutle is probably best described as "light dustings." Consequently, through most of St. Helens' eruptive sequence accumulated ash has been primarily of concern as sedimentation in rivers or as a danger to machinery and plants, rather than a threat to people or structures (although the latter dangers can be significant in heavy ash falls). From a technical standpoint, then, ash is more a persistent nuisance than a major danger. It is probably inappropriate to characterize the eleven respondents who ranked ash fall first among the dangers as representing any serious disagreement with officials' threat assessments. In the first place, each of these respondents ranked flooding as number two behind ash— suggesting some appreciation of flood threats. Second, ash fall was not mentioned by any of the respondents when asked about threats in the open-ended question format. Thus, it is possible that the presence of ash fall on a list of threats reminded people of its nuisance value, and in endorsing it they were acknowledging what they saw as a continuing or frequent threat as an alternative to first citing an event of lower probability (floods or mud-flows) that might actually produce more damage. This interpretation is consistent with research by Slovic and his colleagues which indicates that some people tend to attribute greater negative consequence to threats which are judged to occur frequently (Slovic et al., 1980).

Finally, a few Toutle residents endorsed explosive eruptions (5.8%), forest fires (1.0%) or pyroclastic flows (1.0%) as the most significant volcanic threat. An explosive eruption that would directly impact Toutle would have to be of an extremely large magnitude, much larger than that considered likely by authorities in the spring of 1983. Also, Toutle's distance from the volcanic cone makes it highly improbable that pyroclastic flows would constitute a direct threat. Although slightly more feasible, eruption-ignited forest fires are not seen as a major threat to Toutle by technical experts.

The threat rankings by Lexington residents, like those of their Toutle counterparts, are concentrated in two categories. Flooding was ranked as the most significant threat by 67.7 percent of the Lexington respondents. The next highest proportion of respondents (27.3%) named mud-flows as the number one danger. Although Crandell and Mullineaux (1978) indicate that some historical precedent exists, technical risk assessment indicates that mud-flows of sufficient magnitude to reach Lexington via the Toutle and Cowlitz Rivers are unlikely. If one assumes that Lexington respondents probably also confuse mud-flows with floods, then the twenty-seven people who cited mud-flows are likely to have been focusing upon debris and ashclogged flood waters. If this is the case, 95 percent of Lexington residents can be classified as agreeing with authorities by identifying flooding as a primary threat to their community. Only 2.0 percent mentioned ash fall—more accurately seen as a nuisance—and 3.0 percent named explosive eruptions—which are unlikely to have direct impacts on the community.

On the whole, then, our data tell us that the threat perceptions of Toutle and Lexington residents are highly consistent with the threat assessments of scientists and emergency managers. Indeed, citizens and technical professionals seem to have developed a shared definition of the situational dangers associated with the Mt. St. Helens volcano. In the field of hazard management, this is a relatively rare achievement. Citizen perceptions of hazards, even after elaborate hazard awareness campaigns, routinely differ from those of authorities and technical experts both in the case of natural and technological threats. Generally, citizens have less concern than authorities about dangers associated with natural hazards, particularly floods, tornadoes and hurricanes (cf. McPherson and Saarinen 1977; Davenport and Waterstone 1979; Sims and Bauman 1972; Parker and Harding 1979). On the other hand, there are indications that the public is more concerned about dangers associated with some technological hazards, particularly nuclear technology (Perry 1985; Dierkes et al. 1980; Van Arsdol et al. 1964; Slovic et al. 1980a).

In the case of Mt. St. Helens the congruence of threat assessments by local residents and technical experts seems to have resulted from the continuing salience of the volcanic activity and the shared base of information upon which judgments of the severity of the threat have been derived. These two factors, in turn, depend upon several conditions. The first of these is the extended period of time that volcanic activity has remained an intense and imminent threat to the communities studied. Time is necessary for affected residents to reach agreement with technical experts, but is not in itself sufficient to insure that such agreement will actually emerge. The extended threat, together with periodic eruptions generates a second condition: continuing coverage of the volcano by news media, which has kept the volcano threat salient in the public eye. A third condition may be found in continuing impacts of volcanicity on the economic base of the region and the local communities. Periods of threatened economic collapse due to loss of tourism, occasional boosts related to salvage logging operations, as well as times of anticipated prosperity associated with potential (or planned) tourism have served to link the volcanic activity to citizens' pocketbooks. Fourth, governmental attention to noneruptive threats—like the Spirit Lake debris dam, which sometimes seemed more dangerous than eruptive threats—both reinforced the salience of the volcano and reminded citizens that the threat environment could expand over time.

Finally, the last factor promoting congruence, and undoubtedly the most important, was the assignment of high priority to public education by the Cowlitz County Department of Emergency Services. In hazard management, public education serves two important functions: it provides technically accurate threat information to citizens and it explains the reasoning behind the authorities' assessment of danger. Although hazards researchers have concluded that public education campaigns do not convince citizens of the need for attention to environmental hazards, it should be noted that many such campaigns have failed to teach people how to evaluate threats. The education programs developed by Cowlitz County achieved a balanced emphasis on technical information and threat evaluation. The County public education efforts have been sustained over the years and involve three thrusts: the development of brochures distributed via newspapers and on request; the maintenance of high visibility of emergency management staff through frequent personal contacts with the public; and the effective utilization of mass media as dissemination channels via newspaper articles and "informational spots" on local radio and cable television. The outcome of these efforts has been that local emergency management authorities informed citizens about volcanic threats, established themselves as credible technical experts and "taught" people how to evaluate threats. These three achievements may be seen as the primary bases of creating agreement between citizens and authorities regarding environmental threats, both specifically at Mt. St. Helens and in hazard management generally.

Threat Consequences

While congruence about threat identification is an important first step toward effective emergency response, identifying the events likely to create danger represents a fairly general level of understanding regarding environmental threats. From both the applied management and scientific perspectives, it is also valuable to obtain a measure of the depth of citizens' knowledge about threats that they do recognize. One way researchers can characterize depth is in terms of the extent to which citizens can accurately name consequences of target environmental threats. That is, one asks people to describe the mechanisms through which the threat impinges upon themselves and their property (especially upon the "constructed" environment). To answer such a question requires that a person recognize the threat, possess at least minimal understanding of the actions through which it operates, and be able to link these features of the threat with social patterns to visualize outcomes.

As a practical matter it is necessary to restrict our attention to two specific volcanic threats. In selecting two threats from those listed in Table 2, an attempt was made to account for event probability and likely scope of potential negative consequences. Mud-flows were combined with flooding to form the first targeted threat. The logic for combining these two threats rests upon our data and observations which indicate that respondents tend not to draw a sharp distinction between these two phenomena, but instead use both terms to refer to high water filled with ash and debris. Mud-flow/floods constitute a major threat to both Toutle and Lexington in the sense that the potential for damage is extremely high, even though the actual frequency of the events have been relatively low throughout the current volcanic sequence.

The second threat targeted for measurement is ash fall. Technically speaking, the level of *potential* damage from ash fall is great. Throughout the current eruptive sequence, however, Toutle and Lexington have experienced largely light ash falls. Our interest in ash fall lies not so much in its potential for disruption but in the fact that it is a volcanic threat which has been felt in each community several times throughout the eruptive sequence. Thus, in the experience of local residents, ash fall has been a high frequency threat associated with mild to moderate negative consequences.

The structure of our questioning of respondents regarding the consequences of each threat was open-ended. People were simply asked to name any consequences they could think of that were caused by ash fall and also by mud-flow/flooding. This format forced respondents to rely entirely on their own knowledge without any benefit of cues from the interviewer. Table 3 enumerates the consequences named for ash fall and mud-flow/floods in each community. Since each respondent had the opportunity to mention any (or all) of the consequences recorded in the left-hand column, the percent figures shown tell us what fraction of all respondents from the relevant community named each consequence.

Table 3

Identification of Consequence of Ash Fall
and Mud-flow/Floods by Community

	Toutle[1]		Lexington[2]	
Ash Fall Consequences	N	%	N	%
None mentioned	0	0.0	3	3.0
Personal health danger	49	47.6	45	45.5
Block roads	42	40.8	22	22.2
Reduce visibility	10	9.7	4	4.0
Building damage	99	96.1	68	68.7
Kill plants	22	21.4	29	29.3
Machinery damage	38	36.9	52	52.5
Interrupt electricity/phones	18	17.5	19	19.2
Mud-flow/Flood Consequences				
None mentioned	0	0.0	5	5.1
Building damage	101	98.1	98	99.0
Drown people	26	25.2	23	23.2
Destroy roads/bridges	18	17.5	12	12.1
Destroy personal property	16	15.5	30	30.3
Public health threats	11	10.7	8	8.1
Deposit debris	9	8.7	2	2.0
Interrupt electricity/phones	10	9.7	8	8.1

[1]Percentages for each consequence in Toutle are based on a total sample size of 103.
[2]Percentages for each consequence in Lexington are based on a total sample size of 99.

It is interesting to note at the outset that every respondent from Toutle and all except three from Lexington were able to name at least one consequence of ash fall. The consequences named for ash fall may be grouped into three categories: damages to people, damages to property and interference with social affairs. Approximately half of the respondents in each community named a personal health danger when asked about the consequences of ash fall. Specific items mentioned in this category included breathing difficulty, eye irritations and skin conditions.

Damages to property were often cited as ash fall consequences by residents in each community. Damage to buildings or structures was the most prominently mentioned event, named by 96.1 percent of the Toutle respondents and 68.7 percent of those living in Lexington. Most of these citations were to roofs collapsing under the weight of ash, but also mentioned were blocked chimneys, nonfunctioning sash-type sliding windows and blocked gutters and drains. The second most frequently named type of property damage was to machinery (36.9% in Toutle, 52.5% in Lexington). The majority of these respondents cited automobile engines, painting and farm equipment, chain saws, and gasoline engines which powered water pumps or electrical generators as the targets of machinery-related damage. The third type of property damage stemming from volcanic ash noted by our respondents was plant and vegetation destruction. This outcome was identified by 21.4 percent of Toutle residents and 29.3 percent of Lexington residents.

Finally, residents of both study sites mentioned three kinds of potential ash fall damage whose major consequence was the restriction of human mobility or communication in some fashion. For the most part, these types of consequences were the least frequently mentioned by respondents in both communities. The only exception to this statement can be found among Toutle residents where 40.8 percent named blocked roads as a consequence of ash fall. Only 22.2 percent of Lexington respondents cited the same consequence. It is probable that the mounds of ash that virtually closed all roads into Toutle during the summer 1980 eruptions made a lasting impression on local inhabitants. More equal proportions of Toutle (17.5%) and Lexington (19.2%) respondents listed interruptions of electrical or telephone service as possible outcomes of ash fall. Reductions in visibility were the least frequently mentioned ash fall consequences, noted by 9.7 percent of Toutle residents and 4.0 percent of those living in Lexington.

From these data, one can construct an aggregate picture of the respondents' beliefs about ash fall consequences in each community. They tell us which outcomes come to mind, collectively speaking, when citizens think of volcanic ash. In Toutle, the majority think of building damage, with personal health outcomes being a distant second concern. Blocked roads and machinery damage conclude the kinds of ash consequences cited by proportions in excess of one-third of the Toutle residents. Three of the same four consequences were also most often mentioned by Lexington residents, although their rank order by frequency is different. Like Toutle dwellers, the largest proportion of Lexington residents cited building damage when asked to describe consequences of ash fall. More than half of the Lexington respondents associated ash with machinery damage, followed by dangers to human health and safety and damage to plants and vegetation. This similarity of ash fall concerns in two communities which lie at different distances from the volcanic cone deserves brief comment. It is true that the severity and the nature of the "mix" of volcanic threats which bear upon a place changes as distance from the cone increases. Thus, one should expect that hazard awareness and perceived vulnerability would be different for the same threat—for example, ash fall—at different distances from the volcano. As a corollary, our data indicate that to the extent that two communities are exposed to the same threat and are subject to the same emergency management information (education) networks—in this case the Cowlitz County Department of Emergency Services—their threat perceptions will be similar without regard to geographic location. As we will now see, this conclusion also fits our data on mud-flow/flood threats.

The lower portion of Table 3 lists the mud-flow/flood consequences identified by Toutle and Lexington respondents. The most striking finding here is that almost every person questioned in Toutle (98.1%) and Lexington (99.0%) named damage to buildings as a significant consequence of mud-flow/ flooding. The primary concern here was with private homes; none of the respondents mentioned public buildings and only a handful indicated that farm structures were endangered. Considerably smaller proportions of respondents mentioned two other types of property damage likely to result from the impact of mud-flows and flooding. The potential loss of personal property—furniture, keepsakes, small items of special value—was cited by 15.5 percent of Toutle residents and 30.3 percent of Lexington residents. Damages associated with debris deposited by mud-flow/floods were mentioned by small numbers of respondents in each community (8.7% in Toutle and 2.0% in Lexington). In the case of debris, Toutle residents most often mentioned water-borne logs, rock and ash (which literally buried buildings after the May 1980 eruptions), while Lexington respondents tended to mention mud and silt deposits.

Direct risks to human life such as drowning were cited by 25.2 percent of Toutle respondents and 23.2 percent of those living in Lexington. Similar proportions of Toutle (10.7%) and Lexington (8.1%) residents also associated public health threats with mud-flow/flooding. In almost every case, this concern was manifest as a fear of contaminated drinking water.

As was the case when we inquired about ash fall, our respondents described two consequences of mud-flow/flooding that can be grouped together as factors which interrupt or restrict social interaction. In Toutle, 17.5 percent of those questioned identified the destruction of roads and bridges as a significant consequence, which would create the problem of physical isolation. Similarly, 12.1 percent of Lexington respondents cited the destruction of roads and bridges. Isolation in a different sense--through breaks in telephone and electrical service—was mentioned as a consequence of mud-flow/flooding by 9.7 percent of those questioned in Toutle and 8.1 percent of Lexington respondents.

As was the case for ash fall, there is some correspondence between the two study communities regarding citations of specific consequences of mud-flow/floods. The four most frequently mentioned consequences were the same for each community, although the rank order by frequency of mention varies. Nearly every respondent in Toutle and Lexington named building damage when asked about specific outcomes of mud-flow/floods. In Toutle, the collective vision of mud-flow/flood consequences was completed by threats to personal safety, destruction of roads and bridges, and loss of personal property. After building damage, Lexington residents most commonly cited personal property loss, personal safety and bridge and road damage as consequences of mud-flow/flooding.

These data raise an interesting point when we explore what people define as specific consequences of ash fall and mud-flow/flood threats associated with the volcanic sequence at Mt. St. Helens. The items listed in Table 3 tell us about the range of events citizens have learned to associate with each threat and the frequency of mention of each event tells us how prevalent concern regarding that outcome is in each town. Research by Kahneman and Tversky (1981) suggests that people's retrieval of information from memory is influenced by its availability, which is in turn affected by salience and vividness. Thus, data suggest that people living in Toutle and Lexington have learned about—and think most often about-outcomes of the ash fall and mud-flow/flood threats that deal with property damage rather than personal safety risks or interruptions of social interaction. The evidence for this claim rests on three observations. First, our respondents spontaneously thought of a preponderance of property damage related events when asked to name threat consequences; three of the seven consequences listed collectively for each threat were directly related to property and two others were indirectly related to property. Second, when we compile the four most frequently mentioned consequences for each threat, half of the events named deal with property damage. Third, in both communities and for each threat, the most frequently named consequence was building damage.

One may conclude that at this stage of Mt. St. Helens' volcanic sequence, people associate volcanicity largely with threats to property. As we will see in subsequent chapters, this finding has important implications for the kinds of coping patterns citizens employ and for the ways in which emergency managers go about creating community disaster preparedness. This condition might also indicate that citizens have developed confidence in the eruption detection and warning systems devised by federal, state and local authorities. Confident that such systems will provide adequate forewarning to protect lives, citizens may have focused upon the question of property preservation. In any event, the data presented to this point have documented residents' beliefs about the range of ash fall and mud-flow/flood threats and have developed an aggregate "picture" of expected consequences of each threat. This measure can be used as an indicator of the "depth" of each respondent's beliefs about volcano threats. A further assessment of hazard awareness can be obtained by counting the number of consequences people were able to list for each threat. Table 4 shows the number of consequences listed for ash fall, mud-flow/floods, and the total for each community.

With regard to ash fall consequences, the number of consequences named by each respondent ranges from one to three. Knowledge of ash fall consequences was extensive in both communities, but substantially more Toutle (74.8%) than Lexington (57.6%) respondents were able to list three consequences. Only three individuals, all residents of Lexington, were unable to name any consequences. The number of mud-flow/flood consequences cited ranges from one to three, with the proportion of respondents able to identify three consequences being greater in Toutle (39.8%) than in Lexington (24.2%). The modal category for number of consequences listed was three in Toutle versus one in Lexington. Overall, it should also be pointed out that aggregate knowledge of the consequences of mud-flow/floods is lower than for ash fall. Substantially greater proportions of people in both communities could name more consequences of ash fall than mud-flow/ floods. Also, with respect to both ash fall and mud-flow/floods, the depth of the residents' beliefs is greater in Toutle than in Lexington. This circumstance possibly reflects a greater salience in Toutle which may be a function of more frequent direct experience with the threats in that town. Finally, one can combine the consequences listed for each threat to obtain an index of general beliefs about volcanicity at Mt. St. Helens. Such an index tells us the extent to which citizens have developed specific beliefs about the two most prominent (from a technical risk analysis standpoint) threats posed by the volcano at this stage of the eruptive sequence. The lower third of Table 4 shows that the number of consequences named by Toutle

Table 4

Number of Different Threat Consequences
Identified by Community

	Toutle		Lexington	
Ash Fall	*N*	*%*	*N*	*%*
Zero	0	0.0	3	3.0
One	5	4.9	10	10.1
Two	21	20.4	29	29.3
Three	77	74.8	57	57.6
Mud-flow/Flood				
Zero	0	0.0	0	0.0
One	36	35.0	40	40.0
Two	26	25.2	35	35.4
Three	41	39.8	24	24.2
TOTAL: Ash Fall with Mud-flow/Flood				
Zero	0	0.0	0	0.0
One	0	0.0	1	1.0
Two	4	3.9	7	7.1
Three	18	17.5	18	18.2
Four	19	18.4	34	34.3
Five	21	20.4	18	18.2
Six	41	39.8	21	21.2

respondents ranges from two to six, with the greatest proportion (39.8%) naming six. Only four respondents listed just two consequences, and the remaining cases are fairly evenly spread over the categories of three, four and five impacts. The range for Lexington residents varies between one and six consequences, with the largest proportion (34.3%) naming four consequences. Approximately 40 percent of the respondents could identify either five or six impacts, while the remaining quarter listed three or four.

Now that we have devised a general index of people's extent of beliefs about the threats posed by Mt. St. Helens, it is important to gain a systematic perspective on factors which contribute to these beliefs. Our data clearly show individual variability in the depth of these beliefs; some respondents mention more consequences than others. Some of the variability can be attributed to place of residence. On the whole, slightly greater proportions of Toutle than Lexington respondents can name larger numbers of consequences. When ash fall and mud-flow/flood threats are combined, however, the between-community differences are not substantial—in fact, differences within the sites are nearly as great as those between Toutle and Lexington. This suggests that variables other than simple geographic location must be examined to understand why some people have developed a more elaborate system of beliefs about the volcano threat than others.

Factors in Accurate Threat Knowledge

The way that the concept of depth of threat knowledge has been developed here differs somewhat from the way hazard awareness is usually treated. Hazard awareness may be seen as a global idea, representing an individual's knowledge that some hazard impinges either upon him personally or upon some place (location). Typical ways of measuring awareness involve simply asking respondents to either report whether they know they are subject to a particular hazard ("Are hurricanes a problem where you live?") or respondents who are known to be subject to a hazard are asked to describe the probability of an impact ("How likely is it that flooding would affect you?"). For the most part, such measures yield information about citizens' abilities to *recognize* hazards.

Our strategy for dealing with threat knowledge *assumes* that citizens recognize the hazards and *measures* their ability to describe particular facets of the threat in the form of impact consequences. Thus we obtain a relatively specific measure of what is generally characterized as hazard awareness. In the case of Mt. St. Helens, this approach is made feasible by distinctive features of the volcano threat. These include repeated exposure to eruptive activity over a relatively defined period of time, time for citizens to learn about the threat, and availability of information about the threat. This approach has the advantage of measuring the residents' awareness of the specific threats that affect them directly, instead of being a check on their ability to recognize an event that may affect them only indirectly.

This difference in the specificity of referent regarding awareness implies that one should be cautious in drawing generalizations from the Mt. St. Helens' data. These findings apply to (and can be compared with) situations where awareness was operationalized as "knowledge of consequences" and in settings which approximate the threat environment of volcanos or other multiple impact disasters. The relationships obtained here may not generalize well to single impact disasters or to cases where hazard awareness is measured in a more general fashion. In spite of these differences in emphasis and referent, however, we can still look to the scientific literature on hazard awareness for clues regarding which variables are correlated with our measure of threat knowledge. This literature alerts us to the idea that four classes of variables appear to influence the level of knowledge an individual possesses about environmental threats: experience with the threat, beliefs about personal vulnerability, personal planning activities and social variables.

Volcano Experience

Historically it has been believed that personal experience with a disaster event captures the individual's attention, makes a lasting impression and predisposes the person to attend to the underlying hazard. When dealing with a volcanic sequence the meaning of experience may be defined in two contexts: the period prior to the eruptive sequence and the period of the eruptive sequence itself. Before a given eruptive sequence begins, people's direct experience of volcanic threats would be determined by prior eruptions of that volcano or by prior eruptions during past periods of residence near other active volcanos. Our respondents at Mt. St. Helens were geographically stable—about half reported living at their current address for more than twenty years—and had not previously lived near active volcanos. Since the 1980 eruptions of Mt. St. Helens marked its first activity in 123 years, before the current eruptive sequence all of our respondents reported no previous experience with volcanic threats. One can also consider experience within the context of a given eruptive sequence, which is the case for which our data have bearing. Interestingly, however, since March 27, 1980, all citizens in our samples have "directly experienced" to some varying degree one or more eruptions of Mt. St. Helens.

Perhaps the most commonly utilized measure of experience is to ask people to report whether they have been exposed to the impact of a given disaster agent—a hurricane, tornado, volcanic eruption or flood, for example. Social scientific studies show a variety of conclusions about disaster experience measured in this way. It is known that people who have experience in the recent past are more likely to acknowledge that a threat exists and to describe the probability of disaster impact as high (Whyte 1980, 30). Experience is also positively correlated with citizens' propensities to comply with disaster warning messages (Drabek and Boggs 1968, 442). Unfortunately, general measures of experience are not necessarily correlated with the possession of accurate information about a threat (cf. Windham et al. 1977, 49). Although experience may motivate people to seek additional information, there is always the chance they will tap inappropriate sources (e.g., relatives' or friends' conventional wisdom), thereby obtaining technically incorrect data. Another way of translating experience into incorrect beliefs occurs when people equate their most recent disaster experience with the "worst case" or "typical case" events (Quarantelli 1977). Burton and Kates (1964, 429) were among the first researchers to acknowledge that ". . . the effect of experience as a determinant of technically accurate hazard perception is considerably blurred." Their work continues to suggest that key research concern should be with the way people interpret experience, rather than with the presence or absence of experience itself.

Because the general measures of experience used in other studies yields a constant value, that is, everyone living nearby has "experienced" one or more eruptions, there is no variance between people on the experience dimension. This situation forces the investigator to look critically at the concept of experience to discern which features of being exposed to an event are relevant to the acquisition of threat knowledge. Using this approach we also embrace the suggestion by Burton and Kates to consider people's interpretations of disaster experience.

One tactic for exploring the idea of experience within the context of volcanic eruptions is to ask "experience with what?" A volcanic sequence involves multiple eruptive events and consequently the dissemination of multiple warning messages asking for compliance with emergency measures—in the case of Mt. St. Helens, usually evacuation. One might reason, then, that people who have complied with evacuation warnings in the past would be more sensitive to the seriousness of the danger and correspondingly more motivated to accumulate information. We focus here upon information about the threat as distinct from information about emergency measures. Our data from Mt. St. Helens do not bear out this particular reasoning. People who evacuated in response to the cataclysmic eruption (May 18, 1980) were not able to list significantly more threat consequences than those who did not evacuate. Nor are people who have evacuated in response to warnings since the cataclysmic eruption any more knowledgeable about the threat than those who have not evacuated. Finally, the total number of times a person has evacuated since the volcanic sequence began was not related to possession of accurate threat knowledge. These data indicate that, while past warning compliance may predict future compliance (Perry 1985), it is not useful in helping to distinguish people with extensive threat knowledge from those who are less informed.

A second dimension of experience particularly relevant in a volcanic sequence is the idea of damages linked to eruptive activity. It has been argued that variation in the way people understand threats may be due in part to historical differences in damage experienced (Burton and Kates 1964, 417). Presumably, citizens who sustain higher levels of damage have a qualitatively different experience of the threat than those who feel little or no direct damage. Empirical studies suggest that people who experience high levels of damage remember the event longer, show higher probabilities of sustaining negative psychological outcomes, experience higher levels of social network disruption, and make different demands upon the restorative social system (Barton 1969; Haas et al. 1977, 30-37; Perry 1985, 111-113). A.F.C. Wallace (1956) has reported that extensive property destruction is associated with serious negative psychological consequences for victims, including preoccupation with the threat-agent and changes in world view.

Since sustaining disaster damage appears to be linked to a variety of outcomes, it is necessary to explore how it may be related to the possession of threat knowledge. Drawing upon existing research, one can construct a logical chain which links these two variables. First, it can be reasoned that the experience of damage leads the individual to seek to avoid damage in the future. Then, the desire to avoid harm motivates the person to acquire information about the threat in an effort to understand what dangers are present and what may be done about them. Finally, as part of the information seeking process, one would expect that the individual would accumulate higher levels of threat knowledge, particularly regarding impact consequences. To the extent that this logic is correct, we would expect a positive correlation between level of damage sustained and threat knowledge.

Table 5 shows level of threat knowledge by the degree of damage sustained for Toutle and Lexington residents. In keeping with the literature cited above, our measure of damage relied upon citizen perceptions and beliefs rather than "objective" measures such as dollar costs. On the level of the individual household, dollar values are often inadequate indicators of emotional values associated with possessions. Our subjects were asked to rate the cumulative damage they sustained from volcanicity at Mt. St. Helens since the eruptive sequence began in March 1980. One difference between the communities is immediately evident in our data. Most Toutle residents reported either moderate or severe damage (only slightly less than 10% characterized damage as none or slight), while most Lexington residents rated damage as none, slight or moderate (about 5% of these respondents defined damage as severe). These differentials in citizen perceptions of damage extensiveness are consistent with authorities' estimates of aggregate damages to each community. An important qualification of our data analyses is demanded by this condition: We know little about the threat knowledge of Toutle residents who reported little damage and of Lexington residents who reported severe damage.

Turning to the data in the body of Table 5, it must be acknowledged that level of sustained damage is not strongly correlated with depth of threat knowledge in either community. In Toutle, a smaller proportion of people who experienced severe damage, compared to those reporting moderate damage, could name only one or two threat consequences. More people who believed damage was severe (42.9%) named three or four consequences than those with moderate damage (27.3%). However, 68.2 percent of the respondents citing moderate damage could name five or more consequences compared with 55.1 percent of those with severe damage. When we consider the Toutle data as a whole, we see virtually no relationship between sustained damage and threat knowledge.

Table 5

Threat Knowledge by Level of Damage Sustained

		Damage Sustained					
		None or Slight		Moderate		Severe	
Site	*Number of Consequences*	*N*	*%*	*N*	*%*	*N*	*%*
	One or two	1	10.0	2	4.5	1	2.0
Toutle	Three or four	4	40.0	12	27.3	21	42.9
	Five or six	5	50.0	30	68.2	27	55.1
	One or two	4	7.7	4	9.8	0	0.0
Lexington	Three or four	29	55.8	19	46.3	4	66.7
	Five or six	19	36.5	18	43.9	2	33.3

While most cases are concentrated on the opposite end of the damage continuum, the Lexington data largely echo the results obtained in Toutle. In this situation, relatively similar proportions of people who sustained little damage versus moderate damage were able to name one or two (7.7 versus 9.8%), three or four (55.8 versus 46.3%), and five or more threat consequences (36.5 versus 43.9%). Thus, among Lexington respondents, knowing whether a person experienced little or moderate damage does not enhance our ability to predict how many threat consequences he or she can name. Looking at the Toutle and Lexington data as a whole, one must characterize the magnitude of the correlation between damage and threat knowledge as low.

These data cast some doubt upon the adequacy of the reasoning offered above to link damage with threat knowledge. It is indeed likely that victims do view threats differently than non-victims; this proposition rests upon much empirical support. And, victims may well seek information to protect themselves in the future more ardently than non-victims. Although less directly supported by research, it is widely reported that disaster events initiate heightened information seeking among those subject to the impact (Perry 1985, 67). The inference that this gathering of information necessarily leads to a more extensive knowledge of threat consequences, however, is apparently faulty. It may be that victims focus upon accumulating knowledge of specific protective measures, acquiring knowledge of warning signals, evacuation routes and shelter destination *without* necessarily learning the specific consequences of ash falls and mud-flow/flooding. In a subsequent chapter, we will more specifically address the etiology of such specific adjustments to the volcano threat.

Much of the reasoning which attempts to connect disaster impact experience with either hazard awareness or threat knowledge rests upon the idea that the event has some underlying social psychological significance for individuals which is somehow transformed into knowledge or action. We have seen, however, that creating long chains of logic based upon this assumption to link experience with knowledge does not result in the predicted empirical outcomes. As an alternative to this strategy, one might focus upon the experience of disaster impacts as the individual's basis for assigning importance to the threat. One would then infer that the more important a threat is, the more likely the person is to possess knowledge about it. The individual uses disaster experiences when integrating beliefs about the hazard into his particular world view, that is, when assigning the threat a "priority value" for attention relative to other issues with which the person must deal on a daily basis.

This logic is particularly well adapted to the problem of volcanic eruptive sequences. Here, the individual's experiences of eruptions are personal, recent, and often numerous. Because these events intrude upon the individual's life and are not subject to human control, they intermittently demand attention. Over time, people are forced to attach a psychological meaning to such events; if for no other reason than because ignoring them implicitly involves accepting a risk to personal safety and property. In this way, the threat from the volcano becomes integrated into the priorities of day-to-day living. Social psychologically speaking, when an event is assigned a relatively high priority among the constellation of daily demands upon a person, it is said that the event is *salient*. The essence of our argument is that experience produces salience and salience should be positively correlated with threat knowledge.

Table 6 shows level of threat knowledge by salience of the volcano for each study site. Salience was measured by asking respondents to report about the extent to which they were concerned about threats of Mt. St. Helens on a daily basis. People who said that they thought about the threats "often" or "continuously" were classified as exhibiting "high" salience. Those who claimed to think about the threats "periodically" were assigned moderate salience, and people who reported thinking of the threats "rarely" or "never" were said to exhibit low salience.

The data for Toutle show a positive correlation of moderate strength between salience and level of threat knowledge. Looking at the category representing greatest knowledge (those who named five or six consequences), we see a steady increase in the proportion of citizens herein as we move across salience levels from low (44.0%) through moderate (50.0%) to high (72.2%). Thus, nearly three-quarters of Toutle residents exhibiting high salience showed a high level of threat knowledge compared with half of those with moderate salience and less than half of those with low salience. Also, three of the four respondents who could name only one or two consequences fell into the low salience category. The Lexington data also show a steady increase in the proportion of people with the most extensive threat knowledge as salience increases: 18.2 percent at low salience, 51.7 percent at the moderate level, and 61.5 percent when salience is high. The majority of people for whom salience was low were able to name three or four consequences, while the modal category for those with high salience was five or more consequences.

Table 6

Threat Knowledge by Salience of Volcano Hazard

		Salience of Volcano					
		Low		*Moderate*		*High*	
Site	*Number of Consequences*	*N*	*%*	*N*	*%*	*N*	*%*
	One or two	3	12.0	0	0.0	1	1.9
Toutle	Three or four	11	44.0	12	50.0	14	25.9
	Five or six	11	44.0	12	50.0	39	72.2
	One or two	4	9.1	0	0.0	4	15.4
Lexington	Three or four	32	72.7	14	48.3	6	23.1
	Five or six	8	18.2	15	51.7	16	61.5

In summary, these data support the hypothesis that as the salience of the volcano increases, so does the individual's knowledge of threat consequences. One should be cautious about generalizing this finding to other types of natural hazard settings, however. Residents of Toutle and Lexington have had an opportunity to experience the disaster agent on a firsthand basis. Moreover, this personal experience has been relatively frequent. As the time between events or opportunities for exposure increases, one would expect fewer cases of moderate or high salience. Hence, salience could become a "constant" at the low value and its predictive efficacy regarding threat knowledge would correspondingly decline. It may be expected that the hypothesis would hold fairly well for seasonal threats-floods, tornadoes or hurricanes—but not as well for less frequent events such as earthquakes or tsunamis in the United States.

Perceived Vulnerability

The idea of perceived vulnerability is important in understanding how citizens think about natural hazards. An environmental hazard introduces "uncertainty" into the lives of those subject to it. That is, in the event of disaster impact there is a chance of damage—a risk to the personal safety or property of an individual (family). There is uncertainty, then, in two broad senses: Neither the time nor consequences of an impact are precisely known. People have come to rely upon institutionalized mechanisms (such as detection and warning systems) to reduce uncertainty about the timing of impacts. Reducing uncertainty about the consequences of impact is generally handled through the adoption of mitigation and preparedness measures; by individuals, by governments, or sometimes by both.

For an individual, the adoption of protective measures is preceded by awareness of the risk. Decision analysts have used the term *risk assessment* to refer to the process by which people make decisions about uncertain events that are potentially harmful. Rowe (1977, 25) describes this process as being built around three activities: risk identification, risk assessment and risk reduction. Risk identification involves the "reduction of descriptive uncertainty" through such activities as research, screening and monitoring whereby the individual recognizes and acknowledges potential environmental dangers (Kates 1976). Risk assessment focuses upon individual *beliefs* about potential personal or property injury that would accrue from a disaster impact. Withey (1962, 104) emphasizes that once people recognize a threat, they develop beliefs about ". . . the probability of the impending event occurring and the severity, to the individual, of such a development." Social psychologically, people are deciding, given the existence of a threat, what it *means* for them: "Am I vulnerable?" Finally, risk reduction involves determining what can feasibly be done to reduce the danger or uncertainty to some level that is "acceptable" to the individual (Janis and Mann 1977, 38).

The first part of this chapter addressed risk identification at Mt. St. Helens. Now, and more extensively in Chapter 3, we will examine risk assessment. Chapter four focuses on risk reduction.

Individual beliefs about vulnerability (or perceived personal risk) have been shown to be relevant to a variety of disaster behaviors. People who believe themselves vulnerable have been found to be more likely to comply with warning messages (Menninger 1952; Williams and Fritz 1954; Perry 1979), to engage in adaptive planning (Perry and Mushkatel 1984), and to recognize threats (Burton 1972). It has also been suggested that the way citizens personally define the "catastrophic potential" of different threats should be considered in governmental decisions regarding how resources should be allocated to the management of hazards (Slovic et al. 1980a, 207-209). Given knowledge of these linkages, it is possible to construct an argument that perceived vulnerability should be positively correlated with threat knowledge. People who see themselves as vulnerable to a particular threat in a sense are acknowledging considerable uncertainty about their safety relative to that threat. Sociologists who embrace Emergent Norm Theory have indicated that when uncertainty about appropriate ("normative") behaviors exist, people engage in social milling—an information seeking process (cf. Turner and Killian 1972; Gillespie and Perry 1976). Thus, it is suggested that when individuals feel vulnerable to a threat, they seek to clarify, for themselves, the nature and extent of their vulnerability. One would expect that people would explore what consequences are possible, how likely they are, their probable personal impacts, and possible strategies for protection. Through this process of social milling, citizens should accumulate threat knowledge. It can therefore be inferred that the higher the level of perceived vulnerability, the more intense the milling process, and the greater the extent of threat knowledge.

There are two distinct aspects of the concept of perceived vulnerability: that of risk to personal safety and risk to property. Earlier in this chapter, it was noted that when asked to enumerate impact consequences, respondents from both communities named more events associated with property damage than personal safety. It was speculated that this may indicate that our respondents considered eruptions to be a greater risk to property than to people. The distinction between these two components was maintained when measuring perceived vulnerability. Respondents were alternately asked to characterize the danger posed to property and personal safety by the volcanic activity at Mt. St. Helens. Responses to each question were classified along a continuum ranging from slight, through moderate, to severe perceived risk.

Table 7 shows levels of threat knowledge by perceived risk to personal safety for each community. These data tend to bear out our earlier speculation that citizens were less concerned about personal safety risks: only 15.5 percent of the Toutle sample and 9.1 percent of Lexington residents defined personal safety risks as severe. Indeed, the modal category for safety risk was "slight" for respondents in both Toutle (46.6%) and Lexington (55.6%). These data also show a positive relationship of moderate strength between perception of personal safety risk and threat knowledge. In Toutle, the proportion of respondents who could name five or more threat consequences *increases* as we move from slight (52.1%), to moderate (64.1%), to severe (75.0%) perceived risk. Conversely, the proportions of people who can name *fewer* consequences declines as perceived risk increases. The same relationship is

---

Table 7

Threat Knowledge by Perceived Risk to
Personal Safety and to Property

		Risk to Personal Safety					
	Number of	*Slight*		*Moderate*		*Severe*	
Site	*Consequences*	*N*	*%*	*N*	*%*	*N*	*%*
	One or two	3	6.3	1	2.6	0	0.0
Toutle	Three or four	20	41.7	13	33.3	4	25.0
	Five or six	25	52.1	25	64.1	12	75.0
	One or two	6	10.9	0	0.0	2	22.2
Lexington	Three or four	37	67.3	12	34.3	3	33.3
	Five or six	12	21.8	23	65.7	4	44.4
		Risk to Property					
	One or two	3	13.0	1	3.0	0	0.0
Toutle	Three or four	11	47.8	14	42.4	12	25.5
	Five or six	9	39.1	18	54.5	35	74.5
	One or two	2	7.7	1	3.4	5	11.4
Lexington	Three or four	22	84.6	15	51.7	15	34.1
	Five or six	2	7.7	13	44.8	24	54.5

present in the Lexington data, although the small number of respondents in the severe risk category makes it difficult to generalize about that category. It remains, however, that only 21.8 percent of those who defined risk as slight could name five or more threat consequences versus 65.7 percent of those for whom risk was felt to be moderate. Most of the respondents who believed risk was slight (67.3%) were able to name only three or four consequences. The bulk of respondents defining risk as moderate named five or six consequences, about one-third named three or four consequences, and none were limited to naming only one or two consequences.

Table 7 also shows the cross-tabulation of threat knowledge by perceived risk to property. It is interesting to note that in both communities there is a more even spread of respondents across the three categories of property risk, although the modal category for Toutle and Lexington was "severe" risk. It is clear that dangers to property from Mt. St. Helens are of a greater concern to local residents at this point than dangers to personal safety. These data show a strong positive correlation between perceived property risk and threat knowledge in each study site. The proportion of respondents in Toutle who were able to name five or six consequences increases steadily from slight risk (39.1%), through moderate risk (54.5%), to severe risk (74.5%). None of those who believed that property risk was severe listed as few as one or two consequences, while 13.0 percent of those who defined risk as slight did so.

The Lexington data similarly show an increase in the proportion of people with maximum threat knowledge as perceived risk to property increases: slight, 7.7 percent; moderate, 44.8 percent; severe 54.5 percent. More than nine out of ten respondents who believed property risk was slight named four consequences or fewer. Only about four out of ten defining property risk as severe named as few as four or less.

Our data permit us to make two inferences about perceived vulnerability. First, there is a moderately strong positive correlation between perceptions of personal safety risk and threat knowledge. People who believe that the danger to their personal safety is high tend to be able to accurately name more threat consequences than people who define personal safety risk as lower. Second, there is a strong positive relationship between perceived property risk and threat knowledge. Furthermore, in these data, perceived property risk is a slightly better (statistically speaking) predictor of threat knowledge than perceived personal safety risk, although both dimensions of perceived risk are positively correlated with knowledge.

The greater correlation between perceived property risk and respondents' understanding of threats associated with Mt. St. Helens may be a function of specific characteristics of the volcano hazard. Our respondents have been exposed to many eruptions since 1980. Yet, to date, the principal impacts of the volcanicity have been upon property. Only the May 18, 1980 eruption resulted in loss of life. Also, there is an effective, well-publicized, well-coordinated warning system that allows people to protect themselves (by evacuating) from eruptions and floods. These conditions permit people, in effect, to experience slightly less uncertainty about personal safety. Residents of Toutle and Lexington may be confident that the warning system will provide an alert with sufficient lead time to enable them to take action before their lives are seriously threatened. However, with the exception of small items, one cannot evacuate property. It must be protected "in-place," and even then the level of protection that it is possible to achieve declines with the increasing magnitude of the eruption. Consequently, there are limits on the extent to which a person can reduce uncertainty about property. As a result, greater proportions of people in both communities defined property risk as severe than defined personal safety risk as severe.

Because concern about property risk tends to dominate citizen assessments of risks from volcanicity at Mt. St. Helens, threat characteristics and consequences must be thoroughly examined to define exactly what dangers exist and how they might be mitigated. The process of reducing uncertainty about property risks, then, demands a relatively extensive information gathering activity. By contrast, one can achieve a modest degree of personal safety protection with a minimum of effort by merely paying attention to warning messages. Hence, it is possible to reduce uncertainty about personal injury or loss of life without developing an extensive threat knowledge. This should not be interpreted to mean that property risk is always a better predictor of threat knowledge than is personal safety risk. Rather, one might conclude that in threat environments characterized by a low level of uncertainty about life safety and a high level of uncertainty about property safety, the latter concern will be more strongly correlated with threat knowledge. In other situations, the converse may be true. In dealing with radiation threats from nuclear power plants, evidence suggests that the public focuses more upon the health safety dimension than upon property risk (Perry 1985, 56-57).

Under such conditions, one would anticipate that perceived personal safety risk might be the best predictor of threat knowledge. We will further explore the relationship of personal safety risks versus property risks in Chapter 3 when we examine the antecedents of perceived vulnerability.

Personal Planning Activity

It is possible to identify three different types of agents that conduct disaster planning: individuals, private organizations and governments. One distinction that can be made among these three contexts pertains to the "protective target." Planning undertaken by individuals aims at modifying hazard-related dangers perceived to bear primarily upon individual households. Planning by private sector organizations tends to be directed at preserving organizational resources. Governmental planning may have multiple objectives including the protection of public property and resources, as well as enhancing the ability of citizens to protect their personal safety and private property. It should be noted that individual planning, here labelled "personal planning activity," focuses upon the planning and information gathering activity of individuals, but we acknowledge that individual planning may draw upon or be influenced by the planning activities of organizations and/or governments. It is hypothesized that people who engage in personal planning educate themselves about the threat as part of the planning process. Consequently, individuals who engage in extensive planning activities will also have more extensive knowledge of threat consequences. Our interest in this hypothesis is reinforced by empirical studies which indicate that personal planning activity is correlated with other disaster behaviors, particularly evacuation warning compliance (cf. Perry et al. 1981, 40-43).

Personal planning activity was measured by asking respondents to characterize the extent of their planning efforts to protect themselves from volcano-related dangers. Based upon answers to this question we grouped citizens into three categories in relation to the apparent extensiveness of the planning effort. People who reported that they had engaged in little or no planning, or who had focused on it only in a general way, were described as evidencing a "low" level of personal planning activity. Those who claimed to have engaged in specific planning but focused upon a single protective dimension, such as personal safety or property preservation, were assigned a "moderate" value for personal planning activity. Finally, people who reported specific actions directed at multiple protective dimensions were said to represent a "high" level of personal planning activity.

Table 8 shows the level of threat knowledge by personal planning activity for each study community. It is interesting to note at the outset that substantial proportions of people in each community engaged in what is here called a high level of personal planning: 72 people or 69.9 percent of the Toutle sample and 48 people or 48.5 percent of the Lexington sample. Only 7.8 percent of Toutle residents and 28.3 percent of Lexington residents showed a low level of personal planning activity. This finding contrasts sharply with previous studies of floods, where smaller proportions of people—usually less than one-third at best—claim to have engaged in specific adaptive planning activities (cf. Perry et al. 1981; Perry et al. 1983). It is likely that the relatively higher levels of planning activity at Mt. St. Helens are related to the threat environment of the volcano, particularly salience. The larger proportions of people who engage in high levels of planning in Toutle (as compared with Lexington) may be a function of two motivations for planning that more strongly affect Toutle residents: a history of higher levels of actual damage to the community from eruptions and a closer proximity to the volcano.

These data show a moderately strong positive relationship between level of personal planning activity and depth of threat knowledge in both communities, although the correlation is slightly stronger among Lexington residents than among those living in Toutle. The Toutle data show that the proportion of people exhibiting the lowest level of threat knowledge (naming only one or two consequences) steadily declines as we move from low levels of planning activity to higher levels. The proportion of people with the highest level of threat knowledge is about the same for low and moderate planning (about 50%), but increases for those whose planning activity is high (65.3%). Thus, one might infer that, at least for Toutle residents, a high level of planning activity must be achieved to produce a noticeable effect upon citizens' ability to name threat consequences. Parenthetically, the observed correlation between planning activity and threat knowledge is also consistent with the hypothesis that high levels of threat knowledge motivate planning activity. The Lexington data also show an increase in the proportion of people with the most extensive threat knowledge as we move from low

(17.9%), through moderate (21.7%), to high (60.4%) levels of personal planning activity. Once again there is only a small difference in threat knowledge between low and moderate categories for personal planning. It appears that only a high level of planning activity is significantly related to high levels of threat knowledge.

Table 8

Threat Knowledge by Personal Planning Activity

| | | Personal Planning Activity | | | | | |
| | | Low | | Moderate | | High | |
Site	Number of Consequences	N	%	N	%	N	%
	One or two	1	12.5	2	8.7	1	1.4
Toutle	Three or four	3	37.5	10	43.5	24	33.3
	Five or six	4	50.0	11	47.8	47	65.3
	One or two	5	17.9	0	0.0	3	6.3
Lexington	Three or four	18	64.3	18	78.3	16	33.3
	Five or six	5	17.9	5	21.7	29	60.4

Another factor which may contribute to citizens' threat knowledge that is related to, but not subsumed by, personal planning activity deals with the level of effort that the individual expends in information seeking. Throughout the volcanic sequence, local, state and federal government agencies, as well as private groups, have made publicly available much information which describes the dangers associated with Mt. St. Helens and what can be done about them. In addition, the Cowlitz County Department of Emergency Services has undertaken multiple "outreach" information dissemination programs. Such activities, however, seek to minimize demands upon citizens by providing information in a fashion that requires the least inconvenience and effort from the target audience. In these types of interactions, most of the effort is made by the information sender or disseminator, while the target audience is relatively passive.

Alternately, information may be transmitted in response to requests initiated by citizens. The nature of the information involved in this type of exchange is usually more specific and the content is more idiosyncratic. The nature of this type of exchange may also be seen as having implications for citizen accumulation of threat knowledge. That is, citizen initiated contacts demonstrate more effort on the part of the individual—both in the form of a desire for specific knowledge and sufficient motivation to actively seek that knowledge. It allows us to focus on an action in which the individual controls the accumulation of threat knowledge, rather than looking at dissemination programs which are subject to control outside the individual. It can be hypothesized that citizens who are willing to initiate contacts have adopted an organized approach to acquiring threat information, are willing to assume the burden in the acquisition process, and are consequently more likely to develop an extensive threat knowledge.

Table 9 shows threat knowledge by whether, and how many times, respondents had initiated contacts with authorities which were aimed at acquiring information about volcanicity at Mt. St. Helens. More than half of the respondents from each community (68.0% in Toutle and 55.6% in Lexington) claimed to have initiated one or more contacts with authorities. In Toutle there is a positive relationship of low to moderate strength between initiating contacts and threat knowledge. None of the respondents who initiated contacts were limited to naming only one or two threat consequences compared with 12.1 percent of those who had no history of initiating contacts. Among people who reported initiating no

---

Table 9

Threat Knowledge by Contacts
Initiated with Authorities

Site	Number of Consequences	No Contacts Initiated		One or More Contacts Initiated	
		N	%	N	%
	One or two	4	12.1	0	0.0
Toutle	Three or four	11	33.3	26	37.1
	Five or six	18	54.6	44	62.9
	One or two	6	13.6	2	3.6
Lexington	Three or four	28	63.6	24	43.6
	Five or six	10	22.7	29	52.7

Steam and ash eruption, March 30, 1980. *Photograph by G. Braun*

Dredging operations on the Cowlitz River, summer 1980. *Photograph by M. R. Greene*

Early digging out at Camp Baker. *Photograph by M. R. Greene*

Trees stripped and downed by the eruption blast, summer 1980. *Photograph by M. R. Greene*

Banks of the Cowlitz River show evidence of flooding, summer 1980. *Photograph by M. R. Greene*

Small marina filled with mud and volcanic debris, summer 1980. *Photograph by M. R. Greene*

Barren banks of the Toutle River recall 1980 mud flows more than three years later. *Photograph by R. W. Perry*

Toutle Grocery in peaceful times (December 1983), looking toward cloud-covered Mt. St. Helens. *Photograph by R. W. Perry*

Toutle Filling Station with eruption mural added to west wall (December 1983).
Photograph by R. W. Perry

May 18 eruption seen from Toutle.

Same view as of December 1982. *Photograph by R. W. Perry*

Beginning of reconstruction plans included visitor centers. This photograph was taken in December 1985. *Photograph by R. W. Perry*

View of Spirit Lake before the 1980 eruptions.

View of Spirit Lake after the May 18, 1980 eruption.

Restricted zone warning signs identified limited access areas (summer 1981). *Photograph by R. W. Perry*

The town of Cougar on the south side of the volcano escaped high levels of damage, but was subject to access restrictions anyway. *Photograph by R. W. Perry*

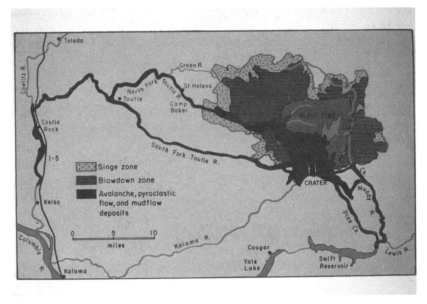

Map indicating damage to ecosystem around Mt. St. Helens.

By 1984, dredging operations on the Cowlitz River had amassed large quantities of volcanic ash and debris. *Photograph by R. W. Perry*

By 1982 emergency warning and information signs were prominently posted throughout the area. *Photograph by R. W. Perry*

To accommodate visitors, evacuation routes were marked by signs in the Toutle area. *Photograph by R. W. Perry*

View of Mt. St. Helens across Silver Lake (south of Toutle) in December 1983. *Photograph by R. W. Perry*

Mt. St. Helens from the south, December 1985. *Photograph by R. W. Perry*

New visitor's center, December 1986. *Photograph by R. W. Perry*

Mt. St. Helens from the south, December 1985. *Photograph by R. W. Perry*

State of Washington emergency command post, June 1980. *Photograph by M. R. Greene*

Mt. St. Helens from the Cougar area (south side), December 1985. *Photograph by R. W. Perry*

contacts, 54.6 percent were able to name five or six consequences versus 62.9 percent of those who made at least one contact. The Lexington data show a higher (moderate strength) correlation between these two variables. Here, the proportion of respondents able to list five or more consequences increases from 22.7 percent of those not initiating contacts to 52.7 percent of those making contacts. Thus, these data tend to support our hypothesis that citizens who initiate contacts with authorities while accumulating information develop higher levels of threat knowledge.

Social Variables

Information about dangers at Mt. St. Helens reaches citizens through a variety of channels. We have just seen that personal planning activities as well as citizen initiated inquiries are positively correlated with threat knowledge. It was pointed out that in these cases we were relying upon the predictive power of *information seeking effort* expended by the population at risk. It was also acknowledged that many agencies and groups made threat information available to citizens through general community-wide dissemination programs. A special case of such dissemination programs may be seen in the information distribution efforts of social institutions which serve specific sub-groups of the community. These distribution efforts deal intensively with a focused population over time. In effect, they make situation specific threat knowledge available to individuals within the *routine context of day-to-day life*.

In connection with volcanicity at Mt. St. Helens, two such special distribution efforts afforded some residents the opportunity to acquire specialized threat knowledge. The first falls within the context of the local economic system and the role of the volcano in it. In Chapter 1 we observed that two sectors of the local economy—logging and tourism—are intimately related to the volcano. Thus, people working in volcano-dependent jobs have special opportunities and motivation to gather threat knowledge. Loggers working on the slopes of the volcano, for example, have a special need to understand both human operated eruption warning systems and environmental cues that might forecast danger. People working in volcano-related jobs have two types of unique opportunities to obtain threat knowledge: through employer-managed training programs and through simple observation of the threat during the workday. Based upon this reasoning it may be hypothesized that people with volcano-related employment should evidence more extensive threat knowledge than those not so employed. The second learning opportunity occurs in connection with the system of public education. Guided by the Cowlitz County Department of Emergency Services, local elementary and high schools have engaged in systematic planning for events that might occur during the school day. This has involved providing information to parents and students regarding threats and protective measures that might be initiated by schools. Through this channel one might expect that parents of school-aged children would accumulate higher levels of knowledge regarding volcanic threats.

Table 10 shows level of threat knowledge by volcano-related employment for both communities. As predicted, there is a positive relationship of low to moderate strength between having a job which depends on the volcano and threat knowledge. Among Toutle residents without a volcano-related job, 55.3 percent could list five or more threat consequences, compared with 64.3 percent of those in Lexington, but one must be cautious because of the small number of people in this sample that reported volcano-related jobs (11 respondents). Given the limited data, the most appropriate interpretation for Lexington is to say that the direction of the relationship is positive, but little can be said about the strength of the correlation.

Table 10 also shows threat knowledge by the presence of school-aged children in the household. These data show a moderately strong positive correlation between having school-aged children and possession of more extensive threat knowledge. In Toutle, 76.0 percent of people with school-aged children could name five or six threat consequences while only 45.3 percent of those without children of school age could name this many. Similarly, 32.5 percent of Lexington residents without children identified five or more consequences compared with 44.1 percent of those with children. Correspondingly, in each community, a greater proportion of people without children than with children listed only one or two consequences. It should also be mentioned that the observed correlation is slightly stronger for the Toutle sample than for Lexington, a result that may be an artifact of differences between school programs in the two communities. All schools in Toutle were subject to volcano threats and consequently conducted emergency planning. Only those Lexington residents whose children attended schools in the flood plain would have been exposed to volcano-related emergency planning. These data do suggest, however, that such institutional—school or work related—information distribution programs can enhance levels of threat knowledge among target populations.

Summary

In this chapter we have examined people's understanding of the threats posed by volcanicity at Mt. St. Helens. It was found that citizens of Toutle and Lexington are able to accurately identify volcanic threats and recognize those most likely to impinge negatively on their lives— mud-flows, flooding and ash fall. When asked to focus upon these particular threats, our respondents were also able to describe a wide range of potential consequences for their communities. Interestingly, more of the consequences named dealt with potential damage to property rather than possible negative outcomes for personal health and safety. Relative to other hazards, we found that our respondents possessed a reasonably extensive knowledge of threats associated with the volcano. Approximately three-fourths of the respondents from both Toutle and Lexington were able to name four or more specific negative consequences associated with ash fall and mud-flow/floods.

Table 10

Threat Knowledge and Employment
and School-Aged Children

| | | Volcano-Related Job | | | |
| | | No | | Yes | |
Site	Number of Consequences	N	%	N	%
	One or two	2	4.3	2	3.6
Toutle	Three or four	19	40.4	18	32.1
	Five or six	26	55.3	36	64.3
	One or two	8	9.1	0	0.0
Lexington	Three or four	49	55.7	3	27.3
	Five or six	31	35.2	8	72.7
		School-Aged Children in Household			
	One or two	4	7.5	0	0.0
Toutle	Three or four	25	47.2	12	24.0
	Five or six	24	45.3	38	76.0
	One or two	6	15.0	2	3.4
Lexington	Three or four	21	52.5	31	52.5
	Five or six	13	32.5	26	44.1

We also explored the question of how people with more extensive threat knowledge were different from those with less knowledge. It was found that a history of compliance with eruption warnings and sustaining eruption damage were largely unrelated to level of threat knowledge. Several variables were found to have moderate to strong positive correlations with threat knowledge. The most highly correlated of these variables were the extent to which one perceived risks to property and the level of personal planning activity. Salience of the volcano, perceived risk to personal safety, the initiation of contacts with authorities, and having school-aged children were all found to have positive correlations of moderate strength with threat knowledge. Finally, employment in a volcano-dependent job showed a low to moderate positive correlation with depth of threat knowledge.

CHAPTER THREE

Acknowledging the Volcano Threat

In examining citizen understanding of the threat posed by Mt. St. Helens, we focused upon the accumulation of technically accurate knowledge and the beliefs that this information generated about personal impacts of the volcano. Interestingly, we found considerable agreement among scientists and technical experts regarding the nature and probability of threats associated with the volcano. This agreement was reflected in our interviews with citizens where, although depth of knowledge varied, there was notable homogeneity regarding the primary threats and their consequences. Now we will turn our attention to the ways in which people *interpret* this threat knowledge.

The way in which humans come to cope with natural hazards in their environment may be conceptualized as a process of interdependent stages (following the work of Kates 1971; White 1974; Burton et al. 1978). Thus people recognize a threat, accumulate information about it, arrive at a definition of vulnerability, and begin a process of surveying, selecting and adopting adjustments. Admittedly these stages represent analytic distinctions; in practice the distinctions may be blurred and some people may seem to "skip" some steps. The stages do provide, however, a framework for viewing in a systematic fashion the ways in which citizens "interact" with environmental hazards. Chapter two addressed the first two stages and essentially dealt with how citizens accommodate the scientific view of the volcano threat with their own experiences. This chapter deals with how citizens personalize this threat knowledge and come to define themselves as more or less vulnerable to the dangers associated with Mt. St. Helens. This process of making decisions about vulnerability is a significant "causal" factor in the willingness of citizens to adopt hazard adjustments.

We will approach the question of perceived vulnerability in two phases. First, the process of gathering information will be scrutinized. Interest here centers upon describing the sources through which people receive information and how these sources are evaluated in terms of their credibility and reliability. An important goal of these analyses is to identify where citizens acquire information about a threat that they have been exposed to for some years. The second phase involves conceptually clarifying what is meant by vulnerability and isolating variables which contribute to the individual's feelings of vulnerability. That is, we are interested in understanding what factors citizens attend to when assessing the extent to which they are vulnerable to harm from Mt. St. Helens volcano.

Sources of Volcano Information

As noted in chapter one, information about Mt. St. Helens' periodic eruptions has appeared in Indian folklore, depictions of the experience of explorers, missionaries and settlers, and the more recent systematic writings of naturalists and scientists. Indeed, to a person who looks for it, there has long been available much descriptive information. Even before the present volcanic sequence began, a considerable quantity of technical data existed regarding the threats posed by Mt. St. Helens for twentieth-century inhabitants of the region surrounding the volcano (cf. Crandell and Mullineaux 1978; Crandell et al. 1975).

The current eruptive sequence has the multiple distinction, however, of being the first to occur since (1) settlements became larger and characterized by higher population densities, (2) strong local governments developed, (3) the technological growth of "modern" earth science, (4) the rise of emergency management as a profession, and (5) the growth of modern mass media, particularly telecommunications. These factors have combined to create an environment in which substantial threat-relevant information is available or can be created, and where a capacity exists to distribute the information. The beginning of volcanicity in March 1980 may be seen in this context as providing the impetus to begin the process of producing and disseminating information about threats associated with Mt. St. Helens.

Whether done in connection with Mt. St. Helens or some other natural hazard, there are many different reasons for disseminating threat-relevant information. From the standpoint of authorities, dissemination programs are undertaken to create knowledge so that citizens recognize and understand threats. There is also the desire to create salience—to help citizens appreciate the importance of the threat. Finally, dissemination programs may seek to stimulate vigilance, and to familiarize people with protective options and strategies. In all, the hope is to induce citizens to "realistically" appraise environmental dangers and to integrate them into their social world in a way that minimizes probable negative outcomes.

While the goals of dissemination may appear clear and straightforward, the practice—and even the study—of dissemination is beset with problems (cf. Knott and Wildavsky 1979). Technical specialists ponder what information should be disseminated, in what form, by whom and how frequently (Douglas et al. 1970; Travis and Reibsame 1979; Metsner 1979). These issues of course impinge upon strategies for disseminating information on natural hazards. It is most profitable at this juncture to focus discussion on the problem of disseminating threat information about Mt. St. Helens. At present, two types or categories of content are routinely disseminated. The first consists of messages about the short-run status of the volcano: eruption warnings, flood warnings and other announcements regarding impending dangers. For the most part such messages are products of prediction or detection technology designed to elicit an immediate response from citizens. The second category represents information of a longer-range nature describing the evolution of threats, warning systems and hazard management programs generally, or explaining protective strategies or tactics available to citizens. It is the long-range information that is of interest here.

In connection with all research on information dissemination, one must consider both a target audience and sources or senders of information. Hazard information is directed at the population at risk, in the specific case of the data in hand, residents of Toutle and Lexington. Information about Mt. St. Helens is made available by a variety of sources, which may or may not coordinate content or style and timing of dissemination among themselves. These sources include private citizens and private groups such as the Red Cross and Mental Health Centers. Other sources are government agencies at all jurisdictional levels such as the Sheriff's Office, county and state emergency services, the U.S. Geological Survey, Army Corps of Engineers, National Weather Service, Federal Emergency Management Agency and the U.S. Forest Service. Obviously both the nature of information routinely provided and the technical authority or expertise of these sources differs radically.

To begin to systematically examine the environment in which volcano hazard information is disseminated, one can choose a focal source as a structuring mechanism. For our purposes, it is most appropriate to select the county level emergency manager. At Mt. St. Helens, it is the county unit that possesses the greatest amount of resources to direct at hazard management (relative to municipalities) and is directly responsible for the safety of the largest number of citizens. From the perspective of the county as the local emergency management authority, the sources of information can be partitioned into several groupings: (1) the county itself; (2) state and municipal organizations that are interested in the public safety and possessing a "local" orientation, (3) agencies with technical expertise charged with monitoring or administering some aspect of the threat or response to it; and (4) interested citizens. The county has complete control (within certain political and technical limitations) of the information it disseminates, some influence (usually through coordination) over that disseminated by state and municipal organizations and technical agencies, and limited influence over information disseminated by citizens. Recognizing that all of these sources may be "sending" at the same time, the dissemination problem becomes one of determining how the local emergency manager can operate to insure timely passage of accurate information to the public at risk.

From the research literature, one can begin to derive a variety of guidelines for addressing this problem. First, one should develop a pro-active dissemination program based on accurate threat data which includes periodical contacts with the public at risk (Quarantelli 1967; Perry 1985). Second, one should coordinate with other information disseminators in an attempt to achieve some consistency of content across messages (Perry and Nigg 1985). Careful coordination, coupled with monitoring of messages delivered by others, also permits a local emergency manager to provide interpretation or qualification of information within the scope of his/her own dissemination efforts. A third suggested practice involves disseminating information through a variety of modes or channels to enhance coverage of the population-at-risk (Perry and Mushkatel 1986). Finally, the local emergency manager should strive to build credibility as an information source through such tactics as maintaining visibility in the community, establishing channels that permit citizen-initiated contacts, and making public the bases of the agencies' assessments of the threat (Dynes et al. 1972; Perry 1985).

Such guidelines are especially useful in an abstract sense because they apply to the management of threat information dissemination in a variety of settings. That is, they are not hazard specific and should apply as well to the case of volcanos as to riverine floods, earthquakes, tornadoes or hurricanes. Our data from Mt. St. Helens provide an opportunity to examine the veracity of some of these claims in the specific context of an eruptive sequence and to extend the guidelines by drawing new inferences from our observations. We shall approach this analysis problem by looking at three dimensions of information exchange in Toutle and Lexington: (1) patterns of citizen information receipt, (2) preferred communication channels, and (3) citizen definitions of source credibility.

It is important to remember that our data reflect the communication patterns which prevailed slightly more than three years into Mt. St. Helens current eruptive sequence. Thus, these patterns represent the more routinized contacts between citizens and sources. Information receipt patterns have clearly changed over the years. In April 1980, at the beginning of the sequence, volcanic threat information was being heavily exchanged. At the time, more than 50 percent of the residents of three communities near the volcano reported they *received* information from some source more than four times each day (Greene et al. 1981). These levels of information receipt declined slightly with the passage of time, but increased again following the cataclysmic eruption of May 18, 1980 (Perry et al. 1980). In turn, this increase was sustained during the period of frequent explosive eruptions (May to August 1980) but gradually declined with declining eruption magnitude and frequency, relatively decreasing mass media attention, and apparent information saturation of the local residents (cf. Earle et al. 1982). Within this context our data represent exchanges derived from the systematic efforts of agencies and organizations with an emergency management mission to keep the population informed, and interchanges among citizens, probably aimed at clarifying, interpreting or simply relaying information.

Table 11 shows sources from whom respondents reported receiving volcanic threat information by the frequency of contact for each of the study communities. It should be mentioned that these reported contacts are based upon citizen perceptions; consequently, they are subject to the social psychological processes of selective retention and selective recall. They may not correspond precisely with actual or "objectively counted" contacts, particularly when the reported frequency of contact is low. They constitute important data, however, because they represent people's memory and reconstruction of the information dissemination process. In this regard, these data allow us to identify which sources people *remem-*

ber interacting with the ones that created an interpersonal impression of some significance.

The data in Table 11 show that the three sources with whom the largest proportions of respondents reported no contact are the same in each community. Among Toutle residents, 95.1 percent reported no contacts with the Federal Emergency Management Agency (FEMA), 94.2 percent reported none with Washington State Department of Emergency Services, and 88.3 percent had no contact with the U.S. Forest Service. Although the proportions of contacts with these agencies were slightly higher in Lexington, they still represent the agencies least often contacted in that community. Thus, 85.9 percent of Lexington residents had no contact with the Forest Service, 75.8 percent had no contact with the State DES, and 75.8 percent claimed to have not received any information from FEMA. Furthermore, in both research sites, the greatest proportions of people who *did* claim contact with these agencies described the frequency of contact as "rare." All of these agencies have general oversight roles relative to the volcano threat at Mt. St. Helens rather than direct responsibility for citizen protection. Earlier in the volcanic sequence, both FEMA and the state occupied more visible roles in the development of emergency response contingency plans where the local citizenry was a primary focus. In recent years, however, the activities of all three agencies have centered upon coordinating with, supporting and providing special resources to other agencies engaged in volcano hazard management. It is therefore not surprising that citizens report very low levels of contact with these agencies.

At the opposite pole, the Cowlitz County Sheriff's Department was the agency with which the largest proportions of citizens in each community reported contacts: 97.1 percent in Toutle and 97.0 percent in Lexington. The frequency of contact with the Sheriff's Department was also uniformly high. In Toutle, 46.6 percent of the respondents reported that contacts occurred "often," and another 46.6 percent described frequency as "sometimes." Only 3.9 percent said they "rarely" had contact with the sheriff and even fewer, 2.9 percent, claimed to have never had contact. Likewise, 43.4 percent of Lexington respondents recall "often" receiving information from the sheriff, while 35.4 percent report being contacted "sometimes" (Perry and Greene 1983). Contacts were reported to be "rare" by 18.2 percent of these respondents, while 3.0 percent reported no contact at all. These data highlight the significant role attributed to the Sheriff's Department in the hazard information dissemination process.

The Cowlitz County Department of Emergency Services was also among the three information sources cited by the largest proportions of citizens in each community. Among Toutle respondents, 26.2 percent reported receiving information from this source "often," 29.1 percent "sometimes," and 13.6 percent "rarely." Slightly less than one-third of the respondents claimed no contact with the County DES. In Lexington, 43.4 percent of the respondents described their contact with County DES as "often," and 37.4 percent received information "sometimes." Only 14.1 percent "rarely" heard from the County DES, while 5.1 percent claimed to have never been contacted by this agency. These high levels of perceived contacts with the County DES are especially interesting in light of the fact that this agency is a part of the Cowlitz County Sheriff's Department.

Since the beginning of the volcanic sequence, the Sheriff's Department has been both very active in managing the threat from Mt. St. Helens and very visible to the public. The staff of the County DES is less than one-tenth that of the Sheriff's Department; the DES draws many resources from the sheriff—including personnel during acute emergencies—and coordinates all planning activities with that department. In social surveys conducted in 1980, relatively small proportions of citizens reported receiving information from the County DES (while larger proportions identified the Sheriff's Department) in spite of the fact the agency had been disseminating information. It was suggested at the time that citizens tended not to draw a sharp distinction between DES and sheriff's personnel, and that citizen recall favored the apparently more visible Sheriff's Department (Perry et al. 1980, 17-19). Since that time, the DES has systematically pursued a structured citizen education program. DES has provided speaker services for community organizations and schools, provided interviews on hazard topics for local mass media, distributed brochures on the volcano threat, as well as a comprehensive flood preparation guide, and effectively deployed limited personnel to achieve the highest possible levels of direct contact with the public at risk (Perry and Greene 1983). The success of these endeavors is reflected in the present data where the County DES is cited as an information source by very large proportions of citizens. Indeed, in Lexington, it is second only to the Sheriff's Department and third in Toutle, behind the Sheriff and friends or neighbors. These findings reinforce the importance of the previously mentioned guidelines for managing information dissemination that emphasize the need for a proactive program involving regular citizen contact.

The last of the three most commonly mentioned sources is friends and neighbors. Approximately three-fourths of the respondents from each community indicated they received some information from this source. The frequency of reported contacts, however, was higher in Toutle than Lexington. Toutle residents who had contact are about equally divided across the three levels of frequency; one-third in each category of often, sometimes and rarely. About half of the Lexington residents who received information from friends and neighbors said it came "rarely." Only eight people characterized information receipt from this source as "often."

Table 11

Information Sources by Frequency of Contact

		Frequency of Contact							
		Often		*Sometimes*		*Rarely*		*Never*	
Site	*Source*	N	%	N	%	N	%	N	%
Toutle									
	Friends/neighbors	26	25.5	26	25.5	27	26.5	23	22.5
	Local police/fire	3	2.9	6	5.8	8	7.8	86	83.5
	County DES	27	26.2	30	29.1	14	13.6	32	31.1
	County Sheriff	48	46.6	48	46.6	4	3.9	3	2.9
	USGS	3	2.9	5	4.9	15	14.6	80	77.7
	Army Corps	1	1.0	7	6.8	21	20.4	74	71.8
	NWS	8	7.8	6	5.8	22	21.4	67	65.0
	FEMA	0	0.0	0	0.0	5	4.9	98	95.1
	Forest Service	1	1.0	4	3.9	7	6.8	91	88.3
	State DES	0	0.0	0	0.0	6	5.8	97	94.2
Lexington									
	Friends/neighbors	8	8.1	28	28.3	35	35.4	28	28.3
	Local police/fire	8	8.1	8	8.1	18	18.2	65	65.7
	County DES	43	43.4	37	37.4	14	14.1	5	5.1
	County Sheriff	43	43.4	35	35.4	18	18.2	3	3.0
	USGS	11	11.1	24	24.2	16	16.2	48	48.5
	Army Corps	11	11.1	21	21.2	27	27.3	40	40.4
	NWS	9	9.1	18	18.2	24	24.2	48	48.5
	FEMA	2	2.0	9	9.1	13	13.1	75	75.8
	Forest Service	1	1.0	3	3.0	10	10.1	85	85.9
	State DES	1	1.0	5	5.1	18	18.2	75	75.8

Research on citizen response to disaster warnings has shown that people routinely receive warning-relevant information from friends and neighbors (cf. Drabek 1969; Perry et al. 1981). A recent study of flooding and hazardous materials incidents also indicates that citizens report friends and neighbors as prominent sources of threat information outside the context of a specific warning, and that such social network contacts are particularly prevalent among some ethnic minority groups (Perry and Mushkatel 1986). Furthermore, previous studies of citizen's sources of eruption response information at Mt. St. Helens revealed that much information was acquired via social networks, especially among Toutle residents (Perry and Greene 1983, 37). Thus, previous research has shown social networks to be important sources of information across a variety of disaster phases and across several different types of hazard. The present data show that social networks persist as threat information sources over time when citizens are confronted with multiple impact or extended duration impact threats from the natural environment.

From the perspective of the local emergency manager, these findings indicate that citizens routinely circulate threat information among themselves. Consequently, the emergency manager should not conceive of dissemination as an activity that just sends information to individuals or families. It should be recognized that disseminated information becomes the subject of discussion among local residents and is passed along through linkages in social networks. It is known that information exchanged in this fashion is subject to distortion and misinterpretation, particularly as the size of the network and number of exchanges increases. Thus technically *inaccurate* information could be circulated within social networks along with accurate information. Such a situation could create an apparent conflict between informal sources such as friends, neighbors and relatives, and official sources such as emergency managers and other technical experts. Of course, local emergency managers have little direct control over information circulated in social networks. As we indicated in the discussion of dissemination guidelines, however, positive measures can be taken by emergency managers that increase the likelihood that information exchanged will be technically accurate. Periodic multiple waves in dissemination programs allow accurate information to be "reinserted" into the social networks. The dissemination of information in written form provides information recipients with a reference base that is less subject to distortion than simple mental recall. Finally, the maintenance of communication channels that lead directly to an emergency manager allows citizens to "confirm" messages and affords emergency managers an opportunity to correct technically inaccurate information.

Following the constellation of most commonly cited sources—the sheriff, County DES, and friends and neighbors—is another group of three sources, also the same in each community. These are the U.S. Geological Survey (USGS), the National Weather Service (NWS), and the Army Corps of Engineers. In terms of the absolute number of contacts, slightly more people reported information receipt from these sources in Lexington than in Toutle. Among Toutle residents, 77.7 percent claimed no contact with USGS, 65.8 percent never received information from NWS, and 71.8 percent reported they received no information from the Corps. In Lexington, only about half of the respondents said they had never received information from each of these sources. Among people who did recall receiving information, the contacts were uniformly infrequent. In Lexington, the modal category of frequency for those who had some contact was "sometimes" for the USGS and "rarely" for the Corps and NWS. The modal category in the Toutle sample was "rarely" for all three agencies. Therefore, one can characterize citizen receipt of information from these agencies as sporadic and not achieving high levels of coverage in the population.

It should be remembered that these are technical support organizations, comprised of personnel with specialized skills and equipment, whose primary mission relative to the volcano is to provide data and interpretations to other agencies. None of these technical support agencies is primarily oriented to disseminating information to the public. Instead, they should be conceived as parts of the larger interorganizational network that manages the threat at Mt. St. Helens (Sorenson 1982, 163). The results of work by these agencies regarding the identification, assessment and reduction of volcanic risks can, of course, reach the public. Typically, this occurs through the efforts of another agency that has a direct public safety mission (County Sheriff, County or State DES, or FEMA). Alternatively, the USGS, NWS and Corps can disseminate information via the mass media which routinely monitor the technical support agencies, as well as other organizations involved in volcano hazard management. Given the mission of these agencies, and the very strong emergency management efforts of the County DES and sheriff, one would expect patterns of citizen information receipt similar to those obtained above. In fact, results are indicative of an appropriate division of labor. Had they indicated that large proportions of citizens routinely received information from agencies like the NWS, USGS or Army Corps, it would raise two kinds of issues. First, one would suspect that there existed competition or overlap in the dissemination efforts of the agencies charged with threat management. Another concern might be that these agencies were being forced to directly disseminate information to the public in an effort to fill gaps created by inadequate programs directed by the primary emergency management agencies. Such situations can arise, but have not prevailed at Mt. St. Helens.

Local police and fire departments were also not frequently cited by our respondents as sources of volcano threat information. In Toutle, 83.5 percent of those questioned claimed to have had no contact with this source. Among the few people who reported contact, the majority characterized the frequency of information receipt as "rare." Approximately 65 percent of Lexington residents reported no contact with local fire and police, and again, most of those who had contact said it occurred "rarely." Particularly in Toutle, these apparently low levels of contact represent structural issues rather than a lack of effort or involvement on the part of municipal public safety departments. Toutle has no police department—law enforcement is provided by the County Sheriff—and a small volunteer fire department. Police and fire protection for the Lexington area is provided by the City of Longview. Aside from these considerations, it should be noted that municipal public safety agencies have not been involved heavily in disseminating Mt. St. Helens' threat information directly to the public. For the most part they serve roles in warning and response operations, and are integrated into the interagency contingency response planning process. The primary resources for citizen education lie with the County DES, however, and that agency has taken the lead in information dissemination.

In summary, most of the respondents from Toutle and Lexington report steady contact with the County DES and sheriff—the agencies with the lead roles, relative to citizens at risk, in managing the threat from Mt. St. Helens. Our data also show an active exchange among citizens themselves, indicating that social networks constitute important channels through which threat information passes. Moderate proportions of people report receiving information from federal agencies—the Geological Survey, Weather Service and Army Corps—with technical support missions in the volcano hazard management process. As would be expected, these contacts were intermittent, probably coinciding with the release of special studies or volcano threat status announcements. Citizens reported the lowest levels of contact with state and federal agencies having general hazard management oversight responsibilities.

Now that we have examined the *sources* people recall receiving information from, we can review the *channels* through which these messages arrive. In particular we are interested in two aspects of communication channels: those through which citizens report they *usually* receive information and the ones through which they *prefer* to receive information. By documenting channels through which people remember hearing threat information, it is possible to identify, among a variety of possible dissemination channels, those with a record of actually reaching citizens. This information, coupled with data on channel preference, allows an emergency manager designing a dissemination program to target effective channels, thereby enhancing the probability that messages will reach the intended audience.

It is sometimes difficult to separate information source from communication channel when dealing with hazard information. The concept of information source concentrates upon the person or agency that constructs the information which forms the message. A communication channel is a mechanism through which a message is transmitted. Emergency management authorities, police, firefighters, friends and neighbors are all clearly *sources*. Messages developed by these sources may be delivered via a variety of channels, including personal conversation (either face-to-face or by telephone), in a public meeting, as a brochure, or using mass media (newspaper, radio or television). The distinction between source and channel is clear analytically, but can become blurred in practice. Indeed, certain channels are commonly used by certain sources. For example, information from friends, relatives or neighbors is almost certain to come via personal conversation, while emergency management authorities are likely to use a range of channels.

The mass media have aspects of both channel and source. Clearly, radio, newspapers and television form channels through which information can be passed to citizens. An emergency manager may formulate a threat status bulletin and choose to disseminate it by releasing it to the mass media with the request that it be reproduced. Mass media can also become sources, particularly in the case of chronic environmental threats or multiple or extended-impact disasters. In such cases mass media fulfill their "normal" news function regarding the environmental threat. A quantity of information is gathered by reporters, assembled, interpreted and disseminated to the public. Such information may include data from emergency managers or technical support agencies, but it is also likely to include a variety of other information subject to the interpretation of writers and editors. In this situation, the channel becomes a source; a constructor of messages. This distinction between the mass media as channels versus sources bears upon our analyses of the Mt. St. Helens' data. We will first focus upon the mass media as channels and subsequently, in discussions of credibility and reliability, focus upon mass media as sources.

Table 12 shows the usual and preferred channels for information receipt for each study community. Respondents were asked to select the single channel through which they usually or most commonly received threat information regarding Mt. St. Helens volcano. In Toutle, the largest single proportion of people (41.7%) identified radio as the usual channel for threat information. Newspapers formed the usual channel for about one-fourth of the respondents and 17.5 percent cited personal conversation. About 10 percent mentioned television and very small proportions cited brochures and public meetings. In Lexington, virtually all of the respondents selected some mass medium as the channel through

TABLE 12

Usual and Preferred Channels of Information Receipt

	Toutle		Lexington	
Usual Channel of Receipt	N	%	N	%
Personal conversation	18	17.5	3	3.0
Television	11	10.7	36	36.4
Radio	43	41.7	17	17.2
Newspaper	28	27.2	42	42.4
Brochure	2	1.9	1	1.0
Public meeting	1	1.0	0	0.0
Preferred Channel of Receipt				
Personal conversation	0	0.0	3	3.0
Television	1	1.0	18	18.2
Radio	22	21.4	13	13.1
Newspaper	54	52.4	37	37.4
Brochure	20	19.4	15	15.2
Public meeting	6	5.9	13	13.1

which information was usually received. Newspapers accounted for 42.4 percent of the selections, television for 36.4 percent and radio for 17.2 percent. Only 3.0 percent cited personal conversation and one person mentioned brochures.

The picture of channel use in Toutle emphasizes radio, with the newspaper and personal conversations serving secondary roles. This seems to reflect a perceived need among Toutle residents for quick responses to imminent threats from the volcano. We have already shown these citizens to be sensitive to mud-flow/flood threats, which would technically—by virtue of close proximity to the volcanic cone—reach Toutle relatively quickly. As a "continual broadcast" medium, radio is capable of providing very current information, and Toutle residents may have gravitated toward this medium with the expectation of maximizing the amount of forewarning. In addition, it should be noted that there are no local television stations serving the area around the volcano. Consequently, those who wish to receive locally relevant information more often than daily (from the *Longview Daily News*), must use the radio. In Lexington, the most common channels for information receipt were newspapers and television, followed by radio. Personal conversations were cited as the "usual" channel for receiving threat information by many fewer respondents in Lexington than in Toutle. Recalling that personal conversation tends to be the channel used when the source is friends or neighbors, this finding reflects the previously reported data wherein the use of friends and neighbors as a source in Toutle exceeded Lexington.

The channels through which citizens *preferred* to receive hazard information differed from those cited as most commonly used. In Toutle, there was a clear preference for information transmitted by newspaper (endorsed by 52.4% of the respondents). The next most frequently selected channels were radio (21.4%) and brochures (19.4%). Very few Toutle residents selected public meetings or television as preferred communication channels and none endorsed personal conversation. The largest single proportion of Lexington residents (37.4%) also preferred to receive threat information through newspapers. Behind newspapers, however, these respondents are much more evenly spread across the remaining channels. Among these selections, television was most often endorsed (18.2%), followed by brochures (15.2%), radio (13.1%) and public meetings (13.1%). Personal conversations were again selected as a preferred channel by very few respondents.

These data show a preference in both sites for channels that transmit information in written form. Nearly three-quarters of Toutle respondents and more than half of those from Lexington who were given a choice elected to receive information via newspapers or brochures. This finding is consistent with other research on citizen preferences for communication channels which shows that people of white ethnic backgrounds opt for written threat information (minority group citizens vary from this pattern; see Perry and Mushkatel 1986, 182). The explanation for such preferences rests primarily upon the idea that information in written form can be examined by the reader at his/her own pace. In addition, such information can be kept and referenced by citizens sufficiently motivated to do so. A preference for radio also emerged in both sites, but particularly Toutle, probably because of ease of access and citizen perceptions of the ability of this medium to transmit information that is both timely and locally relevant. About one-fifth of the Lexington respondents expressed a preference for television, which is as timely as radio but not as locally relevant. Some Lexington residents also endorsed public meetings, which lack the "timeliness" dimension of radio and television, but which permit presenters to add greater depth to information. Public meetings also involve face-to-face contact, and unlike all the other channels discussed, allow two-way communications between the message disseminator and intended recipients. In closing, these data emphasize the diversity of citizen channel preferences and underscore the importance of using multiple channels in connection with threat information dissemination programs.

The third, and last, issue we will explore in connection with information communication at Mt. St. Helens is citizen perception of the credibility of sources. Research has shown that source credibility influences the behavior of citizens in at least two contexts. First, during the emergency response phase when a specific threat is impending, citizens are more likely to promptly comply with warning messages received from sources which are perceived to be reliable and credible (Perry and Mushkatel 1984). Second, during non-emergency times when environmental dangers are present but not imminent, citizens appear to attend more carefully to information and suggestions for protective measures disseminated by credible sources (Perry and Greene 1982; Perry and Mushkatel 1986). Consequently, source credibility affects the way the public acts upon hazard information across multiple contexts. This demands that emergency managers, who constitute only one of many potential sources, attend carefully to credibility issues as a means of enhancing the probability that the public will attend to technically accurate information regarding environmental threats and appropriate avenues for protection. To explore this issue, using the Mt. St. Helens case, we shall seek to identify patterns of credibility attributions and to link these attributions with specific rationales underlying the designation of sources as reliable.

Table 13 shows the sources nominated by our respondents as "most credible" cross-tabulated by the reason offered to justify the selection. In both cases, respondents were asked, using an open-ended question format, to first name the single most credible (trustworthy and reliable) source for volcano information and then to explain the bases of their confidence. The range of sources nominated as most credible was narrow compared to the number of sources available. Only six were named: County DES, County Sheriff, U.S. Geological Survey, Army Corps of Engineers, friends or neighbors, and local mass media. Moreover, only small proportions of respondents mentioned the last four sources. The majority of people in both communities identified the County Sheriff as the most credible source. The Sheriff's Department was selected by 75 Toutle residents (72.8%) and 59 Lexington respondents (59.6%). The County Department of Emergency Services was next in the frequency of nomination of "most credible," accounting for 15.5 percent (16 people) of the Toutle sample and 25.3 percent (25 people) of the Lexington sample. Taken together, then, the sheriff and County DES account for approximately 85 percent of the nominations for most credible source made by respondents from both communities.

In Toutle, people who believed the sheriff was the most credible information source cited two primary reasons for this choice. The first reason, cited by 35 people (46.7%) was that the Sheriff's Department had personnel with special skills and access to technical information which made it a credible source of threat information. The second basis for the sheriff's credibility, cited by 36 respondents (48.0%), centers upon the reliability of information received from this source in the past. A small proportion of the Toutle respondents (5.3%) cited department "integrity" as the reason for selecting the sheriff as most credible. These same reasons were given by Lexington residents who identified the Sheriff's Department as most credible. The majority of these respondents (64.4%) focused upon past reliability when selecting the Sheriff's Department. Fourteen people (23.7%) mentioned possession of special skills and access to technical information to justify their confidence in the sheriff. Finally, 11.9 percent said that the integrity of the Sheriff's Department formed the basis of its credibility.

TABLE 13

Most Credible Source by Reason Chosen
(frequency only)

Site	Reason Chosen	County Des	County Sheriff	USGS	Army Corps	Friends/ Neighbors	TV/ Radio
Toutle	Concerned for citizens	2	0	0	0	0	0
	Special skills/information	8	35	5	2	0	3
	Past reliability	3	36	0	0	2	0
	Integrity	3	4	0	0	0	0
	Total	16	75	5	2	2	3
Lexington	Concerned for citizens	4	0	0	0	0	1
	Special skills/information	14	14	0	2	0	3
	Past reliability	5	38	1	0	0	0
	Integrity	2	7	0	0	4	4
	Total	25	59	1	2	4	8

The reasons given for placing high confidence in the County Department of Emergency Services covered a wider range, proportionally, than those cited for the sheriff. In Toutle, 12.4 percent cited DES's "concern for citizens," 50.0 percent mentioned special skills and information, and 18.8 percent cited each of two other reasons: past reliability and integrity. The majority of Lexington respondents mentioned special skills and information (56.0%), followed by past reliability (20.0%), concern for citizens (16.0%) and integrity (8.0%). It is important to note, however, that the possession of special skills and information is by far the most common basis for a credibility attribution, cited by about half of the respondents in each community.

Our data indicate that with regard to the volcano threat posed by Mt. St. Helens, citizens have come to define the County Sheriff and Department of Emergency Services—the local emergency authorities—as the most reliable sources of information. It was observed above that the establishment of local authorities as a credible source has positive implications for citizen attention to and compliance with hazard related information and protective measures. It should be emphasized here that such credibility attributions are an often cited goal for emergency managers, but are difficult to achieve in practice (Perry 1983). In connection with riverine floods, for example, relatives and friends are sometimes defined as credible sources almost as often as local emergency managers (cf. Perry et al. 1979). Also, during the nuclear reactor incident at Three Mile Island, the mass media dominated citizen nominations for most credible source, with only 2.0 percent of those surveyed identifying local emergency management authorities (Barnes et al. 1979, 14).

Credibility attributions are subjective judgments made by the public. Our data, however, provide a glimpse of this judgment process by identifying the two principal dimensions by which such attributions are made: past reliability and access to special skills and information. When the Toutle and Lexington respondents named a source they believed to be highly credible, large proportions of them justified the choice in terms of the extent to which the organization possessed these characteristics. These dimensions are consistent with some considerations that have been described in previous discussions of credibility in communicating risk information. Lindell and Earle (1983, 245) noted that experimental research on persuasive communications has suggested that there are two principal components of source credibility that are relevant to these types of situations, *expertise* and *trustworthiness*. Expertise is the same as what has been described here as special skills and information. Trustworthiness refers to a willingness and ability to communicate information without bias (e.g., Perry and Lindell 1980). This latter dimension corresponds to the categories of *concern for citizens* and *integrity* listed in Table 13. The emphasis by Toutle and Lexington residents on past reliability can be interpreted as referring to the *basis* upon which an inference of credibility is made rather than to specific aspects (expertise and trustworthiness) of credibility. More generally, there are three different bases upon which a source can be judged to be credible. The first basis is the source's "credentials," usually a job title such as geologist, meteorologist, or hydrologist. Each of these three examples conveys an image of expertise that results from specialized knowledge.

Inferences about trustworthiness can also be made from credentials. A university professor is likely to be considered to be a disinterested party, while a representative of a corporation whose timberlands might be closed is likely to be considered less than completely trustworthy. A second basis of source credibility is the way in which it is treated by other sources whose credibility has already been established. A source of, as yet, unknown credibility is likely to be accepted by the public as credible if it is treated with respect by sources that have already established their credibility. Finally, a source may be considered to be credible because of its past history of job performance. The three-year series of volcanic eruptions at Mt. St. Helens has provided the County DES and Sheriff's Office with an opportunity to establish their credibility by means of continuing test of job performance.

Emergency managers should be aware of factors that influence the public's perception of their agencies. The objective, of course, should not be to create unwarranted visions of agency reliability; it is probably not possible to make a basically unreliable system appear competent for any significant period of time. Instead, the idea is to accurately communicate the strong points and limitations of technical emergency management systems so that citizens can compare information produced by these systems with information derived from alternate sources. Essentially this gives citizens a clearer basis for rejecting inaccurate or inappropriate protective action recommendations generated by sources with faulty or incomplete information about the situation.

In disseminating information, local emergency managers must strive to provide data that are as technically accurate as possible. A chronic problem in emergencies is that hazard monitoring systems break down, data are misinterpreted, and conditions rapidly change rendering data no longer representative of the actual situation. When an emergency manager disseminates information that turns out to be unreliable for any of these reasons (basically outside the department's control), an effort should be made to disseminate follow-up information which corrects the inappropriate message and provides a brief explanation of how incorrect information was disseminated in the first place. The goal here is to avoid permitting an incorrect or misleading forecast or status report to simply stand. By providing an explanation, the emergency manager helps the public to interpret apparent "unreliability" by understanding its genesis. Such treatment converts what would otherwise simply be remembered as an instance of unreliability into an opportunity for the emergency manager to educate the public regarding the limitations of available technology. In effect, such performances demonstrate to the public that emergency managers exercise control over the situation in that errors can be identified, explained and corrected.

Another avenue for enhancing agency credibility can be derived from citizen concern with the special skills and information that may be used by a source in generating threat information. In all dissemination efforts, emergency managers should not only seek to educate the public about environmental threats, but also about the process and practice of emergency management. When threat information is disseminated, emergency managers are describing and interpreting the state of the environment, and *asking* citizens to accept that view. In the special case of disaster warning messages, authorities must not only ask citizens to accept their view of the environment, but also to undertake specific actions consistent with that view. It is well documented that citizens are unlikely to accept on faith the judgments of emergency managers (cf. Quarantelli and Dynes 1972).

Instead, receipt of threat information—from any source—stimulates individuals to collect additional information from other sources, including observations of the environment. This information is used to devise a personal definition of the situation which may or may not agree with the view promoted by the information source. It is therefore important for an emergency manager to not only present interpretations and conclusions, but also to share the bases which underlie them. This includes establishing ethos by describing the kinds of expertise in the form of specialized equipment and personnel available to the emergency manager that were used in evaluating the relevant environmental threat. This tactic has two effects. First, it communicates information about the decision process used by authorities, which in turn increases the chance that citizens will focus their own decision making on similar issues and adopt a similar point of view (Perry 1985, 65-72). Second, it publicly describes special resources available to emergency managers that uniquely qualify them to make pronouncements about environmental threats. Our volcano data indicate that citizens are particularly attentive to such qualifications when making judgments about source credibility.

In closing, it is important to emphasize that establishing credibility is a long process that is difficult to shortcut. Perceptions of credibility flow from many experiences or source/citizen interactions over a sustained time period.

Perceptions of Vulnerability

We have already considered the nature and extensiveness of volcano threat knowledge assembled by our respondents, and described the channels through which such information is passed. Understanding an environmental threat, however, is distinct from feeling personally vulnerable. Feelings of personal vulnerability arise from beliefs about the subset of eruptive impacts that are believed to personally affect the individual. For those living far from the volcano, acquisition and storage of information in eruptive threats can be conceived as primarily a "neutral" process because negative eruptive consequences would not reach them. For those near enough to be affected, perceptions of vulnerability arise from the juxtaposition of their knowledge of a threat in general with their understanding of personal situational factors. These perceptions of vulnerability can be expressed as individuals' beliefs about the certainty and severity of harm they might experience. As we have pointed out above, unlike the acquisition of threat knowledge, perceptions of vulnerability have direct effects upon the individual's propensity to take protective action in connection with environmental hazards. In the sections which follow, we will first carefully scrutinize the concept of vulnerability and then identify specific variables correlated with perceived vulnerability. Chapter four will further explore this logic by examining the role of vulnerability in stimulating decisions to implement protective measures.

Conceptualizing Vulnerability

In the research literature on human behavior in disasters, the idea of vulnerability has been dealt with under the rubric of perceived personal risk. The empirical tradition has been to define personal risk as the individual's beliefs about the likely *personal* negative consequences associated with an environmental threat (Fritz and Marks 1954, 29; Withey 1962, 104; Glass 1970, 64; Kates 1976; Perry 1979). The terms susceptibility (Houts et al. 1984) and danger (Douglas and Wildavsky 1981) have also been used interchangeably with perceived personal risk. Most of the research concern with personal risk has focused upon its antecedent causal status, that is, its predictive efficacy with regard to specific disaster behaviors. Citizen warning compliance and the adoption of protective measures are two types of behavior that are most closely related to the individual's perceptions of personal risk. Comparatively less attention, however, has been devoted to examining factors which produce perceptions of risk or vulnerability (cf. Earle and Cvetkovitch 1983, 5-6).

An initial task in analyzing why people feel vulnerable to environ-mental threats is to ask, vulnerable in what way or at risk from what? Fischoff, Watson and Hope (1983) have noted that there are indeed many possible definitions of risk which vary according to the type of danger being confronted and the values of the people involved. We have already introduced the idea that in connection with disasters, citizens think about risk in two general categories: risk to personal health and safety and risk to property. There is considerable intuitive appeal to partitioning risk in terms of these dimensions. It is logical that individuals would think and act differently towards events which endanger their lives than toward those which exclusively threaten property or those which do both. Furthermore, there is some research evidence that in different situations either endangered citizens or authorities tend to view risk in "personal safety versus property safety" terms.

An approach to risk which emphasizes the property safety dimension can be found in the work of economists on natural hazard management (Dacy and Kunreuther 1969; Kunreuther 1978; Sorkin 1982). Much of this work focuses upon the problem of developing workable approaches to hazard insurance. The objective is to select "countable" consequences of disasters, which usually center on damages expressed as dollar values (death and injury is not necessarily ignored, but may be factored into the equation in terms of economic consequences). On this basis one could ideally examine the number and magnitude (dollar value) of past events at a given place, take into account technical data to estimate future threat conditions, factors in current conditions, and arrive at an estimate of the future likelihood and magnitude of event-related negative outcomes. This strategy forms the basis for both earthquake and flood insurance programs, and essentially defines risk in terms of the probability of an event relative to likely property damages. Of course, some areas may be judged too hazardous to insure—and thus require policy interventions in the form of flood plain management. Nonetheless, it is anticipated that most people will purchase insurance as a hedge against property loss. From this perspective, citizens share the risk and behave rationally by paying premiums to gain compensation from possible property loss. The view of risk which underlies hazard insurance is consequently not designed or oriented to personal safety threats.

In contrast to the economists' emphasis on property risks, research on the perceived risks of technology have shown that citizens emphasize personal health and safety dangers. Lindell and Earle (1983), for example, studied citizen evaluations of risk relative to eight different types of hazardous industrial facilities including nuclear, oil, natural gas, and coal-fired power plants. It was found that facilities considered to be "high risk" were those people believed to have health hazards that were not well understood and less preventable, and liable to affect future generations. Those facilities considered to have the potential for catastrophic accidents were also considered high risk. Research on nuclear power plants in particular suggests that citizen judgments of personal risk are heavily influenced by perceived impacts on life and health, rather than concerns about potential damages to property (cf. Flynn 1979; Lindell and Perry 1983; Houts et al. 1984). Indeed, in an extended study of ninety hazards (not including natural hazards), Slovic, Fischoff and Lichtenstein (1980, 211) conclude that "the perceived potential for catastrophic loss of life emerges as one of the most important risk characteristics." The dominance of the life safety concern is also present in research on the general public's definitions of risk in connection with the threat of nuclear attack (Perry 1982). When defining the personal risks associated with the possibility of an attack or war, people focus on health consequences first, and only secondarily address environmental or property destruction, and even then usually in connection with its impact on the ability of the society or the earth to support life (cf. Katz 1982).

A third group of studies which has focused on behavior in disasters has emphasized the connectedness of people's beliefs about risks to property and risks to persons (Danzig et al. 1958; Moore et al. 1963; Drabek 1969; Perry et al. 1981). Intellectually, such conceptualizations are related to the work of Anthony Wallace (1956) on "mazeway disintegration." Wallace observed that some types of disasters have the potential to take life, disrupt social networks and destroy the human-constructed environment. Thus, as a consequence of some natural or technological threats, both the social environment and the physical environment can be almost "instantly" altered. Wallace labelled situations wherein both environments were radically impacted, mazeway disintegration; in effect identifying such events as ones which create intense citizen reactions because of the cumulative effect of risks to persons *and* property.

This reasoning has inspired several studies in which risk has been conceived and measured in a way that simultaneously incorporates person and property dangers. Particularly in the case of floods, risk measured as a composite has been shown to be a powerful predictor of some warning behaviors, especially evacuation compliance (Perry 1985,

78-79). Certain empirical anomalies have arisen, however, which suggest that people differentially weight the person and property dimensions of risk. For example, in some flood settings, people may define risk to be "high," but refuse to comply with a warning message to evacuate (cf. Perry et al. 1981, 36; Perry and Mushkatel 1984, 60-63). Interestingly, it was found that such people who refused evacuation compliance were often undertaking property protection measures instead of evacuating (evacuating being a measure to protect personal health and safety). Anecdotal evidence obtained throughout interviewer debriefings indicated that some respondents justified their actions by pointing out that they didn't believe they were likely to die in the flood, but were very concerned about the psychological and financial hardships that might accrue from massive property destruction. In essence, these people were behaving consistently with their views of risk. Believing the risk to personal safety was low, they shunned a person protection measure in favor of actions aimed at protecting property, which they believed to be at considerable risk. Thus, the *apparent* inconsistency between high perceived risk and failure to evacuate resulted because the measure of perceived risk was simply tapping two different aspects at the same time.

The literature just reviewed supports three general conclusions about risk perception in environmental threats. First, there is some empirical justification that citizens partition risks associated with disasters into health-safety and property categories. Second, under different circumstances—apparently tied to different characteristics of the threat agent—people place different emphases upon the two dimensions. Finally, when trying to understand hazard response (particularly the adoption of protective actions), the most accurate predictions are made when one matches the nature of the behavior (person protection versus property protection) with the dimension of risk emphasized (person versus property).

From these inferences flows the conclusion that to obtain a complete picture of citizen beliefs about vulnerability, it is necessary to take into account both aspects of perceived risk. This is not to argue that any one of the three approaches found in the literature—insurance purchasing, technological risk perception or warning response perspectives—is inherently better than the others. Each approach is designed to study slightly different issues. What is important is to recognize that if person and property risk are combined in the same measure, it is not possible to subsequently assess their separate effects.

Put differently, perceived risk should be treated as a multidimensional rather than a one-dimensional attribute. Accordingly, researchers and emergency managers should examine beliefs about property danger and person danger when documenting citizen beliefs about vulnerability and when assessing the types of actions people are likely to undertake in connection with an environmental threat. Recognition of the property—person risk distinction raises the question of how the two dimensions are interrelated, particularly in reference to threat-connected behaviors. A broad review of research to date can be summarized as a cross-classification of person with property risk (Table 14), allowing two levels, low and high, for each dimension. The entries in the cells represent hypotheses (derived from the disaster literature) about the modal response to each of the different combinations of perceived risk.

By examining each cell, one can illuminate the relationship between person and property risk and project the implications of the relationship for likely citizen actions. When citizens believe that both risk to property *and* person are low, one would expect that they are likely to not engage in any protective actions. This would include both warning-related actions and the adoption of mitigation measures in general. Such people would not see themselves as subject to any type of negative consequences and would therefore not believe there was a need for protection. Early research on Mt. St. Helens indicated that people living in Woodland, a community at some distance from the volcano, believed them-

---

TABLE 14

Probable Citizen Actions for Combinations
of Perceived Person and Property Risk

Perceived Property Risk	*Perceived Person Risk*	
	Low	*High*
Low	Protective action unlikely	Person protection likely
High	Property protection likely	Person protection likely

selves not at risk from ash or floods or eruptions, and it was found that their interest in protective actions in general was low (Lindell et al. 1982). Similarly, citizens who have been repeatedly exposed to low magnitude seasonal flooding are sometimes characterized by low levels of perceived danger to property and person, and are correspondingly slow to adopt protective actions (cf. Perry et al. 1981).

When risks to person are believed to be low and risks to property are seen as high, citizens are most likely to eschew person protection measures in favor of property protection. Person risks might be defined as low for different reasons. In some cases the nature of the environmental threat may be judged less likely to harm people due to characteristics of the threat agent. This may be either technically accurate or largely a matter of local conventional wisdom (cf. Barton 1970). Often, natural disasters characterized by a gradual onset—which affords the opportunity for detection and forewarning—are not identified as posing high levels of person danger. Riverine floods and hurricanes serve as familiar threats which are sometimes treated in this manner. Property protection is common in the face of such threats, while authorities have often cited difficulties in persuading citizens to comply with evacuation orders (cf. Baker et al. 1976; Windham et al. 1977). Empirical studies indicate that when person risk is perceived to be high, citizens engage in protective measures aimed at health and safety, regardless of the level of perceived property risk. Thus, person risk may be seen as the dominant concern. If they believe there is significant danger to life, individuals focus on that danger and seek to reduce it before dealing with other aspects of risk. The 1979 chlorine tank car derailment at Mississauga, Ontario (Borton et al. 1980) and a 1983 nitric acid spill in Denver, Colorado (Perry and Mushkatel 1984, 115-121), both produced emergencies where property damage was likely to be low, but potential risks to health were judged to be high. During the Three Mile Island nuclear reactor accident, many evacuees felt no conflict between person protection and property protection, even though they believed their homes would be permanently contaminated. It was believed that no actions could be taken that would effectively protect property. In each of these three cases, citizen compliance with person protection measures was far greater than authorities initially anticipated, and interviews with citizens showed that only limited efforts were made to protect property.

When both person risk and property risk are perceived to be high, citizens also concentrate on measures to protect life. Research on citizen response to the May 18, 1980 eruption of Mt. St. Helens indicated that citizens defined property and person risk as high, and consistently engaged in behaviors aimed at protecting life, again with relatively little attention to negative consequences for property (Perry and Greene 1983). The rationale used by these citizens was concisely captured by one of the evacuees who reported: "I figured I could get another house if it was ruined, but I've only got one life."

In considering the implications of the different combinations of perceived person and property risk the focus has been on *perceived* risk. It should therefore be acknowledged that such perceptions (like all perceptions) are subject to change based upon changing information, experience, and circumstances. From an emergency manager's point of view, this suggests that one can shape citizen perceptions of risk to be consistent with technical assessments of risk (cf. Perry and Nigg 1985), thereby increasing the subjective probability that people will comply with protective action recommendations from authorities. From the standpoint of researchers attempting to characterize the way that the general public views risk and the way these definitions of risk result in action, the discussion implies that both dimensions of risk need to be documented and acknowledges that each may be of differential importance in understanding human behavior. This means that a researcher may measure both person and property risk, but subsequently use only one of the dimensions, whichever is most relevant, in understanding human response to the environmental threat.

In chapter two the data showed that property risk was more salient than person risk among our respondents in Toutle and Lexington. Table 15 shows the cross-tabulation of property with person risk. Forty-eight Toutle residents (46.6%) and 55 Lexington residents (55.6%) reported they defined person risks as slight. Most of those remaining believed person risks were moderate; only 9.1 percent of Lexington respondents and 15.5 percent of those living in Toutle believed person risks were severe. On the other hand, large proportions of residents of both communities felt that property risk was more likely. Approximately three-fourths of the respondents in Toutle (77.6%, or 80 people) and in Lexington (73.7%, or 73 people) defined property risk as either severe or moderate. These data may be interpreted to mean that—at this point in time at Mt. St. Helens—people characterize vulnerability largely in terms of dangers to property rather than dangers to person. Thus, in this chapter and chapter four, when risk is examined we will use our measure of property risk as a means of capturing the dimension of risk of greatest concern to our respondents. For analytic purposes, it is also interesting to note that the two dimensions of risk are not strongly correlated. It is true that almost all respondents who believed that person risk was severe likewise defined property risk as severe. However, at slight or moderate levels of person risk, it is more difficult to accurately predict level of property risk. For example, among respondents who believed person risk was *slight*, 39.6 percent of those in Toutle and 34.5 percent of those in Lexington felt that property risk was *severe*. The important point is, that while the two dimensions are indeed positively correlated, they are by no means dependent upon one another. The remainder of this chapter is devoted to identifying the factors which produce these feelings of vulnerability.

TABLE 15

Perceived Property Risk by Perceived Person Risk

		Risk to Person					
	Risk to	*Slight*		*Moderate*		*Severe*	
Site	*Property*	N	%	N	%	N	%
	Slight	20	41.7	3	7.7	0	0.0
Toutle	Moderate	9	18.8	21	53.8	3	18.8
	Severe	19	39.6	15	38.5	13	81.3
	Slight	25	45.5	1	2.9	0	0.0
Lexington	Moderate	11	20.0	18	51.4	0	0.0
	Severe	19	34.5	16	45.7	9	100.0

Classic Risk Determinants

Historically, research on the extent to which people define themselves as vulnerable to environmental threats has concentrated on three determinants: proximity, certainty and severity of the threat (Diggory 1956; Withey 1962; Williams and Fritz 1957; Menninger 1952). Three propositions may be constructed to summarize the results of studies of these variables. First, the closer an individual believes he or she is to the source of an environmental threat or to a likely impact area, the more vulnerable he or she is likely to feel. Second, the more certain it is that an impact will occur, the greater the feelings of vulnerability. Thus, if there is doubt that an event will ever take place or if the probability is quite low, people tend to see it as less dangerous. Third, the more severe the *possible* negative consequences associated with a threat, the more vulnerable individuals are likely to feel.

In a narrow sense, these variables have formed central components for structuring disaster warning messages. The idea is to create a message that accurately conveys vulnerability to endangered citizens in the hope of inspiring action on their part. To accomplish this, warning messages address the issues of "where, when and with what force" regarding the anticipated disaster impact (Williams 1964; Mogil and Groper 1977; Lindell et al. 1980). This information allows recipients of warnings to determine proximity, and assuming the message sender is believed to be a credible source, it also defines the certainty and severity of the threat. In a slightly broader sense, this same logic underlies the development of information designed to enhance both citizen hazard awareness and emergency preparedness (Bolton et al. 1981; Christensen and Ruch 1978). In this context, vulnerability is seen as a prerequisite to citizen recognition and danger reduction behavior, and the information supplied for citizens to judge vulnerability focuses upon identifying the place endangered, the likelihood of an event and the consequences of an event.

Because these three antecedents of vulnerability have been consistently documented by past research, we anticipate that they will again emerge as important in understanding our data on Mt. St. Helens. Table 16 shows perceived vulnerability by proximity to the threat for Toutle and Lexington. We have chosen to not define proximity in terms of respondent distance from the volcanic cone; this dimension is shown by the fact that we have segregated our data by community. Instead, we have focused upon the more specific dimension of respondent proximity to a river. The major dangers facing our respondents accrue from mud-flows and flooding which, of course, follow river systems. Thus, to obtain a measure of proximity, respondents were asked to estimate the distance from their home to the nearest river. In Toutle, the Toutle River was used as a referent; in Lexington distance was calculated to the Cowlitz River. Judgments of distance were grouped into three categories: close (less than one-fourth mile), intermediate (one-fourth to one mile), and distant (more than one mile).

The data in Table 16 show that, for each community, there is a positive correlation of low to moderate strength between proximity to the threat and level of perceived vulnerability. The closer people perceived themselves to the source of danger, the greater the feeling of risk. In Toutle, the proportion of respondents who define risk as severe steadily declines as we move from being close to the river (63.0%), through intermediate (35.5%), to distant (26.9%). Conversely, the proportion defining risk as moderate increases as distance from the river increases. Only 17.4 percent of those close to the Toutle River believed risk was moderate, compared with 38.7 percent of those at intermediate range and 50.0 percent of those who were distant. Similarly, the proportion of Lexington residents who believed risk was severe declines with increasing distance from the Cowlitz River. One-third of those whose homes were distant felt severe risk, compared with one-half of those who were intermediate and nearly three-fourths of those who were close. Again, the proportion of respondents who reported that risk was moderate increases with increasing distance.

TABLE 16

Perceived Vulnerability by Proximity to Threat Source

| | | Proximity to River | | | | | |
| | | Close | | Intermediate | | Distant | |
Site	Risk to Property	N	%	N	%	N	%
	Slight	9	19.6	8	25.8	6	23.1
Toutle	Moderate	8	17.4	12	38.7	13	50.0
	Severe	29	63.0	11	35.5	7	26.9
	Slight	1	14.3	13	26.0	12	28.6
Lexington	Moderate	1	14.3	12	24.0	16	38.1
	Severe	5	71.4	25	50.0	14	33.3

Although the relationship between proximity and perceived vulnerability is in the predicted direction, it was expected that the observed correlation should have been higher, particularly based on the results of studies of riverine floods. The relatively lower correlation found in Toutle and Lexington is probably more a function of mechanical issues, rather than an indication of conceptual problems. First, the magnitude of the correlation is probably affected by a statistical problem called "restriction of range." This occurs when the cases being analyzed are concentrated in one or two categories of a measurement scale, which in effect reduces either the amount of variance to be explained (for dependent, variables) or the variation which can be used in explaining (for independent variables). Such restriction of range exists for the independent variable in Toutle where 44.7 percent of the sample fall into the close proximity category and in Lexington where only 7.1 percent of the sample fall into the close category, resulting in a heavy concentration of cases in the remaining distance categories. In this case, the restriction of range is produced by the location of sample households which were selected on a random basis, so no systematic bias is in evidence. The existence of restricted range, however, does tend to attenuate the magnitude of the observed correlation.

The second reason for the lower observed correlation between proximity and perceived vulnerability in these data centers on the question of terrain and topography in the two study communities. Most studies of flood-plains deal with terrain which is relatively flat, producing a smooth threat gradient in which, for example, the depth and speed of water—and consequently the danger—decreases smoothly with increasing distance from the river. Our two communities are located in foothill areas characterized by sometimes rapid changes in elevation, ravines, and hills. This is particularly the case in Toutle. Under such circumstances it is possible to be geographically close to a river but located on a hill, bank or rise and therefore relatively safe from mud-flows or flooding. On the other hand, it is also possible to be at some distance from a river but located in a valley or low-lying area and consequently at some danger from high water. Thus, the terrain around Mt. St. Helens is such that one would not expect a perfect correlation between proximity and vulnerability on technical grounds.

We are reminded, then, that vulnerability in a technical sense depends on local conditions which vary between study sites. Our data are also subject to interpretation difficulties which stem from the statistical phenomenon of restricted range. The fact that in spite of these problems we found a positive correlation between proximity and perceived vulnerability underscores the importance and strength of the conceptual argument that links the two variables.

Table 17 shows perceived vulnerability by certainty of danger. In

studies of the disaster warning process, certainty has been operationalized in terms of the likelihood that the predicted disaster impact will in
fact occur (Perry et al. 1981). At Mt. St. Helens, we are concerned with
certainty in a broader sense; not just in the context of the likelihood of a
particular impact. Instead, we wish to characterize certainty with respect
to the likelihood that continued volcanic events (of any nature) will pose
dangers for people living near Mt. St. Helens. Thus, we asked respondents to estimate the likelihood that dangerous volcanic events would
occur in the future. Our response format permitted people to define the
probability of future volcanicity as "unlikely," "even odds," or "likely."

TABLE 17

Perceived Vulnerability by Certainty of Danger

		Probability of Future Volcanicity					
	Risk to	Unlikely		Even Odds		Likely	
Site	Property	N	%	N	%	N	%
	Slight	10	55.6	12	23.1	1	3.0
Toutle	Moderate	3	16.7	21	40.4	9	27.3
	Severe	5	27.8	19	36.5	23	69.7
	Slight	22	56.4	2	5.1	2	9.5
Lexington	Moderate	8	20.5	16	41.0	5	23.8
	Severe	9	23.1	21	53.8	14	66.7

Among Toutle respondents, as the probability of future volcanicity
increases, so does the level of perceived risk. The proportion of citizens
who define risk as severe increases from 27.8 percent of those who
believed future volcanicity was unlikely, through 36.5 percent of those
who chose even odds, to 69.7 percent of those who felt future activity was
likely. Most of the people (55.6%) who felt that future volcanic activity
was unlikely (that is, less certain) defined risk as slight. Among those
who believed that the probability of activity was even odds, the largest
proportion (40.5%) placed risk slightly higher at the moderate level. The
modal category of perceived risk for people who felt that future volcanic
events were likely was severe.

The Lexington data are similar to those from Toutle. Again, there is a steady increase in the proportion of respondents who defined risk as severe as the probability of future volcanicity increased from unlikely (23.1%) to even odds (53.8%) to likely (66.7%). Most people who thought volcanic events were unlikely defined risk as slight (56.4%), while only 9.5 percent of those who believed future activity was likely thought risk was slight. In Lexington, people who assigned even odds to future activity did judge risk to be severe more often than their counterparts in Toutle, but the overall pattern of relationships remains the same.

These data indicate that there is a positive correlation of moderate strength between citizen perceptions of the certainty of danger and the level of perceived risk. In connection with Mt. St. Helens, then, people who envision future volcanic activity as more certain also believe risks to be greater. It is interesting to note in closing that in both communities, nearly four years after the first steam and ash eruptions, many citizens believe that still further volcanic threats will materialize. About 80 percent of the Toutle respondents and 60 percent of those in Lexington felt that the probability of dangerous events in the future was either even odds or likely. This suggests that people have become sensitized to the multiple impact nature of volcanic sequences and that they do not subjectively reduce the likelihood of future events on the basis of the apparent length of the volcanic sequence to date. Put simply, the fact that numerous eruptions have taken place does not seem to influence people's judgments about the likelihood of future eruptions. This condition is probably facilitated because the magnitude and frequency of eruptions has varied considerably over time and does not appear to follow either a declining or increasing pattern.

The third of the classic determinants of risk is severity: the magnitude of negative consequences that citizens believe *might* be associated with an environmental threat. In assessing severity in connection with Mt. St. Helens, it was necessary to specify a referent threat for citizens to rate regarding possible consequences. Following the logic developed in chapter two, we chose to focus on ash fall and mud-flow/floods as threats. Respondents were asked to rate the *potential* damages which might result from each of these volcanic hazards as "slight," "moderate," or "severe." The objective was to obtain an estimate of the degree of harm that could be associated with each threat. In this sense we obtained a measure of the perceived severity of ash fall and mud-flow/floods.

Table 18 shows perceived vulnerability by severity of damage for both ash fall and mud-flow/floods. The ash fall table indicates that there is a low to moderate strength positive correlation between severity and perceived risk. In Toutle, the proportion of respondents who define risk as severe increases as citizen estimates of the severity of ash fall increases. Hence, 35.6 percent of those defining severity as slight thought risk was severe, compared with 52.3 percent of those who saw severity as moderate and 57.1 percent of those who believed potential consequences were severe. Conversely, the proportion of people who believed risk was slight decreases as potential damage estimates increase: 37.8 percent of those defining potential damage as slight, 11.4 percent at the moderate level, and 7.1 percent at the severe level. A similar pattern is seen in the Lexington data. The proportion of respon-

TABLE 18

Perceived Vulnerability by Severity of Danger

Site	Risk to Property	Potential Ash Fall Damage					
		Slight		Moderate		Severe	
		N	%	N	%	N	%
	Slight	17	37.8	5	11.4	1	7.1
Toutle	Moderate	12	26.7	16	36.4	5	35.7
	Severe	16	35.6	23	52.3	8	57.1
	Slight	24	35.8	1	3.6	1	25.0
Lexington	Moderate	21	31.3	8	28.6	0	0.0
	Severe	22	32.8	19	67.9	3	75.0

Site	Risk to Property	Potential Mud-flow/Flood Damage					
		Slight		Moderate		Severe	
		N	%	N	%	N	%
	Slight	18	56.3	3	25.0	3	3.4
Toutle	Moderate	9	28.1	6	50.0	18	30.5
	Severe	5	15.6	3	25.0	39	66.1
	Slight	20	80.0	4	30.8	2	3.3
Lexington	Moderate	5	20.0	9	69.2	15	24.6
	Severe	0	0.0	0	0.0	44	72.1

dents defining risk as severe again increases as perceived severity increases from slight (32.8%) to moderate (67.9%) to severe (75.0%). Also, the proportion of people who saw risk as slight decreases generally with increasing perceived severity.

These data need to be cautiously interpreted, however, because of the small number of cases in each community that believed that potential ash fall damage could be severe. Virtually all of the respondents perceived that possible ash fall damage would be either slight or moderate (a perception which is probably technically accurate). It is important to emphasize, though, that the data for the slight and moderate potential damage categories for both Toutle and Lexington do follow the pattern that increases in perceived severity are matched by increases in perceived risk. A conservative interpretation of the ash fall data acknowledges that a low to moderately strong positive correlation exists between the two variables.

The data which use mud-flow/flood damage as a referent threat also show a positive correlation between perceived severity and perceived risk, but the strength of the association is slightly greater than that observed in connection with ash fall threats. Among Toutle respondents, there is a steady increase in the proportion of people who define risk as severe as potential damage estimates increase from slight (15.6%) to moderate (25.0%) to severe (66.1%). On the other hand, the proportion of people who define risk as slight decreases from 56.3 percent at the slight damage level, to 25.0 percent at moderate and 3.4 percent at the severe level. The Lexington data also indicate that people who define potential mud-flow/flood damage as higher tend to perceive risk as higher. Eighty percent of the people who believed potential damage was slight also believed that risk was slight. Most of the respondents who projected likely damage as moderate in turn estimated risk to be moderate (69.2%). Among those who felt that potential damage was severe, nearly three-fourths (72.1%) characterized risk as severe. Once again, however, one must be cautious in interpreting these data. Most of the respondents in both communities felt that potential mud-flow/flood damage should be classified as severe; there was also a concentration of cases in the slight category, and comparatively few people described potential damage as moderate. Of course, the distribution of cases on the potential damage scale does reflect a technically accurate assessment in that mud-flows and floods do in fact carry the potential of severe damage. This situation does result, however, in limiting the variation on the independent variable and consequently places restrictions on the strength of the statistical association. It is important to acknowledge that although there is some restriction of range, the direction and strength of the relationship observed between severity and perceived risk conforms with the results of other studies and with existing theoretical formulations.

To summarize, our analyses indicate that, as predicted, proximity, certainty and severity are all positively correlated with citizen perceptions of risk from Mt. St. Helens. Some qualifications were needed to understand the special characteristics of the volcano threat, but for the most part our findings were consistent with the results of other disaster studies. Interestingly, together these classic determinants may be seen as representing what Slovic et al. (1980b) have called the "disaster potential" of an environmental threat. That is, by addressing these issues, people are characterizing the threat in terms of the personal harm it may be expected to perpetrate. Will the threat really reach me (proximity)? Will danger really materialize (certainty)? Will the negative outcomes really be extensive (severity)? In answering these questions, citizens are determining just what sort of danger they are facing. It should be noted too that these questions all focus upon the nature of the hazard events themselves: the object of interest and assessment is the agent of danger. It is also possible to consider issues which bear upon vulnerability that are not directly connected with the hazard agent. Particularly in the case of volcanicity, people develop a history of interaction with the environmental threat. In the process of "living" with the threat citizens have experiences and form opinions about dangers that have social psychological bases rather than being explicitly tied to characteristics of the threat agent. The following section explores three such social psychological issues in defining risk.

Social Psychological Determinants

Certainly the principal determinants of perceived vulnerability lie with the characteristics of the hazard agent itself. However, since risk is a function of the interaction between people and the environmental hazard, variables other than those related to the threat agent are likely to affect citizen definitions of vulnerability. Although disaster researchers have generated little data which directly bear upon the relationship of such variables to risk, the literature does suggest that three issues in particular merit consideration: prior experience with the hazard agent, the perceived efficacy of protective measures and the impact of family responsibility.

It is reasonable to believe that people's perceptions of danger will be shaped by their experiences with the hazardous event. "Prior experience" is often construed in a broad sense. For disaster threats to which an individual has not been directly exposed—perhaps because of the "newness" of the threat, as one finds with some emerging technological hazards; or because the negative event has a very low probability; or because the individual has simply not had the opportunity to be exposed—experience may be vicarious in a psychological sense. Thus one may develop a vision or definition of the threat on the basis of news media accounts, fiction literature, Hollywood movies, or through accounts given by people who have direct experience (cf. Quarantelli 1982; Perry 1982). Actual exposure to the environmental threat constitutes the alternative to vicarious experience. Actual exposure—the experience of howling wind, torrential rain and the pounding surf of a hurricane perhaps—is likely to create a much more vivid image than any verbal message, book or movie could hope to do. Yet previous investigations (cf. Baker 1980) have argued that prior "actual" experience has little or no effect upon risk perception. Such research findings may exist because there is a wide range of consequences that a person might be exposed to as a function of "being in a hurricane" or any particular disaster event. Some people live the tragedy of seeing friends, relatives or neighbors lose lives or property. For others, such losses were merely statistics seen in the news media.

In particular, this suggests that those who sustain damage have a different experience from those who are subject to an environmental threat but have had no direct damage (Perry and Hirose 1985). Among other things, it is likely that people who feel damage directly remember the event longer, evidence different outcomes, experience higher levels of social network disruption, and make different demands upon both the emergency response systems and the restorative system (Perry and Lindell 1978, 112). Thus, people who are directly exposed should feel higher levels of vulnerability. This logic is particularly suggestive for the eruptions of Mt. St. Helens where all residents have had "actual" experience with the threat, but some have (thus far) escaped personal damage.

Table 19 shows perceived vulnerability by damage sustained for each study community. The Toutle data indicate that only ten respondents reported levels of damage as slight or none; more than 90 percent of the residents estimated damages as either moderate or severe. Concentrating on these latter two categories, there is a moderately strong positive relationship between damage sustained and perception of risk. When damage is moderate, 22.7 percent of the respondents defined risk as severe, compared with 65.3 percent of those reporting severe damage. Also the proportion of people who believe risk is slight *declines* from 36.4 percent when damage is moderate to 6.1 percent when damage is severe.

TABLE 19

Perceived Vulnerability by Damage Sustained

		Damage Sustained					
		Slight or None		Moderate		Severe	
Site	Risk to Property	N	%	N	%	N	%
	Slight	4	40.0	16	36.4	3	6.1
Toutle	Moderate	1	10.0	18	40.9	14	28.6
	Severe	5	50.0	10	22.7	32	65.3
	Slight	14	26.9	11	26.8	1	16.7
Lexington	Moderate	14	26.9	15	36.6	0	0.0
	Severe	24	46.2	15	36.6	5	83.3

The Lexington data set shows a concentration of cases in the lower categories of damage sustained. Only six respondents—6.1 percent of the total—characterized the damage they had sustained as severe. The data for the slight or none versus moderate categories show an apparent negative relationship between degree of damage sustained and level of perceived risk. Almost identical proportions of citizens who experienced slight or damage (26.8%) and moderate damage (26.9%) believed that risk was slight. The proportion of people who believed risk to be moderate increases from 26.9 percent of the respondents who experienced none or slight damage, to 36.6 percent of those reporting moderate damage. There was a decrease in the proportion of people who believed risk was severe from 36.2 percent among those with little damage to 36.6 percent of those with moderate damage.

What we face is an apparent positive relationship between damage and risk perception in Toutle and an apparent negative relationship in Lexington. Particularly because of the distribution of cases which emphasizes different ends of the measurement scale in each community, these findings require very careful interpretation. It is possible, as a general interpretation, that there is a threshold effect for damage sustained as it relates to perceived risk. Thus, sustaining damage may be important in a person's decision about vulnerability *only* if the damage has exceeded moderate levels. That is, experiencing no damage or a slight amount may not have a major impact on the definition of risk; in such cases people may rely on other issues (variables such as proximity, certainty and severity) in assessing vulnerability. However, when damage is moderate or high (when it becomes personally and socially meaningful), then there is a more direct effect upon the individual's conception of vulnerability. If one treats the categories of damage that contain few cases as indicative (or tentatively acceptable for analysis) in Table 19, then our data support the above interpretation. Thus, in both communities, people who described damage as slight or none show a modal category of severe for risk perception, but the variance is great; 40.0 percent of the Toutle respondents at this damage level also defined risk as slight as well as more than a quarter of the Lexington respondents. On the other hand, again for both communities, when we compare the moderate and severe categories of damage, there is an increase in perceived vulnerability as damage increases from moderate to severe. While this interpretation meets the two requirements of fitting the data and being consistent with existing theory, it is admittedly ad hoc. Thus, it will be necessary to await the results of further research to test the hypothesis that damage is positively related to perceived risk only above a threshold level.

Another factor that might be assumed to be relevant to the personal assessment of vulnerability is perceived efficacy of protective measures. If one can have confidence that protective measures may be undertaken that have a reasonable probability of reducing the negative consequences of an environmental threat, then undertaking such measures should result in the reduction of perceived vulnerability. The logic upon which this assertion rests is drawn from psychological research on *locus of control* or self efficacy (cf. Bandura 1977). Studies of human behavior in natural disasters suggest that a person's beliefs about his level of control over natural events is correlated with both perceived danger and the likelihood of undertaking protective actions. Sims and Bauman (1972, 1389) report that the extent to which individuals believe that they can control what happens to them is positively related to their willingness to undertake protective actions in connection with tornado warnings. Subsequent research by Schiff (1977) failed to replicate the findings by Sims and Bauman. One possible explanation for the inconsistent results lies in the conceptualization of self efficacy as an individual's generalized expectancy that his or her efforts will result in a successful performance. Thus, self efficacy is appropriately classified as a characteristic of an individual, that is, a personality trait. Investigation of adjustments to natural hazards should recognize that individuals choose among alternative responses on the basis of the perceived efficacy of those alternatives in accomplishing the goals of personal safety and property protection. Thus, the investigator should be concerned with measuring the perceived efficacy of protective measures—a characteristic of protective actions—rather than self efficacy, which is a characteristic of the individual. In particular, it may be speculated that people who believe that there are measures available which are genuinely protective should also feel less vulnerable.

Table 20 shows perceived vulnerability by the efficacy of protective measures for each study community. The Toutle data show a weak positive relationship between increasing certainty that protective measures will be effective and level of perceived risk. In Toutle, for all levels of uncertainty about the efficacy of protective measures, the modal category of risk perception is severe. People who are uncertain about the effectiveness of protective measures (50.0%) are only somewhat more likely to define risk as severe than people who are reasonably certain (43.6%) or very certain (45.5%). There is a steady increase in the proportion of people who define risk as moderate for increasing certainty about protective measures (uncertain, 38.5%; reasonably certain 32.7%; very certain 22.7%). There is a corresponding decrease in the proportion defining risk as slight as the level of efficacy of protective measures decreases.

The Lexington data show a positive correlation of moderate strength between these two variables. The proportion of respondents who believe risk is severe increases as the perceived efficacy of protective measures changes from very certain (20.7%) to reasonably certain (44.4%) to uncertain (70.8%). Similarly, there is a corresponding drop in the proportion of people who believe risk is slight as the amount of uncertainty about the effectiveness of protective measures increases. Because the direction of the relationship is positive in both communities, one may interpret these data to mean that, indeed, increasing certainty about the effectiveness of protective measures does result in reductions of perceived vulnerability.

TABLE 20

Perceived Vulnerability by Efficacy of Protective Measures

		Certainty Protective Measures Will Be Effective					
		Very Certain		Reasonably Certain		Uncertain	
Site	Risk to Property	N	%	N	%	N	%
	Slight	7	31.8	13	23.6	3	11.5
Toutle	Moderate	5	22.7	18	32.7	10	38.5
	Severe	10	45.5	24	43.6	10	50.0
	Slight	17	58.6	6	13.3	3	12.5
Lexington	Moderate	6	20.7	19	42.2	4	16.7
	Severe	6	20.7	20	44.4	17	70.8

Finally, the third factor which might bear upon citizen definitions of vulnerability is family responsibility. The role of the family is important in understanding a variety of human responses to disasters (cf. Drabek and Key 1985). It is known that in the cases of conflicting responsibilities in a disaster setting, most people opt to account for their family obligations first (Killian 1952). In the response phase in particular, research indicates that families are coherent and tend to define danger in terms of the danger to the entire family unit rather than to individual members (cf. Quarantelli 1960; Drabek and Boggs 1968; Perry 1985). It is reasonable to suspect, then, that one's family obligations may have an impact on the way that vulnerability is defined outside the response phase as well.

We have chosen to characterize family responsibilities in terms of the presence of children in the household. Less than 5 percent of the respondents in each of the study communities listed themselves as "single, never married." Remaining respondents were married, divorced, widowed, or separated, and consequently most had at least the "opportunity" to incur family responsibilities in the form of children living in the household. Our hypothesis is that people who have the responsibility of children are likely to feel more vulnerable to the volcano threat as a function of the obligations which accompany parenthood.

Table 21 shows perceived vulnerability by the presence of children in the household. The Toutle data indicate there is no statistical relationship between having children and perceived risk. That is, the proportions of people endorsing each risk category are approximately the same for those who have children and those who do not. Among Toutle residents, then, the presence or absence of children in the household does not appear to have an effect on citizen perceptions of risk. In this community, the largest proportions of people believe risk to be severe whether they have children (46.0%) or not (45.3%). In contrast, the Lexington data show a positive correlation of moderate strength between having children and perceived risk. Thirty percent of the respondents without children defined risk as severe, compared with 54.2 percent of those with children. Also, fewer people with children (20.3%) defined risk as slight than did those respondents without children (35.0%).

TABLE 21

Perceived Vulnerability by Children in Household

		Children in Household			
	Risk to	No		Yes	
Site	Property	N	%	N	%
	Slight	13	24.5	10	20.0
Toutle	Moderate	16	30.2	17	34.0
	Severe	24	45.3	23	46.0
	Slight	14	35.0	12	20.3
Lexington	Moderate	14	35.0	15	25.4
	Severe	12	30.0	32	54.2

There is no obvious explanation for the difference between the communities regarding the effects of having children on perceived risk. One would be inclined to suggest that differences in the threat environments of the two communities are responsible for differences in the role of family responsibilities. However, this interpretation depends upon the assumption that Toutle residents view risk as higher than Lexington residents. In fact, the proportions of each community judging the risk to be slight (22% versus 26%) moderate (32% versus 29%), and severe (46% versus 44%) are quite similar. Consequently, the appropriate interpretation of these data remains indeterminate pending further research.

Vulnerability appears to be largely determined by citizen views of characteristics of the threat itself; particularly by proximity, certainty and severity. Past victimization through sustaining damage also enhances perceived vulnerability but only among those experiencing moderate or severe levels of damage. It was also found that as citizen perceptions of the efficacy of protective measures increased, their feelings of vulnerability decreased. The strength of this correlation was weaker in Toutle, however, where it was argued that there were no efficacious measures to protect against some aspects of the threat. Finally, family responsibility was positively correlated with perceived risk in Lexington, but no correlation was found for Toutle. Having thus explored the factors which contribute to citizen perceptions of risk, we will now turn in chapter four to the problem of how and why citizens go about reducing risk to acceptable levels.

Adjusting to the Volcano Threat

The relationship between humans and their natural and constructed environments is indeed complex. The study of natural hazards is in large part concerned with the ways in which people interact with the natural environment. In fact, the concept of hazard draws its meaning from the overlap of the human use system and the natural events system (Burton et al. 1978, 20). Hazards or dangers only exist to the extent that humans invade or exploit the natural environment. Up to this point, we have examined the nature of citizen awareness of such hazards, as well as people's perceptions of their own vulnerability. We now turn to the problem of understanding citizen *actions* relative to environmental hazards.

Human existence depends upon our exploitation or manipulation of the natural environment. Our very evolution, as well as our continued survival and ability to prosper, has hinged on our skills for extracting, transforming and effectively using natural resources. Consequently, humans cannot escape the challenge of natural hazards; they have been and are destined to remain parts of our lives. White and Haas (1975) have acknowledged that people must confront natural hazards and observed that there are essentially three tactics in such confrontation. First, man may seek to modify the cause of the hazard—in effect, to make the danger itself disappear. Such approaches fall under the rubric of mitigation or prevention and include measures such as weather modification or cloud seeding to induce rain in drought situations. A second tactic involves modifying human vulnerability to hazards. Vulnerability may be modifying human vulnerability to hazards. Vulnerability may be reduced by altering human use patterns, for example, by avoiding settlement inside flood plains. In some cases, we accept the necessity of exposing ourselves to a hazard and develop preparedness measures to minimize the negative outcomes of exposure. The development of detection and warning systems for floods, hurricanes, and tornadoes constitute attempts to prepare for dangerous events. Finally, for some hazards we must accept both exposure and acknowledge that little can be done to manipulate negative outcomes, so efforts are made to distribute the losses to make them more bearable. Insurance against floods, earth-quakes and volcanic eruptions serve to illustrate the practice of loss distribution.

The aim underlying all of these tactics is to permit people to effectively coexist with natural hazards. The imagery of coexistence is significant here. Particularly in the popular literature, humans are often portrayed as "triumphing" over nature; of imposing human will upon the environment. Even in the social scientific disaster literature we speak of concepts such as recovery, reconstruction and restoration after disasters, implying that such natural events "interrupt" normal activities and that following the event man "reimposes" order on the environment. For some time, however, scholars have questioned this perspective. Anderson (1970) pointed out that post-disaster planning often strives not to restore human systems to pre-disaster levels but to incorporate knowledge and experience acquired through the disaster event to change pre-disaster structures, institutions and attitudes, presumably with the objective of reducing or in some way accommodating future vulnerability. Almost inescapably, disaster impact creates an awareness of a particular environmental hazard, arouses feelings of vulnerability, and demonstrates at least to some degree the kinds of consequences which may exist for humans. It can be argued that these conditions provide an opportunity for individuals, organizations and governments to act positively regarding the hazard in question. Some would say that the conditions *demand* action, but it is well known—particularly in the case of single impact disasters—that many variables may intervene between disaster impact and the implementation of policy or individual measures.

For our purposes, the important point is the idea that humans *change* as a function of experiencing disasters or in response to environmental risks. One doesn't *overcome* risks as much as one simply learns to live with them (cf. Burton et al. 1978, 204-206). Baisden and Quarantelli (1979, 6) emphasize that "change is the essence of the recovery period," and that change may be conceptualized in terms of opportunity to accommodate hazards through disaster mitigation and preparedness. White and Haas (1975, 57) similarly argued that a key concern in understanding human behavior *vis-a-vis* hazards is the idea of *adjustment*: "all those intentional actions which are taken to cope with the risk and uncertainty of natural events."

Although adjustments may be undertaken by a variety of societal actors simultaneously—by individuals, families, organizations, governments—our attention in this chapter will focus upon individuals. That is, we are interested in the conscious actions undertaken by citizens which, in their view, reduce the risks of living near Mt. St. Helens volcano to an "acceptable" level. It is acknowledged that "acceptable" may have different meanings for different people, just as we saw in Chapter 3 that different people defined vulnerability differently. What remains, however, is that most people have in some way sought to "adjust" to the volcano hazard, and these attempts at risk reduction may be documented. The remainder of this chapter is structured around two issues. First, we wish to describe the types of specific protective measures that people have undertaken and to identify individuals' sources of information regarding such measures. Second, we are interested in devising an indicator of the extent of citizen adjustment and determining what variables and characteristics are correlated with adjustment.

The Adoption of Protective Measures

The kinds of individual actions that afford protection from volcanic eruptions tend to be a function of the nature of the threats and the state of technology. Worldwide, volcanoes are situated in relatively well-defined zones. Furthermore, a volcano's location is correlated with its eruptive characteristics. In mid-ocean areas, such as Hawaii, volcanoes tend to be characterized by effusive (nonexplosive) eruptions which generate mixtures of gases and lava. Volcanoes that lie along the Pacific Rim, sometimes called the "ring of fire," tend to erupt explosively and are characterized by the production of ejecta (ranging from ash fall and pumice through volcanic bombs), pyroclastic flows and mudflows (cf. Leveson 1980, 179). The Cascade volcanoes, including Mt. St. Helens, fall into this latter category of explosive volcanoes that confront humans with dangers from ash fall, violent explosions, and mudflows with associated flooding.

The avenues available to people to deal with these explosive threats are influenced by the available technology. That is, nothing may be done to prevent or stop a volcanic eruption. Thus, two general options exist for achieving protection: the development of systems for eruption detection and alert or directly attacking and manipulating the agent of danger (lava, ash, etc.). Both of these options are largely structured in terms of the state of technology.

For example, the efforts of rural Hawaiians to control lava flows often depended upon prayer and sacrifice to volcano deities. More technologically advanced—though not necessarily more successful—approaches to the manipulation of lava flows include diversion through artificial channels or bombing and surface treatments to allow shorter-term use of land covered by lava (MacDonald 1972, 419). Similarly, observation has formed the basis of eruption detection systems for some time. Yet technology affects the precision and extent of such observation. Following the 1919 eruption of Mt. Kelud which killed 5,000 people in Sumatra, the Dutch East Indies established a "volcanological watching service" that deployed a staff to observe volcanoes and provide warning of eruptions (Padang 1960, 181). Modern detection systems have replaced human "watchers" with instruments to assess seismicity, fumarole gas temperature, composition and volume, tumescence, and heat (cf. MacDonald 1972, 415-419.

The primary threats posed by Mt. St. Helens in its present phase stem from light ash fall, mudflows and flooding. Our approach to these dangers benefits from advanced technology available to our highly industrialized society. As preface to a discussion of protection against Mt. St. Helens' threats by local citizens, it is instructive to briefly examine specific types of measures which have been successfully used to reduce danger at similar volcanoes. Following this overview of "possible" protective measures we will look at traditional protections used by people to cope with historic eruptions of Mt. St. Helens and then turn attention to citizen adjustments during the current volcanic sequence.

One can divide the dangers to individuals from ash fall into two general categories, medical and structural. Medical threats to people center on respiratory difficulties arising from ash inhalation and irritation of the eyes, throat and skin (Blong 1984, 83). Historically, measures taken to protect against medical threats from ash are the use of goggles, breathing masks, and skin coverings. Use of goggles or eyeglasses and protecting skin with light clothing or umbrellas dates back at least to the turn of the century; these measures were employed during the 1906 eruptions of Vesuvius volcano (Lacroix 1906, 223-248). The nature of breathing masks has varied from a wet or dry cloth held over the nose, to surplus military gas masks, to modern filtration masks (Blong 1984, 93). These measures are designed to deal with acute, short-term medical dangers. There is some evidence that heavy and sustained exposure to respirable ash may be connected with some chronic bronchitic conditions, but the protections against development of such conditions appear to be the same as those for short-run conditions (cf. Green et al. 1981, 217). Specific studies of exposure to ash during the 1980-1981 eruptions of Mt. St. Helens indicated that the negative medical effects significantly declined with the passage of time (Bernstein et al. 1982, 212).

Structural threats from ash fall include collapsing buildings from the weight of accumulated ash, buildings that become buried, and destruction of flora from either the acidity or weight of ash. Volcanic ejecta, of course, potentially include material much larger than ash (volcanic bombs can weigh several pounds) which might not only be crushing, but also hot, thereby posing a fire hazard. Aside from a few incidents of large ejecta in connection with the May and June 1980 eruptions, such materials have not been problematic at Mt. St. Helens, and consequently are not addressed here as a "likely" or high probability threat.

It should be emphasized, too, that ash fall in the communities near Mt. St. Helens' cone has been light to moderate. The heavy ash which can bury entire areas, such as that experienced at Pompeii (Kraus and Von Matt 1973), Iceland's Kirkjufell (Grove 1973) or Mexico's Paricutin (Rees 1970), has not materialized. Furthermore, the ash from Mt. St. Helens has not proved to have sufficiently high pH factor to cause significant surface damage to either people or plants. Thus, accumulation of ash has been the threat against which to protect. Accumulated weight endangers structures and the abrasiveness of ash damages finishes (paint, siding, roof coverings) on buildings, vehicles and machines.

Shovels, brooms and water pressure have proven effective means of ash removal designed to eliminate structural threats from light and moderate ash fall. Light intermittent ash falls from Irazu volcano in the early 1960s were effectively removed with periodic sweepings and washings (Clark and Lee 1965). Accumulated ash can likewise be removed from plants by gentle shaking with brooms or poles; water pressure is not recommended for plants because the additional weight engendered by wetting ash can sometimes break limbs. When ash fall is steady and/or continual, removal is not feasible; some structural buttressing of roofs may be used to maintain building integrity until removal is possible (cf. Blong 1984, 214; Bruner 1974).

Volcanic mudflows and associated flooding also pose dangers to both people and structures. Dangers to humans from these events come both from water and from water-borne debris such as ash, boulders, trees and other material. Deaths may accrue from people being buried and drowned in their homes as was the case at Mt. Agung on Bali in 1964 (Surjo 1965) or from being simply washed away either with their homes or attempting river crossings like the approximately 300 who died following the April 1966 eruptions of Kelud (Jennings 1969). There are very few measures for protection from mudflow/floods that lie exclusively in the control of individual citizens. Commonly used flood protections such as sandbagging, structural strengthening and diversion canals are rarely effective because of the destructive impact of the debris associated with volcanic events. Escape from the impact—achieved through the development of a detection and evacuation warning system at the community level— appears to be the most feasible avenue for significantly reducing deaths and injuries from volcanic mudflows and floods.

Interestingly, isolation may be seen as a threat which may arise as a function of mudflows and floods. Typically, such events follow river systems around volcanoes. As a consequence, even if one is not threatened directly by mudflow/flooding, the transportation systems which connect people and communities to regional supports often fall victim. Loss of roads, bridges, and railways frequently leads to the isolation of otherwise unharmed citizens. As such isolation becomes extended; it can become life- or health-threatening in itself. Protective measures against isolation include maintaining food and water supplies, storage of gasoline and purchase of generators to produce electricity, and purchase of radio sending and receiving equipment.

Structures are particularly vulnerable to volcanic mudflows and flooding; they may be knocked down, buried, or foundations may be undercut or otherwise weakened. From the standpoint of individual self-protection, only limited measures may be taken in connection with mudflows and flooding, and these are most likely to be effective only when sediment levels and water volume are low. Thus, to a certain extent one can reinforce structures, raise foundations, provide drainage, and create diversion channels to protect private homes and buildings. In the case of severe impacts, however, such measures are marginally useful.

There are two general approaches to protecting against the negative effects of mudflows and flooding: reduce the amount of sediment in the water and keep the water contained in river systems. One advantage in dealing with this threat is that mudflows/floods follow the topography, keeping to low areas and following rivers. Thus, places of high risk may be identified in advance. Measures to accomplish the above mentioned protections, however, tend to be major projects that require a collective effort on a community or regional scale. For example, sedimentation dams and barriers are currently being used at Mt. St. Helens and also in connection with the river systems influenced by Kelut volcano (Zen and Hadikusumo 1965). Channels may be dredged and levee systems built to restrict floods and mudflows to existing rivers or designated areas (Smart 1981). Another technique used at Mt. St. Helens (at Spirit Lake) and at Ijen volcano on Java (MacDonald 1972, 173) involves draining or reducing the levels of lakes formed by volcanic structures or other reservoirs to preclude the possibility that such bodies of water may be displaced and add to flood potential.

Many of the protective measures for ash and mudflow/flooding discussed above have been recommended, and some used, in connection with the current volcanic sequence at Mt. St. Helens. Historically though, simple avoidance of the volcano has been a primary coping mechanism. As we pointed out in Chapter 1, settlers of European origin only recently came to the area around St. Helens; there were still relatively few such settlers even during the eruptive activity of the 1840s. For these eruptions, and those which came earlier, the relevant local inhabitants were Northwest Indian tribes. Over the generations, passed down through the oral tradition of legends, these people evolved a strategy of avoidance no doubt based on observation and experience of St. Helens during its eruptive phases. The strength of this avoidance "policy" is reflected in the writings of white observers in the 1800s.

> Even our half-civilized Indians . . . cannot be induced, by hope of reward or fear of punishment, to approach the snow-covered peaks in their midst, whose actual manifestations of volcanic energy must exist in their minds as dim traditions. (Emmons 1877, 45)

Emmons was writing less than 30 years after the then most recent eruptive sequence, and in describing volcanic experience as a dim tradition also apparently failed to comprehend the Indian's accumulated experience with volcanicity. Initially though, white settlements were located at some distance from the volcanoes (from 1830-1870) so they were spared direct experience with eruptions. The stage was set for whites to begin to need to understand St. Helens, however, in the late 1800s and early part of the twentieth century when heavy exploitation of timber resources and immigration resulted in permanent settlements and greater population density, both closer to the volcano and along river systems. This growth which created a "volcanic hazard" for the whites was facilitated by the absence of volcanicity at St. Helens from approximately 1857 through 1980.

By 1980, people were living in close proximity to the volcano and the use of the area's resources—for timber, tourism and recreation—was intense. Beginning with the March 27, 1980 eruptive activity, strategies had to be developed by governmental officials and ultimately by individuals to achieve some degree of protection if not complete security, in the face of Mt. St. Helens. As the eruptive sequence has drawn on, authorities have adopted two general management tactics: (1) develop detection and warning systems to evacuate in the event of explosive eruptions, mudflows, flooding, or other serious volcanic events; and (2) educate local citizens about the hazard, providing both motivation and information to achieve self-protection against chronic threats.

The remainder of this section is devoted to exploring the effects of these management tactics; to identifying the extent to which citizens have assimilated protective suggestions.

In documenting the kinds of protective measures undertaken by Toutle and Lexington residents, our initial interest focused upon identifying those measures of which citizens were most conscious. The various threats from the volcano were not new; the respondents had been living with them for a period of years. Consequently, we wanted to know which protective measures had also become a central concern for citizens in that they had become a part of routine life. We therefore asked people, without prompting from the interviewers, to simply name specific measures they had taken to protect themselves from any of the threats associated with Mt. St. Helens volcano.

Table 22 shows the protective measures enumerated by the respondents in each community. The maximum number of protective measures named by any single respondent was three and all respondents were able to name at least one measure they had undertaken. In Toutle, 83.5 percent of the respondents reported they had developed an evacuation plan as a means of minimizing negative impacts of volcanicity. Moreover, some type of evacuation preparation was the first measure mentioned by most of the respondents who named more than one protective measure. In part, the prominence of evacuation plans as a protective measure in Toutle is no doubt a function of past experience. Beginning with the May 18, 1980 blast, multiple evacuation warnings have been issued for Toutle. Also, the nature of the devastation in that community, particularly from mudflows, made it clear to the residents that under severe eruptive conditions evacuation was a most feasible—if not absolutely necessary—means of insuring personal safety. Thus, a history of evacuations coupled with evidence of its importance in past eruptions has apparently contributed to extensive adoption of evacuation plans as a primary protective measure. Certainly it is the only measure spontaneously named by nearly all of the Toutle respondents.

The two protective measures named with the next greatest frequency by Toutle residents (32.0% in each case) are the purchase of equipment and storage of food and water. Equipment purchases were for one of three items: "police scanner" radios, gasoline powered electrical generators, and manually operated water pumps. All of the equipment items as well as storage of food and water may be seen as measures against the negative consequences of isolation. While a police scanner could be a source of current evacuation warning information, it would also provide an isolated citizen with information on prevailing conditions at the volcano. The other measures are more directly oriented to sustaining life and property in the event escape was not possible and outside resources (e.g., electricity, etc.) were blocked.

TABLE 22

Protective Measures Adopted by Community

	Toutle[1]		Lexington[2]	
	N	%	N	%
Purchased insurance	22	21.4	61	61.6
Stored gasoline	20	19.4	3	3.0
Evacuation plan	86	83.5	55	55.6
Possessions to safety	24	23.3	31	31.3
Arranged emergency shelter	20	19.4	42	42.4
Purchased equipment	33	32.0	3	3.0
Involved in neighborhood plan	14	13.6	3	3.0
Stored food and/or water	33	32.0	16	16.2
Emergency checklist	29	28.2	27	27.3

[1]Percentages for the Toutle sample are calculated on a base of 103 respondents.
[2]Percentages for the Lexington sample are calculated on a base of 99 respondents.

An emergency checklist—usually comprised of a listing of things to remember in the event of an eruption—was mentioned as a "protective measure" by 28.2 percent of Toutle respondents. While one would not technically consider such lists themselves as protection, they are included here because they can reduce response time and because so many citizens mentioned them in answer to our query. It should also be pointed out that people who mentioned checklists tended to do so in the context of discussing evacuation preparations. Usually this involved a list of items to remember when leaving, such as turning off gas, water and electricity, or packing medicine or personal papers. It is appropriate to infer that the checklists prepared by Toutle residents were protective in the sense they were intended to support evacuation-related measures.

Four additional protective measures were mentioned by about 20 percent of the respondents: moving possessions to safer places (23.3%), purchasing flood insurance (21.4%), storing gasoline (19.4%), and making shelter arrangements (19.4%). In the mudflows and floods which followed the May 1980 eruptions, a number of Toutle Valley residents lost virtually all of their possessions and also had their homes completely destroyed. A previous study of response to the May 18, 1980 eruption (Perry et al. 1980), indicated that people were deeply concerned not only with property devastation in general, but particularly with the loss of family keepsakes, heirlooms, photographs and other highly personal and irreplaceable possessions. This concern has apparently persisted over the years and is now manifest through nearly one-fourth of Toutle residents choosing to move at least some "irreplaceable" items to safe storage. In most of these cases, respondents reported moving jewelry, photographs or other small objects to safe-deposit boxes in banks. The purchase of flood insurance may be similarly seen as an effort to protect the individual's economic position even if the property itself cannot be protected. It is interesting that, although volcano insurance has been available for some time, all of our respondents reported purchases only of flood insurance. The remaining two measures—storing gasoline and arranging shelter—may be seen as evacuation-connected measures. Shelter arrangements were of two types. Some respondents reported they planned to evacuate in a family-owned recreational vehicle, usually a pickup with camper. As part of the planning process, these potential evacuees reported driving probable routes of egress and selecting several possible campsites at safe distances. Another commonly reported shelter arrangement involved contacting friends or relatives living in nearby— but unthreatened—communities and making agreements to seek refuge in their homes if an evacuation of Toutle was ordered.

Finally, 13.6 percent of the Toutle respondents said that one of the protective measures they had undertaken was involvement in a neighborhood emergency plan. In most cases this took the form of a "mutual assistance" pact with one or a small handful of neighbors. The most common arrangement involved parents in families with children agreeing to "look after each other's kids" in the event of an evacuation warning. Other arrangements that were mentioned included checking property in the event a family was out of town during an emergency, and agreements between two or more families to help each other with temporary property protection measures which would be undertaken just prior to an evacuation. Although neighborhood plans were mentioned as a protective option by the smallest proportion of Toutle residents, it is a development worth notice.

It has been argued for some years that community emergency preparedness depends both upon the skill and motivation of authorities and upon the vigilance and involvement of citizens. Informal grouping of citizens planning to help each other constitute one type of citizen participation. Early research on disaster subcultures (Anderson 1965; Weller and Wenger 1972) posited the existence of groups of citizens who band together to deal with a recurring disaster event or chronic threat. Wenger and his colleagues (Wenger et al. 1980) recently questioned the conceptualization of disaster subcultures on the grounds that their research indicated that general knowledge of disaster myths and social behavior in emergencies was not significantly higher in areas characterized by subcultures than in those without subcultures. These scholars did find, however, that collectives did exist in subculture communities whose instrumental knowledge and ability to cope with great danger were high.

Without arguing about the extensiveness or cohesiveness of "subcultural" knowledge or awareness, our data are consistent with these latter findings in that informal collectives of citizens have formed in Toutle to deal with the volcano threat. Whether these arrangements constitute a subculture or not is problematic; our research design was not oriented to the detection or analysis of subcultures. We do argue, though, that such arrangements are a manifestation of subculture while admitting that participants appear to have primarily instrumental knowledge of only the volcanic hazard. The groups observed in Toutle tend to resemble more closely emergent accommodation groups (Quarantelli 1970) except that they are oriented to future events and have an extended life span. In spite of our inability to comment on the theory of subcultures, we believe that the presence of mutual-aid neighborhood planning groups have important implications for the conduct of emergency management. That is, the existence of such groups apparently has positive implications for the level of community emergency preparedness.

In Toutle, the groups appear to have developed spontaneously. Several conditions prevailed in the community that might be isolated as contributory: (1) it is a small community, somewhat isolated; (2) it has had multiple recent experiences with the impact of a disaster agent; (3) the threat of disaster is chronic; (4) there have been high levels of involvement of local emergency authorities with the members of the community; and (5) relatively large proportions of citizens have experienced more than low levels of damage from disaster impacts. From a social scientific perspective, one would look for the development of such spontaneous groups in communities where the above conditions were present. From the standpoint of emergency management authorities, the evolution of such groups is a pattern worth promoting in the interest of community emergency preparedness. This might be accomplished by a range of activities, from simply acknowledging that such "cooperative" efforts are valuable in emergency preparedness information normally disseminated to the public, to explicit guidance on how such groups might be formed and information disseminated through meetings sponsored for interested citizens (similar to "block watch" meetings held for community crime prevention programs).

In summary, citizen perceptions of appropriate protective measures in Toutle are dominated by evacuation planning. The single measure remembered by the greatest proportion of respondents (more than 80%) as an important protective action they had undertaken was the development of an evacuation plan. The defining characteristics of these plans were the choice of routes of egress and safe destinations. Furthermore, three of the remaining eight protective measures mentioned—checklists, storage of gasoline and shelter arrangements—can be seen primarily as activities which support evacuation compliance. A second theme among the protective measures undertaken in Toutle (mentioned by about one-third of our respondents) relates to the problem of isolation. In this instance, people sought to store food and water and purchase equipment (to generate electricity, maintain some contact with the outside world, or insure access to well water) as a way to enhance both comfort and survival chances. Smaller proportions of our respondents used the common tactic of risk sharing through the purchase of insurance, and the somewhat less conventional tactics of moving irreplaceable possessions to safe places and banding together with other families.

The pattern of protective measure adoption in Lexington is distinct in some ways from that observed in Toutle. The single protective measure most frequently adopted by Lexington residents was the purchase of flood insurance (61.6%). These respondents also eschewed volcano insurance-presumably on rational grounds owing to their distance from the volcano, the relatively minor impacts of ash fall, and accurate concern for flooding on the Cowlitz River. Still, they preferred the more formal and less personal approach of insurance, which involves financial compensation for losses that have been sustained. Social scientifically, it can be noted that this adjustment requires less effort and cost invested in protection than was evident in Toutle where there was considerable emphasis upon personal action before the event. Thus, fewer people in Lexington reported involvement in neighborhood preparedness planning (3.0%), in acquiring equipment (3.0%), and in storing food and water (16.2%). Of course the relatively lower proportions of people adopting the latter two measures may also be related to lower levels of public concern with isolation. This practice would be realistic in Lexington, which lies adjacent to the main north-south transportation route in western Washington; one would not imagine that authorities would allow the area to remain "cut off" for any significant period of time, particularly since emergency and recovery resources would have to enter the area along this transportation route.

The very low levels of neighborhood preparedness planning in Lexington also deserve comment. The absence of such subcultural manifestations appears to hinge on the absence of community and threat characteristics in Lexington which prevail in Toutle (where planning group participation was about four times as common). Particularly in the past three years, Lexington has received at least as much official attention as Toutle; there has been one major flood event and several light ash dustings, and there has been a chronic threat of volcano-related flooding. However, there are three features that distinguish Lexington and appear to correlate with the absence of spontaneous "mutual aid" planning groups. First, while Lexington's population is only somewhat larger than Toutle's, Lexington residents do not view themselves as isolated. Lexington is near two moderately sized towns, Kelso and Longview, and is also near Interstate Highway 5, the Burlington Northern Railroad, and shipping on the Cowlitz River. In this context, Lexington is a more urbanized place whose residents typically work outside the community and where physical access is seldom a difficulty. Toutle, on the other hand, is more rural with only two roads leading into town, and is sometimes distinguished largely as a "stopping place" for Mt. St. Helens' tourists and recreationists. Hence, the psychological sense of community (Sarason 1974) which characterizes Toutle is at best much weaker in Lexington.

Another factor which distinguishes Lexington is that in the immediate past, volcano-related damages have been of lower magnitude and experienced by proportionately fewer people than in Toutle. Thus, the feelings of "shared victimization" which arise in Toutle are less evident in Lexington; there are fewer bonds between citizens which stem from mutual suffering from Mt. St. Helens. Finally, a third factor lies in the idea that the level of threat, as assessed by technical experts, is somewhat less in Lexington than in Toutle. Although both communities live under the chronic threat of flooding, the *likely* magnitude of such events is greater in Toutle.

Taken together, these factors appear to mitigate against the spontaneous formation of neighborhood planning groups in Lexington. That is, the esprit de corps which characterizes Toutle and is less dominant in Lexington apparently depends somewhat on these issues of shared victimization, shared community, and a common and high level of shared threat. This is not to say, however, that neighborhood planning groups could not be encouraged or created in Lexington or other communities with similar characteristics in connection with a systematic approach to emergency management. Instead, it suggests that emergency managers who sought to encourage such groups in communities like Lexington should pay special attention to the problem of defining for potential participants the issues of shared community and shared danger.

Overall, Lexington residents were concerned with evacuation plans as personal protective measures. Evacuation plans were mentioned in 55.6 percent of those questioned in Lexington. While this number constitutes about 30 percent fewer than in Toutle, 42.4 percent of Lexington respondents (about twice the number in Toutle) reported they had made arrangements for shelter should an evacuation be ordered. The kinds of shelter arrangements mentioned by Lexington respondents were essentially the same as those described by Toutle residents. Two variations are worth noting, however. Unlike their Toutle counterparts, Lexington residents more frequently claimed to have a public shelter as a destination, and very few of the Lexington respondents reported they intended to "find a safe place to park a recreational vehicle" as a shelter arrangement. The storage of gasoline, which we have identified as an evacuation supporting protective measure, was mentioned by only 3.0 percent of Lexington residents. This low percentage should not be interpreted as a lack of interest in evacuation, but as an indicator of assumed ready access to this resource by Lexington residents. Gasoline is not difficult to find in Lexington, while there are only two filling stations within the town of Toutle itself.

The proportion of people who reported devising an emergency checklist in Lexington (27.3%) was approximately the same as the Toutle figure. Checklists formed by Lexington respondents also tended to be oriented to evacuation related matters such as remembering to turn off utilities, take along prescription medicines and battery operated radios, and so forth. Finally, slightly more people in Lexington than in Toutle mentioned they had moved possessions to a safe place; 31.3 percent of Lexington respondents cited this protective measure. For the most part, items mentioned fit the same description as those named in Toutle: small keepsakes judged irreplaceable or difficult to replace private papers. Those in Lexington who claimed to have used this option usually mentioned bank safe-deposit boxes as the "safe" place.

In summary, while Toutle residents focused on measures to facilitate evacuation and combat isolation, Lexington respondents concentrated on purchasing insurance and preparing for evacuation as ways of mitigating the negative effects of volcanicity at Mt. St. Helens. Lexington residents tended not to be involved in neighborhood "self-protection" groups, and—perhaps appropriately—did not adopt many measures against the problem of isolation.

Now that we have described the range of protective measures which were most salient to our respondents, a logical question to pursue is that of source of information. That is, how did people first hear of these protective measures? In Chapter 3 we reported that, with respect to the volcano hazard in general, people in both communities reported their "usual" sources of information were emergency authorities (Cowlitz County Department of Emergency Services and Sheriff's Office) and social network contacts. Our interest here is in linking citizens' memories of specific sources with concrete protective measures that have been adopted.

Table 23 shows the tabulation of citizen reports of the "source from which you first heard about the adopted protective measures" for each community. Answers to this question were also solicited in "open-ended" fashion; respondents were simply asked to name the single source which provided the original impetus to explore the protective measures they ultimately adopted. The source of protective measures cited by the single largest proportion of Toutle residents was "personal judgment" (31.3%). Most of these people simply claimed they thought of and devised the protective measures on their own—they analyzed the danger, considered a variety of solutions, and adopted one of them. In these cases, adoption decisions seemed to hinge on the cost of undertaking the measure and the extent to which the individual believed it would "really be effective" in reducing danger.

TABLE 23

Original Source of Information Regarding
Protective Measures

| | Toutle | | Lexington | |
Original Source	N	%	N	%
No single Source	1	1.0	1	1.0
Newspaper articles	30	29.1	31	31.3
Radio Programs	1	1.0	6	6.1
Personal judgment	32	32.1	16	16.2
Friends/neighbors	15	14.6	9	9.1
Relatives	5	4.9	4	4.0
Local emergency authorities[1]	19	18.4	32	32.3

[1]Reference is made here to the Cowlitz County Department of Emergency Services or Sheriff's Department

In relying on personal judgment in choosing volcano hazard protections, Toutle residents may be seen as similar to people who live in communities facing a chronic flood threat (cf. Perry et al. 1983, 203). It should be mentioned, however, that it is difficult in such situations to separate personal choice from past experience. It is likely that citizens who reported "analyzing the situation and taking appropriate action" structured their reasoning in terms of their past experience and accumulated knowledge of the threat. The setting for both chronic flood threats and the volcano threat at Mt. St. Helens involves extended periods of time in which citizens have an opportunity both to experience impacts of the hazard agent and to discuss with a variety of sources the nature of the hazard and potential protections. It is likely that the process leading up to actual adoption of a particular measure is characterized by numerous contacts with many people, as well as reflection and analysis on the part of the individual adopter. People who cite personal judgment as the primary source of protective measure information are consequently claiming they depended extensively on their own powers of assessment judgment, as well as their own inventiveness, in ultimately choosing measures. It would be inappropriate to suggest that these respondents were reporting that, independent of past experience and input from others, some protective measure was devised and adopted. Toutle residents in particular have experienced intensive contacts with representatives of a variety of government agencies (beginning with workshop-type neighborhood meetings with USGS in early 1980, through dissemination campaigns run up to the present by Cowlitz County agencies) describing and urging adoption of a wide range of potential protective measures; inevitably more measures than any single family could or would adopt. It is therefore likely that Toutle residents who cited personal judgment were describing their choice process as one in which they developed their own decision criteria in deciding which of a range of possible protective options wholly to adopt, or to modify and then adopt.

Newspaper articles were cited as protective action idea sources by the next largest portion of Toutle citizens (29.1%). Social network contacts (friends, neighbors, and relatives) provided original suggestions for protective actions for 19.5 percent of the respondents, and 18.4 percent credited local emergency authorities with first suggesting protective actions that were ultimately adopted. Interestingly, radio programs were rarely cited as the place where protective action ideas originated, and no one mentioned television programs. This is undoubtedly because the nearest television stations are in Portland, Oregon, more than fifty miles distant from the communities. It is also interesting that only one individual was *unable* to identify a dominant source of ideas for protective measures. The largest proportion of Lexington residents cited local emergency authorities (32.3%) and newspaper articles (31.3%) as the first source for information regarding "adopted" protective measures. These sources were followed in frequency of citation by personal judgment (16.2%) and social network contacts (13.1%) Although more people mentioned radio programs in Lexington (6.1%) than in Toutle, this source was still the least frequently mentioned.

When we ask "where do people remember first hearing about protective measures that they actually adopted," the answer remains the same for both Toutle and Lexington. Namely, original ideas for protective action came from newspaper articles, local emergency authorities, and personal judgment. While newspaper articles remained prominent sources in both communities, personal judgment was more often cited in Toutle, while local emergency authorities were mentioned more frequently in Lexington. It is important to note that social networks, in the form of contacts with friends, neighbors, and relatives, although not primary sources, were clearly significant in people's memories as places where one learns about protective measures.

It should be remembered that these data tell us only about people's attributions of where ideas for protection originated. When we specifically asked respondents to name the "most important" sources for information regarding protective measures in general, citizens from both communities invariably named local emergency authorities. In Toutle, 42.7 percent of those questioned named the Department of Emergency Services and 54.4 percent named the Sheriff's Office as the most important source. In Lexington, 30.3 percent cited the Department of Emergency Services and 68.7 percent identified the Sheriff's Office as the single most important source of protective measure information. Thus, after continued exposure to the volcano hazard and to a variety of information sources, citizens in each community agreed that local authorities constituted the most reliable and credible place to turn for guidance when seeking information about protection.

Volcano Hazard Adjustment

Up to this point we have focused our discussion on protective measures that citizens reported undertaking when asked in a "free answer" format. Thus the picture of protective actions assembled is one of those foremost in respondents' minds. The actions mentioned by people were diverse and in some cases people described multiple protections adopted against the same threat. As described in the introduction to this chapter, the idea of hazard *adjustment* implies something more systematic and organized than a listing of disparate protective actions. To examine hazard adjustment, one must attend to the constellation of measures that citizens have adopted to make life near the volcano more tolerable. In essence, we want to construct a view of the specific measures undertaken to reduce susceptibility to potential negative impacts associated with volcano threats.

We have chosen to characterize hazard adjustment by listing the range of volcanic threats identified by geologists, and selecting major groupings of protective measures available to individuals for coping with such threats. This analysis process leads to the delineation of five categories of activity, each composed of one or more specific actions, chosen on the basis of their utility in addressing some component of the volcanic hazard. The first of these categories is the purchase of insurance (either volcano or flood insurance). This risk sharing strategy represents primarily a protection against large-scale property damage. We added a restrictive time frame such that the insurance had to be purchased *after* the May 18, 1980 eruption to insure a connection between insurance purchase and volcanicity at Mt. St. Helens. It is here noted that 85.1 percent of the Toutle respondents and 90.9 percent of the Lexington sample reported they did not have such insurance before the May 18 eruption.

The second category of adjustment behavior was the development of an evacuation plan. In this case, we introduced the constraint that, to be defined as having an evacuation plan, a respondent must be able to identify distinct routes of egress as well as a "safe" destination. In this way we sought to separate citizens who had only casually thought about evacuation from those who had engaged in serious planning. At Mt. St. Helens, evacuation is the primary means of minimizing dangers of death and injury in the event of a major eruption or similarly catastrophic event such as the collapse of the debris dam at Spirit Lake.

The purchase of equipment was identified as a third category of adjustment behavior. We were specifically interested in the acquisition of "expensive" equipment, defined as that which costs more than $150.00. Three items form the bulk of such purchases: electrical generators, police scanner radios, and mechanical water pumps. Our purpose was to identify people who had chosen to expend nonnegligible resources on equipment whose primary use was disaster relevant. As we argued above, such equipment may be conceptualized largely as a protection against isolation, though its presence may also insure against other volcanic threats. We chose not to include stockpiling of food and water in this category on the grounds that it may be done for reasons unrelated to volcano threats (religious beliefs, or for the economy of volume purchasing, for example) and because—even when done for disaster purposes—such items tend to be consumed over time and can easily become a daily living pattern not consciously connected to volcanicity.

The fourth and fifth categories of adjustment behavior focus upon the implementation of specific protective measures against ash fall and mudflow/floods. To identify a respondent as having taken ash protective action, we accepted any one or more of the following measures: possession of square-nosed shovels or long-bristle brooms for ash removal, protective tarps, or breathing masks. A person was designated as having taken mudflow/flood protections if he or she reported stockpiling sandbags, constructing diversion channels, stockpiling caulking materials, or undertaking structural reinforcement on either a home or out-buildings.

Collectively, these five categories of action may be seen as constituting "adjustment" to the threat of volcanicity at Mt. St. Helens. Of course they do not exhaust all possible measures for protection that one could conceivably undertake but they do cover the full range of individual adjustment options available to residents of Toutle and Lexington. Each represents a different dimension or aspect of adjustment; one is not necessarily "better" or more protective than another, they simply deal with different protective strategies for different threats. Since they are summative, one can argue that a person who has adopted several such actions has "adjusted" to a greater degree than one who has adopted fewer actions.

Throughout the analyses that follow, our measure of adjustment will be the sum of the number of categorical measures (ranging from one to five) that the individual has undertaken. Unlike our measure of protective actions in the previous discussion which was elicited on a spontaneous basis from respondents, specific questions were used to determine whether respondents had satisfied the minimum requirements for each adjustment category. The purpose of the subsequent analyses is to identify the factors which are correlated with successful adjustment, defined as participating in greater numbers of the adjustment category actions. The analyses have been grouped into explorations of social psychological determinants, the role of social networks, and demographic correlates.

Social Psychological Determinants

Individuals may be motivated or predisposed to adjust to natural hazards because they understand the threat, feel vulnerable, or have had encounters with the agent of threat in their past experience. Four specific variables may be proposed to represent these conditions: salience of the volcano threat, level of threat knowledge, level of perceived property risk, and level of past eruption damage sustained.

One would expect that the more salient the volcano threat is for an individual, the more likely that person is to adopt adjustments. People to whom the volcano is important and relevant to their personal lives are presumably those who attend to its associated dangers and consequently would place a premium on protecting themselves. Table 24 shows volcano salience by the number of hazard adjustments undertaken. For Toutle residents, there is a moderately strong positive relationship between salience and adopting adjustment measures. The proportion of people who have made three or more adjustments steadily increases as we move from low (20%), through moderate (33.3%) to high (59.3%) salience. Conversely, the majority of people making only one adjustment registered low salience (48.0%); only 20.8 percent of those reporting moderate salience and 5.6 percent of high salience respondents engaged in a single adjustment.

In Lexington, there is a somewhat weaker magnitude, but still positive relationship between salience and adjustment. Once again, most respon-

---

TABLE 24

Hazard Adjustments by Volcano Salience

		Salience of Volcano					
	Hazard		*Low*		*Moderate*		*High*
Site	*Adjustments*	*N*	*%*	*N*	*%*	*N*	*%*
	One	12	48.0	5	20.8	3	5.6
Toutle	Two	8	32.0	11	45.8	19	35.2
	Three or more	5	20.0	8	33.3	32	59.3
	One	18	40.9	2	6.9	3	11.5
Lexington	Two	16	36.4	15	51.7	13	50.0
	Three or more	10	22.7	12	41.4	10	38.5

dents who reported low salience undertook a single adjustment (40.9%). There is little difference, however, between moderate and high salience respondents with respect to the number of adjustments adopted. Among those with moderate or high salience, few people reported a single adjustment (6.9% and 11.5%, respectively). The majority of these respondents adopted either two (51.7% and 50.0%) or three or more adjustments (41.4% and 38.5%). The pattern remains that low salience is associated with fewer adjustments and an increase to moderate salience increases the number of adjustments, but a movement to high salience does not add an increment to adjustments in the way observed with Toutle respondents.

As predicted, volcano salience is positively correlated with the number of adjustments adopted by citizens. Parenthetically, it might be noted that salience as measured here in connection with a chronic or multiple impact threat is at least conceptually comparable to general measures of hazard awareness used in connection with single impact threats. The threat context of volcanoes involves long periods of inactivity with interspersed periods of activity characterized by repeated eruptive threats and/or chronic noneruptive threats. During such periods of activity, salience measures the extent to which people are "aware" or conscious of the threats coupled with a subjective assessment of the importance or social significance of such threats. As we pointed out in Chapter 2, traditional measures of hazard awareness generally ask respondents if they "know about" environmental threats to which they are presumably subject. In so doing, salience is indirectly assessed in the sense that— when dealing with single impact events outside the context of a particular impact—people are being asked to indicate the importance of a hazard relative to other issues which might capture their attention. Traditionally, these types of measures have not been found to be closely correlated with the adoption of individual protective measures or with the concept of hazard adjustment (Sorenson 1983).

The positive correlation found between salience and adjustment in the case of a volcano threat may therefore be a function of special character-istics of the volcano threat setting. In contrast to most single impact threats, when dealing with active volcanoes, the citizen is forced to be "aware" of the threat by the presence of unmistakable environmental cues—usually eruptive activity—which are used to define the onset of volcanic activity. Furthermore, volcanic threats are associated with distinct periods of "elevated" probability of volcanic events and also are unusual enough to capture the attention of news media which serve to intensify the volume and frequency with which volcanic hazard information is disseminated to the public. These conditions create a setting wherein the hazard issue is clearly raised for the public in such a way that personal attention is devoted to defining the danger in the context of everyday life. That is, from an emergent norm perspective (cf. Turner 1964), the intrusion of the hazard upon people's "cognitive space" demands that it be considered meaningfully in light of other issues of daily living and assigned some priority for action that is consistent with the perceived likelihood that it will become a problem. Under such conditions of reflection and personal analysis, people assign different levels of salience,which one would expect to correlate with adjustment behavior. We would anticipate that hazards that create similar conditions would also be ones in which salience was positively correlated with adjustment.

A second variable which may be related to volcano hazard adjustment is threat knowledge. Recall that our measure of threat knowledge is highly specific: the number of outcomes of ash fall and mudflow/floods that a respondent was correctly able to name. It is assumed that in order to protect oneself from specific volcanic threats,a respondent must first be able to identify those threats. Thus, it is predicted that lower levels of threat knowledge will be associated with fewer hazard adjustments. Table 25 shows hazard adjustments adopted by levels of threat knowl-

---

TABLE 25

Hazard Adjustments by Threat Knowledge

		Threat Knowledge					
		One or Two Outcomes		Three or Four Outcomes		Five or Six Outcomes	
Site	Hazard Adjustments	N	%	N	%	N	%
	One	3	75.0	7	18.9	10	16.1
Toutle	Two	1	25.0	20	54.1	17	27.4
	Three or more	0	0.0	10	27.0	35	56.5
	One	3	37.5	19	36.5	1	2.6
Lexington	Two	4	50.0	25	48.1	15	38.5
	Three or more	1	12.5	8	15.4	23	59.0

edge for each community. It should be pointed out that these data show some restriction of range with regard to threat knowledge. That is, few people in either Toutle or Lexington fall into the lowest level of knowledge; namely those able to list only one or two outcomes or consequences. Analytically, this means that our data do not allow us to address the case of people with little threat knowledge. Our interpretations focus upon citizens who have more than minimal knowledge and compare respondents familiar with three or four outcomes with those who were able to name five or six outcomes.

Our data do indeed indicate that there is a positive correlation between threat knowledge and hazard adjustment. In Toutle, 27.0 percent of those with knowledge of three or four outcomes had undertaken three or more hazard adjustments, compared with 56.5 percent of those who could name five or six outcomes. More than half of the moderate threat knowledge respondents (54.1%) undertook two adjustments versus only 27.4 percent of the respondents with higher threat knowledge. Interestingly, there was only a slight difference between moderate and high knowledge citizens who adopted a single adjustment (18.9% versus 16.1%), but the difference was in the predicted direction: more people with a lower level of knowledge adopted one adjustment. This pattern of relationship is present in the Lexington data as well. Among citizens who named three or four adjustments, 15.4 percent adopted three or more adjustments compared with 59.0 percent of those who could name five or six outcomes. Conversely, 36.5 percent of the moderate knowledge respondents adopted a single adjustment versus only 2.6 percent of those with high threat knowledge. In summary, in both communities, the more extensive a person's knowledge of the volcano threat, the more likely one is to have adopted multiple adjustments.

Perceptions of risk or vulnerability should also shape an individual's propensity to engage in volcano hazard adjustment. In particular, higher levels of perceived risk should be expected to inspire people to make a systematic effort to achieve protection from the hazard agent. Table 26 shows the cross-tabulation of hazard adjustments with perceived risk for Toutle and Lexington. In both communities there is a positive correlation of moderate strength between risk perception and hazard adjustment. Among Toutle residents, the proportion of people who engaged in three or more adjustment increases as we move from slight risk (21.7%), to moderate risk (36.4%), to severe risk (59.6%). Conversely, the proportion of people who adopted only one adjustment decreases from 34.8

percent of those defining risk as slight, to 21.2 percent among moderate risk and 10.6 percent among high risk. Similarly, the proportion of Lexington respondents with three or more adjustments increases as the level of perceived risk increases: 15.4 percent at slight risk, 31.0 percent at moderate risk and 43.2 percent at severe risk.There is a corresponding decrease in the proportion of people who undertook a single adjustment as we move from slight (38.5%), through moderate (20.7%), to severe risk (15.9%).

TABLE 26

Hazard Adjustment by Perceived Risk
(Vulnerability)

		Risk to Property					
		Slight		Moderate		Severe	
Site	*Hazard Adjustments*	*N*	*%*	*N*	*%*	*N*	*%*
	One	8	34.8	7	21.2	5	10.6
Toutle	Two	10	43.5	14	42.4	14	29.8
	Three or more	5	21.7	12	36.4	28	59.6
	One	10	38.5	6	20.7	7	15.9
Lexington	Two	12	46.2	14	48.3	18	40.0
	Three or more	4	15.4	9	31.0	19	43.2

Finally, it may be hypothesized that, in general, people who have sustained damage from a disaster impact are more likely to adopt adjustment. The reasoning behind the claim focuses upon the idea that damage represents a socially significant negative outcome which underscores the necessity of action on the part of the individual to prevent similar future outcomes.

Table 27 shows hazard adjustments by damage sustained. One is again reminded of the different damage distributions in our two study sites. Most Toutle residents are concentrated in the moderate and severe damage categories, while the majority of Lexington respondents have experienced either slight or moderate damage. For purposes of interpretations, this means that our Toutle data represent a site characterized by heavy damage, with Lexington representing a situation wherein damages have been lighter.

TABLE 27

Hazard Adjustments by Damage Sustained

Site	Hazard Adjustments	Slight		Damage Sustained Moderate		Severe	
		N	%	N	%	N	%
	One	4	40.0	9	20.5	7	14.3
Toutle	Two	4	40.0	18	40.9	16	32.7
	Three or more	2	20.0	17	38.6	26	53.1
	One	10	19.2	12	29.3	1	16.7
Lexington	Two	26	50.0	14	34.1	4	66.6
	Three or more	16	30.8	15	36.6	1	16.7

In Toutle, the data show a moderately strong positive correlation between level of damage sustained and number of adjustments adopted. When we compare moderate versus severe damage, we find that the proportion of people who adopted three or more adjustments increases from 38.6 percent to 53.1 percent. On the other hand, there is a decrease in the proportion of people who adopted only one (20.5% to 14.3%) adjustment or only two adjustments (40.9% to 32.7%) as we move from moderate to severe levels of damage. Parenthetically, although there are too few cases for meaningful analysis, it should be mentioned that people who sustained slight damage fit into the pattern of having a small proportion who engaged in three or more adjustments and most people undertaking two or fewer adjustments.

The Lexington data also show a positive correlation between sustaining damage and adopting adjustments, but the magnitude of the relationship is much weaker in Toutle. Most people who experienced moderate damage had engaged in three or more volcano adjustments (36.6%). However, the modal category for people who defined past damage as slight was to undertake two adjustments (50.0%). Consequently, we see a contradictory pattern: the proportion of people who undertook three or more adjustments increases as we move from slight to moderate damage, but so does the proportion of people who adopted only a single adjustment. Statistically, this leaves us with a positive correlation, but one which approaches zero in magnitude.

One can attempt to interpret this apparent discrepancy between communities by recalling that the same situation arose in Chapter 3 when we examined the relationship between damage sustained and perceived vulnerability. In both cases it is likely that we are detecting a threshold effect for sustained damage. That is, *above a certain minimal level of damage*, there appears to be a positive relationship between sustaining damage and undertaking hazard adjustments; hence is the case in Toutle. Some support for this view can be found in the work on urban snow hazards by Earney and Knowles (1974) who found that the more permanent the nature of damage sustained (and consequently the more severe), the more likely people were to undertake adjustments. When damage levels are lower, and by inference damage is less socially and personally meaningful, there appears to be no correlation between damage sustained and the adoption of adjustments. In general, then, our data indicate that sustained damage, both as a factor in the way people define vulnerability and as a motivation for undertaken protective measures, becomes important in understanding human behavior in disasters only when the levels of damage are considerable. This finding must be treated cautiously, however, until it can be replicated on other populations facing volcano threats and verified through research on other natural and technological hazards.

Social Networks

It is well known that social networks—a person's universe of contacts with kin and friends—serve important social support functions for the individual in society. With regard to adopting adjustments in connection with natural hazards, it may be posited that an important aspect of these networks is to afford information on the efficacy, cost, time requirements and barriers to implementation of different protective options. This claim rests upon a series of assumptions about how citizens act upon protective action information.

The most important contention here is that the actual adoption or implementation of protective measures is a social process. People hear about potential adjustments from a variety of sources. Our data indicate that most Toutle and Lexington residents cite newspapers, local emergency manager and personal judgment as the original sources of protective ideas. From Chapter 3 we also know that the range of sources for both general volcano hazard information and protective measures in particular is broad and includes social network contacts, government agency sources and mass media. One may say, then, that many different protective ideas, from myriad sources, reach individuals residing in threatened communities.

What happens next? The research literature on citizen warning response has documented over many years that citizens discuss the warnings they receive. Such discussions include contacting officials, friends, neighbors, and relatives to "assess" the validity of the warning, the efficacy of suggested protections, and the logistics of suggested protections. Such exchanges have been subsumed under the rubric of *warning confirmation* (cf. Perry 1985). A now classic example of the outcome of the confirmation process is Drabek's (1969) discovery of the "evacuation by invitation" phenomenon in connection with flooding in Denver, Colorado. A flood warning was issued with the suggestion that citizens evacuate as a protective measure. Among several post-warning processes detected, Drabek found that some residents of the area targeted for evacuation initiated or received telephone contacts with friends or relatives living outside the danger area. In the course of such discussions, outsiders "invited" sometimes reluctant potential evacuees to visit their homes until the danger passed; the data indicated numerous people accepted such invitations who might have otherwise not adopted the target protective measure of evacuation. The importance of this example lies in its illustration of the idea that people received information about a protective measure, initiated a social milling process to evaluate both the threat and the suggested measure, and took action based upon a collection of knowledge, some of which came from social network contacts and some from authorities and mass media. In this particular case, some of the evacuees were clearly heavily influenced by the parts of information which came from social networks.

Of course there are obvious differences between adopting a protective measure in connection with a specific disaster warning and adopting hazard adjustments. One is the pressure of time in the warning response context. Another is that warnings usually involve undertaking a single, short-term protective measure, while hazard adjustment typically involves multiple, interrelated measures with a "longer-run" time frame. There is reason to believe, however, that processes of social influence operate similarly in both settings.

In connection with Mt. St. Helens, we have found that people tend to hear about protective measures from a variety of sources. Indeed, people often report hearing at different times about the same measures from different sources. We know also that people discuss measures among themselves. They report talking about the sources, the measures themselves, and about how much work and cost is involved in a given measure. Ultimately we know that these discussions include contacts with authorities, particularly local emergency managers. The role for emergency managers in this process appears to be fairly distinct; citizens look to them often for original ideas, and also as a "final court of appeal" on the implementation tactics and likely effectiveness of protective options, without regard to the source.

There also appears to be a distinct role for social contacts as well. In deliberating about the adoption of a particular adjustment, people report considering what their neighbors and friends have done, how its was accomplished, how many people are using the adjustment and what other adjustments are used in conjunction with it. All these social interchanges may be seen not only as having an impact on *which* measures are undertaken, but on *how many* are undertaken. Our concern with hazard adjustment is the number of interrelated measures undertaken, and encompasses both of these issues. If the above reasoning is correct, one would expect that the more hazard adjustment information people report receiving from social network contacts, the greater the number of adjustments that are actually undertaken.

Table 28 shows hazard adjustments by information from relatives and from friends or neighbors. It is important to note that in both communities, the majority of respondents reported predominantly low levels of information coming both from relatives and from friends or neighbors. One statistical consequence of this condition is that our analyses focus upon the effect of receiving "little" versus "some" information; too few people reported they received "most" information from either sources to permit meaningful analysis. It should be remembered though that this does not mean that these sources were not important or "as important" as we have argued above. Our previous point was that social networks were part of the social process of adopting adjustments, but not necessarily a central part. Our interest is in capturing what role, if any, such contacts play in adjustment adoptions.

In Toutle there is a positive relationship of moderate strength between the amount of information accepted from relatives and the number of adjustments undertaken. Three or more adjustments were adopted by 34.9 percent of those who received little information from relatives; however this proportion increases to 61.8 percent among those who claimed to have received some information from relatives. Conversely, the proportion of people who adopted single adjustment decreases as we move from little information (25.4%) to some information (11.8%). A similar decrease is seen when we move from little (39.7%) to some (26.5%) information for people who adopted two adjustments. The Lexington data follow the same pattern seen in Toutle. The proportion of people who adopted three or more measures more than doubles as we move from little information (23.0%) to some information (54.5%). We also see related decreases in the proportion of citizens who adopted one or two adjustments as the amount of information from relatives increases from little to some.

TABLE 28

Hazard Adjustments by Information
from Relatives, Friends or Neighbors

Site	Hazard Adjustments		Information from Relatives				
			Little[1]		Some[2]		Most[3]
		N	%	N	%	N	%
	One	16	25.4	4	11.8	0	0.0
Toutle	Two	25	39.7	9	26.5	4	66.7
	Three or more	22	34.9	21	61.8	2	33.3
	One	20	27.0	3	13.6	0	0.0
Lexington	Two	37	50.0	7	31.8	0	0.0
	Three or more	17	23.0	12	54.5	3	100.0
			Information from friends or Neighbors				
	One	14	25.9	4	9.1	2	40.0
Toutle	Two	23	42.6	13	29.5	2	40.0
	Three or more	17	31.5	27	61.4	1	20.0
	One	18	29.5	5	14.3	0	0.0
Lexington	Two	27	44.3	16	45.7	1	33.3
	Three or more	16	26.2	14	40.0	2	66.7

[1]Little information includes respondents who reported receiving less than one-fourth of all hazard information from the source indicated.
[2]Some information includes respondents who reported receiving one-fourth to three-fourths of all hazard information from the source indicated.
[3]Most information includes respondents who reported receiving more than three-fourths of all hazard information from the source indicated.

The other types of social network contacts of interest here are friends or neighbors. Again, it is clear in both communities that as the proportion of information received from these sources increases, so do the number of adjustments adopted. The proportion of Toutle residents who adopted three or more adjustments increases substantially as we move from those who received little information from friends or neighbors (31.5%) to those who received some information (61.4%). There is a correspondingly large drop in the proportion of people who adopted a single measure as the amount of information from friends or neighbors increases from little (25.9%) to some (9.1%). The same pattern holds for Lexington, although the strength of correlation is slightly lower. A total of 26.2 percent of those who received little information from this source adopted three or more adjustments, compared with 40.0 percent of those who received some information. A smaller proportion of citizens who received some information (14.3%) adopted a single protection compared with those who reported receiving little information (29.5%).

In summary, we have posited that a social influence process operates in connection with citizen adoption of hazard adjustments in connection with volcanoes. Our data indicate that in Toutle and Lexington, the absolute quantity of information from social network contacts is not high. But it is clear that the amount of hazard relevant information received from relatives and friends or neighbors is positively correlated with the adoption of multiple hazard adjustments. It should be reiterated that social networks constitute but one segment of actors involved in the adoption process, all of which may be seen as sources of ideas and feedback about adjustments. Our analyses simply underscore the claim that, among these actors, social networks do have a positive impact upon adjustment behavior.

Demographic Correlates

Although historically not many demographic variables have been found to be correlated with the undertaking of hazard adjustments, we will briefly examine four such variables that have been previously examined. These variables are employment in a volcano-related job, school-aged children in the household, age, and income.

We previously reported that people who held volcano related jobs were more likely to have higher levels of threat knowledge than those who do not. Since we have already seen that threat knowledge is positively related to the number of adjustments undertaken, this raises the question of whether adjustments may also be directly affected by employment status. It may by hypothesized that people with volcano-related jobs find themselves confronted with the volcano on a daily basis and may readily be drawn into discussions of protective measures with co-workers. The top portion of Table 29 shows volcano adjustments by employment status. In both communities there is a positive but low magnitude correlation between have a volcano-related job and undertaking a greater number of adjustments. In Toutle, the proportion of people undertaking three or more adjustments is approximately 10 percent higher among those with a volcano-related job (48.2%) than among those without such employment (38.3%). On the other hand, fewer people whose work is connected with Mt. St. Helens (16.1%) adopted only one measure than those people with jobs independent of the volcano (23.4%). Likewise, in Lexington 31.8 percent of those with jobs unrelated to Mt.

TABLE 29

Hazard Adjustments by Employment
and School-Aged Children in Household

| | | Volcano-Related Job | | | |
| | Hazard | No | | Yes | |
Site	Adjustments	N	%	N	%
	One	11	23.4	9	16.1
Toutle	Two	18	38.3	20	35.7
	Three or more	18	38.3	27	48.2
	One	21	23.9	2	18.2
Lexington	Two	39	44.3	5	45.5
	Three or more	28	31.8	4	36.4
		School-Aged Children			
	One	8	15.1	12	24.0
Toutle	Two	26	49.1	12	24.0
	Three or more	19	35.8	26	52.0
	One	10	25.0	13	22.0
Lexington	Two	21	52.5	23	39.0
	Three or more	9	22.5	23	39.0

St. Helens engaged in three or more adjustments compared with 36.4 percent of those with volcano-related jobs. Only 18.2 percent of those with volcano-related employment adopted a single adjustment versus 23.9 percent of those without such employment. Thus, while the pattern of relationship is consistent between the two communities, the magnitude of the correlation is sufficiently low to suggest that employment status has no direct impact on the number of adjustments adopted.

A second demographic variable of interest is the presence of school-aged children in the household. Research on earthquake preparedness has shown that households with school-aged children are more likely to be aware of the earthquake threat and to have specific knowledge of preparedness measures (Turner et al. 1979). The logic behind the importance of children in the household is that (1) they constitute a reason for parents to assume a responsible role relative to environmental (and other) dangers, and (2) that they bring home information from school on protective measures and on the "wisdom" of vigilance. The lower portion of Table 29 shows hazard adjustments by the presence of school-aged children in the household. Once again, in both communities we see a positive but relatively low magnitude relationship between having children and adopting a greater number of adjustments. The proportion of people who undertook three or more adjustments in Toutle increases from 35.8 percent for those without children to 52.0 percent for those with children. Also, while the proportion of people adopting two adjustments declines as we move from children absent to children present (49.1% to 24.0%), the proportion who adopted a single measure increases (from 15.1% to 24.0%). In Lexington, the proportion adopting three or more adjustments increases with the presence of children (from 22.5% to 39.0%) and those adopting two adjustments decreases with children (from 52.5% to 39.0%). The proportion of people who chose only a single measure stays about the same, however, without regard to the presence of children. Consequently, we again find ourselves in a situation where the relationship is positive and consistent between study sites, but of a low magnitude. In this case, we acknowledge our empirical results, but believe the magnitude of the relationship is so low that in the absence of a compelling theoretical logic for doing otherwise, the presence of children in the household should not be included as a relevant variable when attempting to explain hazard adjustment.

In connection with a study of the purchase of flood insurance, Kunreuther and his associates (Kunreuther et al. 1978) reported that older people are more likely to buy insurance than younger people. It should be noted that this finding rests upon a study of only one type of hazard adjustment: insurance. Our measure of adjustment includes insurance, but is broader in aim, seeking to describe a distinct constellation of measures which together constitute adjustment to Mt. St. Helens volcano. The top portion of Table 30 shows hazard adjustments by age category. Perhaps the most striking inference from this table is that in neither community do we see either a strong magnitude of relationship or even a consistent pattern. In Toutle, the modal category of adjustments for people under 35 and from 45 to 54 was to undertake three or more measures. The mode for those between 35 and 44 and those over 55 was to undertake two adjustments. There is little difference between age groups in the proportion of people who chose to adopt a single adjust-

TABLE 30

Hazard Adjustment by Age and Income

Site	Hazard Adjustments	Under 35		35-44		45-54		55 or Older	
		N	%	N	%	N	%	N	%
	One	4	17.4	5	25.0	3	10.7	8	25.0
Toutle	Two	5	21.7	10	50.0	10	35.7	13	40.6
	Three or more	14	60.9	5	25.0	15	53.7	11	34.4
	One	8	24.2	2	8.0	5	21.7	8	44.4
Lexington	Two	10	30.3	12	48.0	13	56.5	9	50.0
	Three or more	15	45.5	11	44.0	5	21.7	1	5.6

		Income							
		Under $10,000		$10,000-$20,000		$20,000-$30,000		More Than $30,000	
		N	%	N	%	N	%	N	%
	One	3	37.5	5	15.2	5	14.7	7	25.0
Toutle	Two	3	37.5	12	36.4	9	26.5	14	50.0
	Three or more	2	25.0	16	48.5	20	58.8	7	25.0
	One	2	50.0	9	25.0	8	21.6	4	18.2
Lexington	Two	2	50.0	15	41.7	18	48.6	9	40.9
	Three or more	0	0.0	12	33.3	11	29.7	9	40.9

ment. In Lexington, there is a slight decline in the proportion of people who undertook three or more adjustments as age increases. This is somewhat balanced statistically, however, by the fact that the modal adjustment category for all groups over 35 is the adoption of two measures. The modal adjustment category for people under 35 is to undertake three or more adjustments which suggests there is a very slight negative correlation between age and number of adjustments. However, the correlation is so small that we conclude that hazard adjustment, when defined as multiple, interrelated measures, is not significantly related to age.

Finally, it has been suggested in the theoretical literature that income might be related to the adoption of hazard adjustments. This reasoning reflects the idea that some adjustments involve incurring costs which may be more readily borne by higher income people. Interestingly, in connection with the purchase of flood insurance coverage, it has been found that income is uncorrelated with possession of hazard insurance (Kunreuther 1978). Our data, shown in the lower portion of Table 30, tend to support a more general conclusion that income is unrelated to the adoption of a variety of adjustments. In both of our communities, there are too few respondents in the under $10,000 per year category to permit any meaningful analysis. In looking at incomes above $10,000 though, we again find no significant correlation or identifiable pattern of relationship between income and the adoption of hazard adjustments. In both Lexington and Toutle similar proportions of people engaged in a single adjustment across all three levels of income. In Lexington, there is a slight increase in the proportion of people adopting three or more adjustments among those with incomes greater than $30,000, but this is balanced by the fact that the modal adjustment category is two measures for all three of the income groupings. Toutle shows a conflicting pattern wherein the proportion adopting three or more adjustments drops in the highest income category. Take altogether, the appropriate interpretation for these data is to acknowledge general absence of a patterned relationship and report that we detect no significant relationship between income and the number of adjustments undertaken.

Summary

In closing, we found that social psychological and social network variables were important in accounting for hazard adjustment, while demographic variables (employment status, children in the household, income, and age) were not highly correlated with the number of adjustments adopted. Three social psychological variables were found to have positive correlations of moderate strength with the number of adjustments: perceived risk or vulnerability, level of threat knowledge, and salience of the volcano hazard. Another such variable, damage sustained in the past, was found to be important in the adjustment adoption process only in Toutle, where levels of damage tended to be high. Finally, the proportion of hazard information received from relatives and from friends and neighbors was found in each case to be positively correlated with the number of adjustments undertaken.

Living With the
Volcano Threat

As we were completing the last phases of our interviewing in Toutle, an older grocery store clerk offered an interesting assessment of volcanicity at Mt. St. Helens: "That volcano is here to stay—if we stay, too, we have to learn to live with it." The remark was made with a sigh and obvious resignation. It represents an interesting, and some would say inevitable, sentiment probably embraced by many residents of the area and a "fact of life" even for those who might have less insight or who are not inclined to acknowledge openly that they share life with the forces of nature. Indeed, our analyses document that people are both affecting the volcano and being affected by it. People have divided the area around the volcano into controlled access zones, mapped recreational and educational use areas, begun to use fallen timber, initiated reforesting efforts, undertaken flood control and sedimentation control, and devised means of monitoring volcanic activity. In a sense, all these activities represent human efforts to "mold" the volcano into a more tolerable partner for co-existence. We have also seen that people have been affected; they have become aware of the volcano hazard, developed technical knowledge of specific threats, developed contingency plans for emergencies, and learned about and undertaken protective measures.

In closing our study of citizen adaptation to Mt. St. Helens, we want to address two matters. First, we want to carry our examination of the consequences of the volcano for people one step further. Considerable attention has been given to specifying impacts of the volcano upon *individuals*. We will now turn our analysis attention to the matter of impacts upon the community, or more specifically upon people's perceptions about life in the community. Thus, we will review community changes, alterations in standards of living, perceptions of changes in tourism, and degrees of household disruption that people attribute to the volcanic activity at Mt. St. Helens.

The second matter of interest is retrospective in focus. Most of our analysis attention has centered on understanding three (dependent) variables: threat knowledge, perceived risk or vulnerability, and hazard adjustment. In each case, our search for understanding has taken classic social scientific form: drawing upon the findings of existing studies of related topics, we chose variables believed to be associated with our dependent variables and empirically checked for these posited relationships in our data from Toutle and Lexington. With regard to each dependent variable, we have assembled a "family" of predictors, each of which has been found to be *individually* related to the relevant dependent variable. As a means of summarizing this information—and of beginning the construction of a model—we will close this chapter by examining through regression analysis the *collective* power of each family of predictors to explain the respective dependent variables. It is emphasized here that the theoretical literature of hazards research contains *no* formalized models of threat knowledge, vulnerability or hazard adjustment in connection with volcano threats. In fact, we do not view the product of our analyses here as formal models. Instead, our work is intended as an initial step toward the ultimate development of such models. While our efforts begin to specify broad parameters for model construction, they need to be followed with conceptual refinement, the identification and introduction of new predictors, and the development of a structure of causal priority or antecedence among the predictors.

Perceptions of Community

With regard to people's beliefs about the impacts of Mt. St. Helens' volcanicity on their lives as part of a collectivity, we are interested in two broad areas: change in the community and change in quality of life. In both cases, however, the goal is to identify those changes which were specifically linked—in the minds of our respondents—to the volcano. Our approach to community change was purposely unstructured; the idea was to allow citizens the greatest possible latitude to define and report on community trends believed to have arisen in response to Mt. St. Helens. To obtain information on quality of life impacts, we selected three dimensions of life near the volcano and asked for respondent comment: standard of living, tourism, and household disruption.

General Community Change

Much of the research on post-disaster community change has focused upon delineating changes in the community defined from the perspective of either an outside observer or the government. It is equally important to begin to isolate and describe changes that citizens notice and attribute to the disaster. Table 31 shows changes identified by residents of Toutle and Lexington, accompanied by an evaluation of each: positive, negative, or largely neutral. The column marked total shows the number and proportion of all respondents who mentioned each choice in response to our request to name the "most important changes in your community brought about by the eruptions of Mt. St. Helens."

Only 5.8 percent of the Toutle residents felt that no important changes in the community could be linked with the volcanic eruptions. The single

TABLE 31

Community Changes Attributed to Volcanic Activity

		EFFECT							
		Positive		Negative		Neutral		Total[1]	
Site	Change	N	%	N	%	N	%	N	%
Toutle									
	No change	0	0.0	0	0.0	0	0.0	6	5.8
	Citizens anxious	0	0.0	7	77.8	2	22.2	9	9.3
	Declining property values	0	0.0	5	50.0	5	50.0	10	10.3
	Shrinking population	5	25.0	7	35.0	8	40.0	20	20.6
	Neighbors closer	30	93.8	0	0.0	2	6.3	32	33.0
	Preparedness higher	5	83.3	0	0.0	1	16.7	6	6.2
	Worse economy	1	8.3	4	33.3	7	58.3	12	12.4
	More tourists	2	25.0	4	50.0	2	25.0	8	8.3
Lexington									
	No change	0	0.0	0	0.0	0	0.0	8	8.1
	Citizens anxious	2	6.9	21	72.4	6	20.7	29	31.9
	Declining property values	4	17.4	12	52.2	7	30.4	23	25.3
	Shrinking population	1	25.0	2	50.0	1	25.0	4	4.4
	Neighbors closer	13	92.9	1	7.1	0	0.0	14	15.4
	Preparedness higher	10	76.9	1	7.7	2	15.4	13	14.3
	Worse economy	2	28.6	5	71.4	0	0.0	7	7.7
	More tourists	0	0.0	0	0.0	1	100.0	1	1.1

[1]Base numbers for Toutle percentage totals are 103 for those reporting no change and 97 for all specific changes; in Lexington the base for no change is 99 and 91 for all other choices.

change listed by the largest proportion of respondents (33.0%) was the idea that neighbors had been brought closer together by the experience. Apparently the shared adversity of bracing against volcanic eruptions creates a consciousness of linkages among some citizens. Indeed, particularly since May 18, 1980, Toutle residents have faced a severe and common outside threat; one that potentially affects all citizens without regard to socioeconomic status, age, education, or other ascribed or achieved statuses. From this viewpoint, the eruptions have apparently encouraged a degree of solidarity in Toutle similar to that documented during wartime in populations faced with frontal attacks from outside (Fritz 1971).

From a social psychological standpoint, numerous factors may be cited as contributing to the feelings of increased solidarity. First, the setting itself is important: Toutle is a small town where citizens have high levels of face-to-face contact, anonymity is relatively low, periods of residence are long, and a large proportion of the total work force engages in similar occupations. Second, the kinds of protective actions which can be employed against the eruptions are limited in number, meaning that citizens are called upon to engage in the same kinds of protective behaviors. This means that citizens can sense a shared response to a shared danger. It should be noted, too, that 93.8 percent of the citizens who identified this increased solidarity as an important community change also believed it has a positive effect upon community life. Interestingly, the feelings of social solidarity seem to be minimizing the perception among community members that citizens are "anxious" in connection with the volcanic threat; only 9.3 percent of the respondents cited visible anxiety as an identifiable community change.

The community change cited by the second largest proportion of Toutle residents (20.6%) was a declining population. Permanent residents have left Toutle for a variety of reasons. Especially after the May 18, 1980 eruption, people who experienced very high levels of material losses in mudflows and flooding relocated to nearby towns—usually temporarily, but some permanently—or because they were part-time (seasonal) residents of Toutle. Some also left to escape future threats from the volcano. It is important to mention that the absolute number of people who left Toutle is very small. The exodus has never been such that the community was in danger of becoming a ghost town; for the most part, the "normal" levels of in- and out-migration resumed quickly after the initial cataclysmic eruption. It is not difficult to understand, however, why more than one-fifth of the population would cite the apparently low level of out-migration as a "significant" community change. In a place where long residence is common and social solidarity runs high, migration is very visible without regard to the extent of the migration.

Furthermore, citizens are widely distributed regarding the valence associated with the perceived out-migration. Nearly half (40.0%) of the respondents reported that the shrinking population constituted neither a positive nor negative impact on the community. The overall impact of citizens leaving Toutle was judged to be negative by 35.0 percent of those identifying migration as an important community change. The remaining 25.0 percent of the respondents thought that losing population had a positive effect on community life.

The next two most frequently mentioned concerns deal with economic conditions. The idea that the local economy was worse since the eruptive sequence began was mentioned by 12.4 percent of the Toutle respondents. Another 10.3 percent of the citizens identified declining property values as the most important volcano-related change in the community. Almost all of the residents who reported either of these changes evaluated the impact as either neutral or negative; neither of these changes was generally viewed as positive. Two qualifications should be mentioned here. First, the referent for both of these types of change is abstract, not personal. Respondents were not necessarily reporting on their personal economic experiences, but were describing what they believed were conditions that prevailed in the community as a whole. Second, there is a wide gap between the proportions of citizens who mentioned social solidarity and declining population as community changes and the proportions who identified these general economic issues. Thus, when assessing the most visible or pervasive changes, the economic sector received significantly less emphasis than issues in the social sphere.

Finally, the two community changes mentioned by the smallest proportions of respondents were an increase in the number of tourists (8.3%) and an increase in citizens' ability to cope with disaster threats (6.2%). In Toutle, tourism is generally treated as a "mixed blessing" by the townspeople. On the one hand, it does boost the local economy, but, on the other, it brings visitors who crowd local facilities and roads, and potentially threaten the pristine beauty of the countryside (cf. Perry and Greene 1983). Indeed, 50.0 percent of those who mentioned increased tourism as an important change felt that it was negative in character. The remaining respondents were evenly split on the issue, 25.0 percent saying the change was positive and 25.0 percent pronouncing its effects neutral. In interpreting these findings, one should bear in mind that, in this instance, the only people making an evaluation of tourism are those for whom it was sufficiently salient to be mentioned as the "most important" volcano-linked community change. We will examine the views of tourism held by the population as a whole in a subsequent section.

A small proportion of Toutle residents perceived that an increase in the ability of citizens to protect themselves from eruption threats represented an important community change. Since early 1980 when Mt. St. Helens resumed activity, the Cowlitz County Department of Emergency Services has been engaged in an intense effort to manage the threat at the volcano. These efforts have included an extensive hazard awareness program which has been effective in disseminating knowledge of a variety of protective techniques to the general population. Furthermore, the emergency services department maintains a high level of visibility in the county and coordinates an extensive volcano warning and information system. The fact that more than 6 percent of the Toutle respondents identified a product of these educational efforts—higher citizen emergency preparedness—as a most important community change attests to the effectiveness of the public information program. Also, higher disaster preparedness on the part of citizens was widely seen as having a positive impact on the community as a whole.

The community change cited by the largest proportion of Lexington respondents (31.9%) was the presence of general anxiety on the part of community residents. Respondent sensitivity to collective anxiety in Lexington is possibly, in part, an artifact related to the timing of data collection. The Federal Emergency Management Agency had released a report on mudflows and flood hazards along the Cowlitz River prepared by the U.S. Geological Survey (Swift and Kresch 1983). The report included mudflow inundation maps showing the severe probable magnitudes of damage in several towns along the Cowlitz River, and indicated that Lexington would be subject to considerable danger. This report received a great deal of attention in the local news media and became the focus of concern on the part of community residents. The purpose of the report was to project the consequences of a "worst case" failure of the debris dam at Spirit Lake, so the levels of projected destruction were quite high. From informal discussions with citizens and a review of the content of news reports, it is likely that many citizens did not fully understand the "worst case" nature of the projections, particularly not initially. At least some citizens interpreted the report and news stories to mean the level of danger to Lexington was substantially greater than previously believed. The subsequent "upward" adjustment of the level of perceived risk in the minds of citizens was accompanied by public expressions of frustration, fear and concern.

It took a relatively long period of time for these heightened levels of general concern to decline. Since data collection began in Lexington a few weeks after the incident, the recently released information was especially fresh and, consequently, respondent perceptions of community-wide concerns may have been temporarily elevated. It is possible that perceptions of collective anxiety will continue to be high in Lexington in spite of the fact that the FEMA report also detailed very high magnitude damages from mudflows for Toutle. In fact, an eruption would result in considerably more destruction for Toutle than Lexington. Toutle citizens, however, had known themselves to be collectively at tremendous risk from volcanic threats since the cataclysmic eruption of May 1980. The January 1983 report did not require that these citizens revise upward their perceptions of danger. At worst, the report simply confirmed and added scientific precision to dangers they already knew existed. Also, while the psychological impact of the report in Lexington was anxiety provoking, it could be seen in Toutle as a more positive experience; it provided additional evidence that the protective measures citizens had been undertaking for more than three years were justified.

Declining property values were mentioned as a volcano-related change by 25.3 percent of the Lexington respondents. Concern with declining property resale values is also probably not wholly independent of the salience effects mentioned in connection with perceptions of collective anxiety. A component of this anxiety is no doubt associated with the frustration of being confronted by a threat that is difficult and costly to escape. Specifically, one could avoid remaining subject to the flood hazard by relocating. In the wake of the release of the flood hazard report, however, citizens realized that the sale of property in Lexington would be difficult and not at premium prices. After all, a person buying Lexington property would be subjecting themselves to a flood danger the owner was trying to avoid, so presumably such a purchase would be only at bargain prices. It is interesting, though, that the market value of property can only be determined when a sale is made at an agreed price, and the proportion of homes on the market in Lexington has remained fairly constant for some years. There were no rushes on real estate offices to sell homes, so apparently the property value question remained hypothetical for most Lexington residents. There is, of course, an element of accuracy in the belief that hazard-prone properties have depressed values. Our concern here has been to temper this point and offer the caveat that the psychological component of property values played some role in its identification as a community change by such a substantial proportion of our respondents.

While collective anxiety and declining property values were seen as predominantly negative community changes, the two changes listed next most frequently were defined as positive changes. Closeness to neighbors and higher levels of citizens emergency preparedness were cited as volcano-related changes by 15.4 percent and 14.3 percent of our respondents, respectively. Thus, citizens in both study communities perceived an increase in social solidarity. Community solidarity in the face of disasters has been documented by many researchers in response to a variety of disaster agents (Fritz 1961a; Fritz 1961b; Fritz 1968; Midlarsky 1968; Wilmer 1958). These studies note that disaster impact has an integrative effect upon the "community of sufferers" and in the short-run promote cohesion among victims and between victims and non-victims in the larger community. Quarantelli and Dynes (1976, 141-144) have specified conditions for such social solidarity and noted that community consensus tends to decline as time passes after the disaster impact. Our data on Toutle and Lexington indicate that in multiple impact disasters where the threat is present for a long period of time, social solidarity tends to persist. This finding supports the contention by Quarantelli and Dynes that citizens' identification with the community will remain strong as long as the acute environmental threat continues to exist.

As we found in Toutle, Lexington respondents also cited apparent increases in citizens' emergency preparedness as being a positive consequence of the volcanic eruptions. Once again, it is likely that the prominence of an increased ability to deal with disaster in the minds of those we questioned is largely a function of the dissemination efforts of the Cowlitz County emergency services authorities. By disseminating written emergency plan information to citizens and maintaining a high profile in threatened communities, emergency managers have succeeded in making citizens aware of the dangers, what can be done for protection, and consciousness of the collective efforts of community members to adopt officially sanctioned protective measures.

Three other community changes attributed to the volcano were mentioned by a relatively small proportion of the Lexington residents. In descending order of endorsement, these were: a worse economy (7.7%), shrinking population (4.4%), and the presence of more tourists (1.1%). For the most part, all these changes were seen as negative or neutral for the community. The fact that each of these changes were mentioned by substantially smaller proportions of citizens in Lexington than in Toutle is probably related to the slightly different economic conditions which prevail in each place. Lexington, being considerably more distant from the volcano, has an economy that is less dependent upon volcano-related industry than Toutle. Also, tourists themselves may have indirect positive consequences for Lexington's economy, but they are not normally drawn to that community.

Quality of Life Changes

In the preceding discussion we examined respondent observations about general changes in their communities they attributed to the activity at Mt. St. Helens. Our purpose was to discover citizen perceptions of broad trends which affected the nature of each community. Now we wish to turn our attention to citizen beliefs about how the volcanic eruptions influenced factors which relate to an individual's quality of life. Three issues are specifically addressed: changes in personal standards of living, perceptions of tourism, and the degree of disruption of household routines.

Table 32 shows perceived changes in the living standards for each of the four communities. The largest proportions of citizens in Toutle (44.7%) and Lexington (62.0%) indicated they have experienced no change in their standard of living since the eruptive sequence began. Another 17.5 percent of the respondents in Toutle and 26.3 percent of those in Lexington reported their standard of living had grown better or worse, but they did not believe the changes were related to the volcano. As one might anticipate, given Lexington's greater distance and lower relative dependence on Mt. St. Helens, residents of that community, for the most part, feel their standard of living is either not affected by the volcano or simply hasn't changed. Of the Lexington residents who did believe their living standard was changed by the volcano, ten saw it decline and only one believed it had gotten better. In contrast, nearly 40 percent of the Toutle residents believed the volcanic activity had contributed to changes in their personal standard of living. Of these respondents, 26 people believed their living standard was worse while 13 thought they were doing better. This split is probably related to differential distribution of damages in the community and to changes in job opportunities (some jobs eliminated and others created) by the cataclysmic eruption of 1980 and its aftermath.

TABLE 32

Changes in Standard of Living by Community

| | Toutle | | Lexington | |
Change in Living Standard	N	%	N	%
Better due to volcano	13	12.6	1	1.0
Worse due to volcano	26	25.2	10	10.1
No change	46	44.7	62	62.0
Better or worse not related to volcano	18	17.5	26	26.3

Many families who lived adjacent to the Toutle River completely lost their homes and most personal possessions in the flooding and mudflows that devastated the area. Sometimes even the land itself was buried under volcanic ash and debris that was carried into the area, making massive and costly cleanup necessary before the land could be used again. To families affected in this fashion, even with the help of private aid programs and low interest government loans, the period required for financial recovery was extended. Without doubt such families will maintain lower relative standards of living for some time to come.

The cataclysmic eruption felled thousands of acres of timber, both on federal land and on the private property of logging companies. Some of the timber was incinerated or buried under many feet of ash. Much of it, however, was stripped of branches and simply uprooted or blown over by the hurricane-force winds from the eruption. This timber was considered salvageable by the timber companies who have mounted a massive recovery effort projected to continue for some time. The salvage effort has employed many loggers and auxiliary logging personnel. Thus, for citizens who are employable in this industry, it is possible that the salvage effort has provided much steady work that may result in better living standards.

Government officials in both communities see tourism as an important mainstay of the local economies. As we mentioned earlier, the citizens of both study communities did not mention tourism in any great proportions when they were asked to describe important volcano-related community changes. Yet, in each community, there was much attention given to perceptions of general economic decline as a function of the volcanic activity. To further understand citizen conceptions of tourism in their communities, we queried our respondents about the growth of tourist industries.

Table 33 shows citizens' perceptions of tourism in Toutle and Lexington. Our first concern was with beliefs about the impact of reduced tourism experienced in each town to date. Almost all of the Lexington respondents (99.0%) reported the decline in tourism since 1980 had little effect on them personally. This is not a surprising finding because, historically, tourists have had few direct impacts on commerce in that town. Certainly the area as a whole benefits economically, but, in the past, few livelihoods in Lexington were directly related to visitors and recreationists. Interestingly, in Toutle, which is more directly benefited by tourist trade, the results are only slightly different. Here, 81.6 percent of our respondents expressed the belief that the presence of fewer tourists

TABLE 33

Perceptions of Tourism by Community

Effects of Reduced Tourism	*Toutle*		*Lexington*	
Due to Eruptions	N	%	N	%
No opinion	3	2.9	0	0.0
Fewer tourists was helpful	12	11.7	0	0.0
Fewer tourists had no effect	84	81.6	98	99.0
Fewer tourists hurt me	4	3.9	1	1.0

Will Increased Tourism be	*Toutle*		*Lexington*	
Good for Community?	N	%	N	%
No opinion	0	0.0	1	1.0
Yes. More tourists yields positive effects	36	35.0	49	49.5
More tourists will have no effect	28	27.2	34	34.3
No. More tourists yield negative effects	39	37.8	15	15.2

had no personal impacts. Only 3.9 percent of Toutle residents felt the decline in tourism was harmful. In fact, 11.7 percent of our sample claimed fewer tourists in the area was helpful. This finding reflects the reasoning used by some longtime area residents who argue that tourists "cost more than they are worth." They increase use of public facilities, contribute to over-fishing of streams and lakes, tax the road system, and, since the volcanic activity began, they represent more people who would have to be accounted for in an emergency. It is difficult to estimate the true prevalence of "tourist antagonism" in the population, but those who are opposed seem ardently so.

In shifting to a future orientation, we asked citizens what effect projected increases in tourism would have for their community. It is widely known that Washington State, as well as county and local town authorities, anticipate increases in tourism in coming years and that elaborate planning is underway to take best advantage of this development. When it comes to forecasting the future, fewer citizens in both communities believe that increased tourism will have no effect on their lives. This opinion was held by 27.2 percent of those people living in Toutle and by 34.3 percent of the Lexington residents. The nature of the anticipated effect, however, is in opposite directions. The largest proportion of Toutle residents (37.8%) fear more tourists will have overall negative effects for the community. In Lexington, 49.5 percent of the respondents believe an increase in tourism will be beneficial. It should be noted that part of this difference between towns may lie in the way impacts are projected. Tourism to Lexington citizens tends to mean a boost to the regional economy from which everyone will benefit; it is doubtful that hotels will appear near town or that crowds of tourists will appear. In Toutle, tourism is more directly felt and seen. The economic benefits are realized certainly, but some perceived costs are involved. Still, the view for increased tourism in Toutle is not entirely one-sided; 35.0 percent of the respondents believed tourism will ultimately yield positive consequences for the community. While Toutle residents do not completely share the optimism of Lexington citizens, the situation is not viewed as altogether without promise.

Finally, the last quality of life indicator explored focused upon the extent of household disruption that citizens believed stemmed from the volcanic activity. The idea was to attempt to estimate, at a reasonable personal level, just how much the presence of a volcanic threat interfered with citizen lives. Certainly people had changed both their thinking and behavior over the years since Mt. St. Helens resumed activity, but to what extent do people see these changes as disruptive and penetrating deeply enough to affect something as basic as household routine?

Table 34 shows the degree of household routine disruption attributed to the volcano for Toutle and Lexington. In Toutle, 12.6 percent of the respondents believed that their household routine was *significantly* disrupted as a function of the volcano threat. The majority of respondents in this community (35.9%) described their routines as moderately disrupted, while 27.2 percent characterized disruption as slight. Only about one-fourth of the Toutle residents (24.3%) claimed that their household routines were unaffected. In Lexington, on the other hand, more than half of the respondents (55.6%) said that household routines were not impacted at all. Among those who acknowledge that there was some impact, most described the effect as slight (25.3%), while 19.2 percent believed their household routine was moderately disrupted. None of the Lexington residents felt a significant disruption of routine.

Overall, then, Toutle residents are far more likely to believe that volcanicity has disrupted their daily routines than Lexington residents. Furthermore, Toutle respondents felt that such disruption has penetrated their lives to a greater *degree* than those who live in Lexington. The intrusion of the volcano felt in Toutle may in part be attributed to objective characteristics of the volcano's impacts. A greater proportion of Toutle residents sustained higher levels of damage than was the case for Lexington. Indeed, the effects of volcanicity have seriously touched the lives of many Toutle residents. Also, there are numerous tangible signs of the volcano in Toutle that have become a part of daily living. For example, as one drives through town, as one sees signposts marking evacuation routes, describing warning signals, and denoting radio channels which broadcast emergency information. As we pointed out in Chapter 4, there is also a noticeable amount of cooperative emergency response planning among neighbors in Toutle. All these factors may be seen as contributing to a consciousness of the volcano threat—manifest through individual adjustments of attitude and behavior—that residents would define as having a "disruptive" impact on household routine. In effect, these data tell us that, particularly for Toutle residents, living near a volcano and maintaining "peace of mind" demands changes in lifestyles that deeply penetrate, even to the daily routine; vigilance is not a part-time endeavor.

TABLE 34

Degree of Disruption of Household Routine Attributed
to Volcano by Community

	Toutle		Lexington	
Degree of Disruption	*N*	*%*	*N*	*%*
Routine significantly disrupted	13	12.6	0	0.0
Routine moderately disrupted	37	35.9	19	19.2
Routine slightly disrupted	28	27.2	25	25.3
Routine not affected	25	24.3	55	55.6

Retrospect: Coping with Volcanicity

The character of our research on citizen reactions to the extended volcanic activity at Mt. St. Helens has been largely exploratory. To date, studies of human behavior in connection with volcanos have tended to focus upon response to a single eruption, often the first event in a given volcanic sequence. Only a handful of studies have attempted to empirically examine citizen behavior in light of extended exposure to volcanic threats and many of those studies have dealt with nonindustrial societies (Nolan 1972; Keesing 1952; Rees 1970; Pilles 1979). Thus, in studying citizen coping with Mt. St. Helens, we found that we lacked the advantage of prior volcano studies and systems of texted hypotheses (not to mention formalized models) with which to structure our research efforts. Our approach to the problem, then, was built upon the existing theoretical literature on hazard adjustment and adaptation, and upon empirical studies of longer-term citizen coping with hazards other than volcanos, as well as the small but relevant literature on volcano response.

Our study centers upon a particular setting and problem: citizen strategies for dealing with the threat (and reality) of continued volcanicity at Mt. St. Helens. From the theoretical and empirical literature mentioned above, we selected for study three important coping dimensions for individuals. First, we were interested in threat knowledge— defined as technically accurate information regarding the volcano hazard. Because of the nature of the volcanic sequence, traditional and more general measures of hazard awareness (knowledge of the existence of a hazard) were not suited to our study at Mt. St. Helens. Instead, we measured citizens specific knowledge of the consequences of two important volcanic threats: ash fall and mudflow/flooding. The second dimension of interest in understanding coping behavior in the face of volcanicity was vulnerability. Hence, we sought to explain how people perceived themselves to be at risk (or in danger) of negative outcomes in connection with the volcanic activity at Mt. St. Helens. Finally, we were interested in the extent of hazard adjustment achieved by citizens living near the volcano. Concern here was not just with the adoption of protective measures. By hazard adjustment, we referred to the adoption of a constellation of interrelated protective actions that collectively addressed the range of both threats to and protective options available for citizens.

Given the identification of these three key dimensions, the social scientific problem is one of determining what factors contribute to or create accurate threat knowledge, perceived vulnerability and hazard adjustment. Again, drawing upon the theoretical and empirical literature, we assembled lists of (independent) variables or predictors hypothesized to be related to each of the selected dimensions or dependent variables. We then proceeded to measure all of the relevant variables and examine the relationship (for each study community) between each predictor and the relevant target dimension (dependent variable). This approach is classic in survey research (cf. Babbie 1973), and enables the investigator to isolate a collection of predictors that are correlated with a given dependent variable.

From the standpoint of social scientific explanation, however, this accomplishment represents only a first step in the process of "explaining" a given phenomenon. That is, we have identified a family of variables which *taken individually* are all related to the dependent variable. The analyses are bivariate—looking at the relationship of each predictor, considered alone, with the dependent variable. Thus, to this point we have identified three groups of variables each of which is correlated with threat knowledge, perceived vulnerability, or hazard adjustment.

The next question of interest, which constitutes another step in the process of explanation, is to examine the *collective* predictive power of each group of independent variables relative to each dependent variable. In this case we want to know how all of the independent variables act together to help us understand the relevant dependent variable. Multiple regression analysis provides an appropriate statistical tool for pursuing this query (cf. Blalock 1979). Multiple regression constitutes (or quantifies) a means of assessing two issues of interest in the present analysis: (1) it provides an index (R^2) of the amount of variation in the dependent variable explained by all of the independent variables acting together, and (2) it offers an index (b) of the relative contributions of each independent variable to the total explained variation. Each of the following sections reports the results of a regression analysis for one of the three dimensions of volcano coping behavior; threat knowledge, perceived risk (vulnerability) and hazard adjustment.

Threat Knowledge

In Chapter 2, seven variables were identified as important in understanding the level of volcano threat knowledge developed by citizens: perceived risk, damage sustained, volcano salience, volcano-related employment, school-aged children in the home, contacts initiated with hazard information sources, and personal planning activity. The bases for the selection of these variables rests upon theoretical formulations from disaster research, empirical studies of volcano hazard awareness, and empirical studies of hazard awareness in connection with other natural hazards. In the context of our exploratory study, then, we have chosen this particular constellation of variables as our working model. That is, based upon the best available theoretical and empirical evidence, we will treat these variables as the "relevant" predictors of citizen's threat knowledge.

Having formed a working model, much of Chapter 2 was devoted to an examination of the relationship between each predictor and threat knowledge using cross-tabulations. At this point, we will turn to regression analysis as a means of examining the power of all the independent variables taken together to predict level of threat knowledge. Table 35 shows the results of a multiple regression analysis with threat knowledge as the dependent variable for each study community.

The zero-order (Pearson's r) correlation coefficients for each independent variable with threat knowledge reflect the patterns revealed in our previous cross-tabular analyses. Values of Pearson's r vary between -1.0 (perfect inverse relationship), 0.0 (no relationship), and +1.0 (perfect positive relationship). Thus, perceived risk shows a positive relationship with threat knowledge in both communities, but the strength of the correlation is greater in Toutle. Likewise, the presence of schoolaged children in the household is positively related to knowledge in both sites, although much stronger in Toutle. Volcano salience shows a positive correlation of moderate strength in each community. On the other hand, personal planning, contacts initiated, and volcano employment all show positive correlations with threat knowledge which are stronger in Lexington than Toutle. Only one variable, damage sustained, showed a correlation coefficient approaching zero in both communities.

These data show that taken individually, each variable with the exception of damage sustained is positively related to threat knowledge in our data. Certainly the strengths of the correlation coefficients vary, but at least six of the seven variables do behave as we predicted. At this point, differences in the size of correlation coefficients may be interpreted as reflecting different conditions (explained in Chapter 2) affecting each community. Based upon the near-zero correlation with threat knowledge in each community, we will eliminate damage sustained as a variable in further analyses. This is not to say that damage is unimportant to the development of a theoretical model of threat knowledge. Indeed, further tests of the damage-knowledge relationship would be necessary before one could justify eliminating the variable from theoretical thinking. It is clear, however, that the two variables are unrelated in our data from Toutle and Lexington, and retention of damage sustained in further analysis would only complicate the problem of interpretation.

Table 35 shows the unstandardized regression coefficients and beta weights for each independent variable, the Multiple R summary measure for all variables and the corresponding F ratio is a test of statistical significance for each community. Taken alone, R is a difficult statistic to interpret; only the anchor values of zero and 1.0 have clear meaning. It has been demonstrated, however, that when squared (R^2), R may be interpreted as the proportion of variation in the dependent variable "explained" by all of the independent variables acting together. Called the coefficient of multiple determination, R^2 provides an index of the goodness of fit of our data to the working model. For the Toutle data, we obtain R = .53, indicating that 28 percent of the variance in levels of threat knowledge is explained by the constellation of independent variables. In Lexington, R = .55; 30 percent of the variation in knowledge is explained by perceived risk, salience, employment, children in the home, contacts initiated and personal planning. In each case the F ratio for R is statistically significant. These statistics indicate that the data for each community fit our tentative or exploratory model reasonably well. It is also worth pointing out that our independent variables explain approximately the same proportion of variance in each study site.

The variables which comprise our theoretical model were chosen on the basis of their applicability to the general case; the factors included were those believed to explain citizen threat knowledge without regard to the type of hazard involved or any particular place (location). Our data,

TABLE 35

Regression Analysis for Threat Knowledge

	Toutle			Lexington		
	Unstandardized Regression Coefficient	*Beta Weight*	*Zero-order Pearson's r Knowledge*	*Unstandardized Regression Coefficient*	*Beta Weight*	*Zero-order Pearson's r Knowledge*
Perceived risk	.14*	.19*	.33*	.11	.14	.27*
Damage sustained	—	—	.02	—	—	.02
Volcano salience	.15*	.22*	.28*	.01	.01	.28*
Volcano employment	.05	.05	.08	.24	.12	.24*
School-aged children	.41*	.36*	.34*	.12	.09	.19*
Contacts initiated	.16	.13	.17*	.36*	.29*	.32*
Personal plan	.04	.04	.19*	.23*	.32*	.38*
Multiple *R*	.53	—	—	.55	—	—
F Ratio	6.07*	—	—	6.66*	—	—

*Coefficient statistically significant, p < .05.

of course, deal with a volcano threat and focus on two communities that have experienced different threat environments. Consequently, even though our model explains similar proportions of variation in each community, we expect different variables in the model to contribute differently to the total explained variation. To pursue this line of thinking requires that two questions be raised: (1) What is the relative importance of each variable in each community? (2) Within each community, what is the relative contribution of each variable?

The first question involves comparing each independent variable *between* communities. This may be accomplished by examining the unstandardized regression coefficients, symbolized as the parameter b (Blalock 1968). Values of *b*, sometimes called the partial regression coefficient, give the average change in the dependent variable associated with a single unit change in one independent variable when all other independent variables are held constant or "controlled." The units of change are whatever unit by which the variable was measured. For example, the unit of change in our variable "school-aged children at home" is one child. Partial regression coefficients for the same variable may be appropriately compared across different data sets (or communities in this case) because they are expressed in comparable units. Except for general comparisons of magnitude, the specific value of b has no statistical interpretation (that is, it is not a correlation coefficient).

The unstandardized coefficients shown in Table 35 indicate that one variable, perceived risk, was approximately equally important in Toutle (.14) and Lexington (.11). The amount of change in threat knowledge associated with risk (when the other variables are controlled) is similar. Two variables have a greater impact on threat knowledge in Toutle than in Lexington: volcano salience and the presence of school-aged children in the home. This latter finding is consistent with our inference in Chapter 2 that the greater attention to school evacuation and hazard information in schools that characterized Toutle should influence threat knowledge in that community. The three remaining variables show greater importance in Lexington than Toutle. Thus, having a volcano-related job is less common in Lexington and people so employed are distinctly different in that community in that their threat knowledge is enhanced. Also, initiating contacts with hazard information sources and engaging in personal emergency planning were more prominently associated with higher levels of threat knowledge in Lexington than in Toutle.

Comparisons of particular variables between communities by necessity raise the question of the relative importance (or contribution to R^2) of all the variables *within* each site. Which variables are accounting for the largest part of the explained variation? Again, we expect different variables to contribute differently because of unique aspects of the threat environment at each site. It is important to note that at this exploratory stage, one will not use differential contributions to R^2 as a means of "sorting out" or eliminating variables from our theoretical model. The theoretical model represents the general case of variables believed to be important across many settings and hazards. The analyses which follow are only designed to document differences in relative importance of variables which prevail in the communities we selected for study.

Before beginning these analyses, a technical statistical problem must be addressed. Recall that in our discussion of the partial regression coefficient (b), it was pointed out that each coefficient reflected the units in which each variable was originally measured. For example, the b's for school-aged children reflect a change of one child and perceived risk uses units of one level of risk. Consequently, the importance of risk, for example relative to contacts initiated is difficult to assess because different measuring units were used. This situation is somewhat similar to comparing kumquats with pineapples. It is possible, however, to standardize each variable (by converting its values into standard deviation units) and in so doing express each variable in comparable measuring units. This procedure yields a coefficient called a beta weight (b^*), equivalent to a partial regression coefficient except that it reflects common measurement units. It is this last characteristic that allows us to compare different variables (from the same sample) in a meaningful way. Note, too, that because the standardization procedure involves using values unique to a given data set, one would not attempt to compare beta weights across different data sets.

In Toutle, the variable which contributed most to change in level of threat knowledge was the presence of school-aged children in the household (.36). Salience (.22) and perceived risk (.19) were the next two largest contributors, followed by contacts initiated (.13). Employment in a volcano-related job and personal emergency planning efforts had only small impacts on threat knowledge. For citizens living in Toutle, then, having children in school, believing that the volcano hazard was salient, and believing themselves to be vulnerable were most closely associated with the development of higher levels of threat knowledge.

In Lexington, personal planning activity (.32) and initiating contacts with information sources (.29) were associated with the largest changes in level of threat knowledge. Perceived risk (.14) and volcano-related employment (.12) make a lesser, but similar, contribution. In this data set, the presence of school-aged children and salience of the volcano hazard have the smallest effects on threat knowledge. Therefore, our data indicate that perceived risk and initiating contacts with hazard information sources are associated with higher levels of threat knowledge in both communities. In addition to these two variables, threat knowledge in Toutle is enhanced by the presence of children and perception of the volcano hazard as salient. On the other hand, threat knowledge among Lexington residents was more strongly affected by personal planning activities and employment in a volcano-related job.

Perceived Risk

The theoretical model developed for predicting citizen perceptions of risk or vulnerability is composed of six variables. By examining the zero-order correlation coefficients shown in Table 36, we can review the nature of the relationships between these variables and level of perceived risk. At this stage of analysis, the degree of damage sustained in past eruptions is positively correlated with perceived risk, although the strength of this relationship is much stronger in Toutle than in Lexington. Both the probability of future volcanicity, and likely severity of ash fall threat are positively correlated (at about the same magnitude) with perceived risk in both Toutle and Lexington. Again in both communities, we see that proximity is negatively correlated with risk such that the greater the distance an individual lives from an affected river, the lower is his or her level of perceived risk. Perceived efficacy of undertaking protective actions was negatively correlated with vulnerability in each study site; the less effective people believe protection to be, the more at risk they feel. Finally, perceived severity of the mudflow/flood threat was positively correlated with perceived risk in Toutle and Lexington.

Taken together, these variables are powerful predictors of perceived risk. For the Toutle data, they yield a statistically significant multiple R of .69, thereby explaining 46 percent of the variation in level of perceived risk. The Lexington data set yields a multiple R of .83 ($p < .05$), indicating that 69 percent of the variation in risk is explained by the collective action of our six independent variables. These results suggest that fit of our data to the theoretical model is good. Hence, based upon our research on volcano hazards at Mt. St. Helens, we have confidence that our theoretical model identifies many of the variables relevant to citizen perceptions of risk.

By examining the unstandardized regression coefficients, we can begin to assess between community differences in the relative importance of each variable in the model. Comparing the coefficients in Table 36, we see three variables have similar impacts on perceived risk in both Toutle and Lexington: perceived efficacy of protection, proximity to the threat, and severity of the ash fall threat. Sustained damage has a stronger

---

TABLE 36

Regression Analysis for Perceived Risk

	Toutle			Lexington		
	Unstandardized Regression Coefficient	Beta Weight	Zero-order Pearson's r with Risk	Unstandardized Regression Coefficient	Beta Weight	Zero-order Pearson's r with Risk
Damage sustained	.15	.12	.35*	.04	.03	.05
Efficacy of Protection	-.14	-.12	-.11	-.19*	-.18*	-.45*
Proximity	-.09	-.08	-.20*	-.09	-.05	-.22*
Certainty	.27*	.23*	.42*	.11	.11	.46*
Severity (ash)	.18*	.16*	.27*	.11	.07	.33*
Severity (mud/flood)	.41*	.48*	.60*	.63*	.66*	.79*
Multiple R	.69	—	—	.83	—	—
F Ratio	14.16*	—	—	34.19*	—	—

*Coefficient statistically significant, p < .05.

effect on perceived risk in Toutle than in Lexington. In Chapter 3 we argued that this was probably due to the more extensive damage experienced in Toutle (which implies the presence of a "floor" effect for damage below which its effects on perceived risk are minimal). Similarly, certainty of future volcanicity had a greater effect on perceived risk in Toutle than in Lexington. On the other hand, perceived severity of mudflow/flood threats shows a much stronger effect in Lexington than in Toutle.

To the focus upon the data within each site, we can assess the relative effects of each independent variable (statistically controlling the others), by examining the beta weights. In the Toutle sample, perceived severity of the mudflow/flood threat (.48) has the largest single impact upon change in perceived risk. This is followed in relative importance by perceived certainty of the threat (.23) and perception of the severity of ash fall danger (.16). Damage sustained and perceived efficacy of protection each produce similar and slightly lower (.12) effects on perceived risk or vulnerability. Proximity to the threat produced the smallest change (.08) in levels of perceived risk. Citizen perceptions of the severity of the mudflow/flood threat (.66) were also responsible for the largest change in perceived risk in the Lexington data. This variable was followed at some distance by perceived efficacy of protection (.18) and perceived certainty of the threat (.11). Perceived severity of the ash fall threat, proximity and sustained damage each produced a small change in perceived risk.

To briefly summarize, at least four of the variables from our theoretical model are important in *both* communities in the sense that they are associated with changes in perceived risk. Three of these variables represent two of the classic risk determinants: severity of the threat (the more important being perceived severity of mudflow/floods, but to a lesser extent ash fall as well) and perceived certainty of the danger. A social psychological dimension, perceived efficacy of undertaking protection, was also a contributor to level of perceived risk in both communities. Finally, as we anticipated in Chapter 3, sustained damage affected risk perception to a far greater degree in Toutle than in Lexington.

Hazard Adjustment

The working model developed to explain citizen adoption of hazard adjustments is composed of six variables. Table 37 shows the zero-order correlation coefficients for each variable with hazard adjustment. Three variables show a positive relationship with hazard adjustments and produce values of Pearson's r which are similar in each community: perceived risk, threat knowledge and proportion of protective information received from relatives. Salience of the volcano threat is also positively correlated with perceived risk, although the correlation is stronger in Toutle than in Lexington. In Toutle, sustained damage was positively correlated with hazard adjustment, but this relationship approaches zero in the Lexington data set. Finally, protective information received from friends was positively correlated with undertaking hazard adjustments in both communities, but the magnitude of the correlation was greater in Lexington.

Collectively, our six independent variables perform well as predictors of hazard adjustment. For the Toutle data set we obtain a multiple R of .59 ($p < .05$), indicating that 35 percent of the variation in hazard adjustment can be accounted for by the independent variables acting together. The Lexington data yield a multiple R of .57 ($p < .05$), which may be interpreted as showing that 33 percent of the variance in hazard adjustment has been explained. Again, it is encouraging to note that the overall model (all variables taken together) explained similar proportions of total variation in each data set.

Turning to between community differences, the unstandardized regression coefficients indicate that two variables—perceived risk and protective information from friends—have similar impacts on hazard adjustment in each community. Salience of the volcano hazard, on the other hand, was responsible for a much larger change in hazard adjustment in the Toutle data set than in Lexington. Likewise, sustained damage produced a much larger effect in Toutle than Lexington. Threat knowledge and protective information from relatives each produced a somewhat larger effect in Lexington than in Toutle.

In the Toutle data set, salience of the volcano hazard shows the largest effect on hazard adjustment (beta weight = .32). In relative importance, salience is followed by level of threat knowledge (.19) and protective information from relatives (.18). Damage sustained (.14) and perceived risk (.11) produced smaller but still notable changes in hazard adjustment. Protective information received from friends (.01) shows the smallest effect on hazard adjustment. Turning to the Lexington data set, threat knowledge (.40) and protective information from relatives (.27) are responsible for the greatest changes in hazard adjustment. These are followed at some distance by perceived risk (.08) and salience (.07). Protective information from friends and sustained damage each produced a small change in hazard adjustment.

TABLE 37

Regression Analysis for Hazard Adjustment

	Toutle			Lexington		
	Unstandardized Regression Coefficient	Beta Weight	Zero-order Pearson's r with Adjustment	Unstandardized Regression Coefficient	Beta Weight	Zero-order Pearson's r with Adjustment
Perceived risk	.14	.11	.38*	.08	.08	.25*
Volcano salience	.38*	.32*	.47*	.07	.07	.25*
Threat knowledge	.33*	.19*	.35*	.52*	.40*	.48*
Damage sustained	.21	.14	.27*	-.04	-.03	-.03
Contacts: relatives	.30*	.18*	.25*	.42*	.27*	.36*
Multiple R	.59			.57		
F Ratio	8.40*			7.26*		

*Coefficient statistically significant, p < .05.

In closing, we again see overlap between the two data sets regarding the relative importance of specific variables. In both communities, level of threat knowledge and protective information received from relatives produced noticeable changes in hazard adjustment. Salience of the volcano threat was also an important predictor in both data sets, but its effect on hazard adjustment was much greater in Toutle. Perceived risk made a small contribution, but the effect was present in both communities. Sustained damage created a noticeable change in hazard adjustment in the Toutle data set, but not in Lexington.

Summary

As a means of bringing together and summarizing our theoretical thinking, it is possible to link the working models for threat knowledge, perceived risk and hazard adjustment. This linking is shown graphically in Figure 1. The working model itself may be expressed as a series of propositions. The propositions are stated in their most general form and grouped by relevant dependent variables. Following each grouping of propositions, we have listed qualifications derived from our analyses of the Toutle and Lexington data sets.

I. Perception of Risk

    A. The closer a person lives to the source of danger, the higher the level of perceived risk.

    B. The higher the judged probability of future disaster impacts, the higher the level of perceived risk.

    C. The greater the perceived magnitude of negative consequences associated with the threat, the higher the level of perceived risk.

    D. The higher the level of damage sustained in the past, the higher the level of perceived risk.

    E. The less confidence one has in the efficacy of protective measures, the higher the level of perceived risk.

Two annotations may be made to these propositions based upon our analyses of data from Toutle and Lexington. First, in terms of relative importance, our data indicate that severity and certainty of the threat are particularly important in determining level of perceived risk. Second, there is evidence that damage sustained is correlated with perceived risk only when levels of damage are moderate or high. There appears to be a threshold effect below which past damage is uncorrelated with perceived risk.

II. Threat Knowledge

    A. The higher the level of perceived risk, the greater the level of threat knowledge.

    B. The more salient the hazard, the greater the level of threat knowledge.

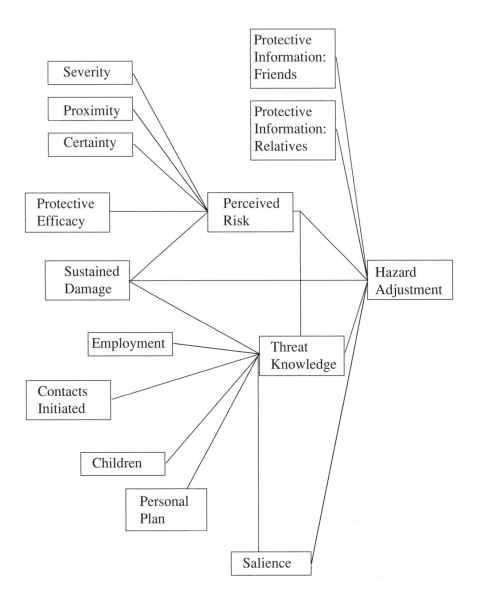

Figure 2
Combined theoretical model for hazard adjustment, perceived risk and
threat knowledge (arrows represent posited relationships, either direct or
inverse).

C. Employment in a hazard-related occupation is associated with higher levels of threat knowledge.

D. The presence of school-aged children in the household is associated with higher levels of threat knowledge.

E. The greater the level of damage sustained in the past, the higher the level of threat knowledge.

F. Citizens who initiate contacts with hazard information sources develop higher levels of threat knowledge.

G. Higher levels of personal emergency planning effort are associated with higher levels of threat knowledge.

The principal qualification to be offered regarding these propositions again centers upon damage sustained. There is, as we pointed out in Chapter 2, some theoretical and empirical support (largely from flood studies) for the idea that past victimization or damage sustained should be correlated with higher levels of threat knowledge. However, in both of our study communities, we found that past levels of eruption damage were uncorrelated with threat knowledge. We acknowledge that it is likely that eruption victims do view volcanic threats differently than non-victims. Victims may indeed seek knowledge of protective measures more ardently than non-victims. The information gathered, however, may educate volcano victims about specific protective measures but at least in Toutle and Lexington, it did not result in the enhancement of threat knowledge measured as information on specific consequences of volcano threats. One negative case in connection with one type of natural hazard is, of course, not sufficient reason to eliminate the proposition from the model. It does justify caution, however, in making generalizations pending a more thorough empirical testing.

III. Hazard Adjustment

A. The higher the level of perceived risk, the greater the degree of hazard adjustment.

B. The greater the proportion of protective information received from relatives, the greater the degree of hazard adjustment.

C. The greater the proportion of protective information received from friends, the greater the degree of hazard adjustment.

D. The greater the level of damage sustained in the past, the greater the degree of hazard adjustment.

E. The more salient the hazard, the greater the degree of hazard adjustment.

F. The greater the level of threat knowledge, the greater the degree of hazard adjustment.

Two qualifications may be offered regarding our propositions which address hazard adjustment. First, our data again show a threshold effect for damage sustained. That is, in the Toutle data set, characterized by moderate and high levels of damage, there was a positive correlation between sustaining damage and adopting hazard adjustments. The Lexington data, characterized by predominantly lower levels of damage yielded a correlation of approximately zero between damage and adjustments. Second, while information about protective measures received through social networks was positively correlated with hazard adjustment, information received from relatives was substantially more important than that received from friends or neighbors.

The primary value of our working model lies in the fact that it is an attempt to integrate a variety of research findings regarding different aspects of hazard adjustment along explicit theoretical lines. As such, the framework identifies important variables, conditions and relationships that pertain to the process of hazard adjustment. As we have stressed throughout, our research is largely exploratory and the resultant model tentative. Future research must deal with the problems of identifying additional variables, refining measurement strategies, and elaborating relationships reported here.

BIBLIOGRAPHY

Anderson, Jon.
1968. Cultural Adaptation to Threatened Disaster, *Human Organization* 27 (Winter): 298-307.

Anderson, William A.
1965. *Some Observations on a Disaster Subculture*. Columbus: Disaster Research Center, Ohio State University.

_____.
1969. Disaster Warning and Communication in Two Communities, *Journal of Communication* 19 (June): 92-104.

_____.
1970. Military Organizations in Natural Disasters, *American Behavioral Scientist* 13 (3): 415-422.

Bailey, R. A., P. R. Beauchemin, F. P. Kapinos and D. W. Klick.
1983. *The Volcano Hazards Program*. Reston, Virginia: U.S. Geological Survey, Open-File Report 83-400.

Baisden, Barbara and Enrico Quarantelli.
1979. The Recovery Period in U.S. Disasters: Problems and Opportunities, *Proceedings of the National Public Policy Forum for Disaster Relief*. Racine, Wisconsin: National Voluntary Organizations Active in Disasters.

Baker, Earl, J. C. Brigham, A. J. Parades and D. Smith.
1976. *The Social Impact of Hurricane Eloise on Panama City, Florida*. Tallahassee: Florida Research and Environmental Analysis Center.

Bandura, Albert.
1977. *Social Learning Theory*. Englewood Cliffs, New Jersey: PrenticeHall.

Barberi, R. and P. Gasparini.
1976. Volcanic Hazards, *Bulletin of the International Association of Engineering and Geology* 14: 217-232.

Barnes, Edward and Donna Haupt.
1985a. Volcano Reborn: The Remarkable Healing of Mt. St. Helens, *Life* 8 (10): 20-26.

Barnes, K., J. Brosius, S. Cutter and J. K. Mitchell.
1979. *Response of Impacted Populations to the Three Mile Island Nuclear Reactor Accident*. New Brunswick, New Jersey: Rutgers University Press.

Bartley, Bruce.
1980. Concern Grows in Nearby Cougar, *Seattle Times*, p. A1, March 28.

Barton, Allen.
1970. *Communities in Disaster*. New York: Anchor Books.

Bates, Frederick, C. Fogleman, V. Parenton, R. Pittman and G. Tracy.
1963. *The Social and Psychological Consequences of Natural Disaster*. Washington, D.C.: National Academy of Sciences.

Beach, Horace D. and Rex Lucas.
1960. *Individual and Group Behavior in a Coal Mine Disaster*. Washington, D.C.: National Academy of Sciences, National Research Council.

Belshaw, Cyril.
1951. Social Consequences of the Mt. Lamington Eruption, *Oceania* 21 (June): 241-252.

Bernert, E. H. and F. C. Ikles.
1952. Evacuation and the Cohesion of Urban Groups, *American Journal of Sociology* 58 (September): 133-138.

Bernstein, R. S., M. A. McCawley, M. D. Attfield, F. Green, D. D. Dollberg and J. R. Merchant.
1982. Epidemiologic Assessment of the Risk for Adverse Pulmonary Effects from Persistent Occupational Exposures to Mt. St. Helens' Volcanic Ash. In S. Keller, ed., *Mt. St. Helens: One Year Later*. Cheney: Eastern Washington University.

Blong, Russell J.
1984. *Volcanic Hazards: A Sourcebook on the Effects of Eruptions*. New York: Academic Press.

Bolin, Robert.
1976. Family Recovery from Natural Disaster, *Mass Emergencies* 1: 267277.

Bolt, B. A., W. Horn, G. MacDonald and R. Scott.
1977. *Geological Hazards*. New York: Springer-Verlag.

Bolton, Patricia, Marjorie Greene, and Michael Lindell.
1981. *Public Information Programs Accompanying Emergency Plans at Nuclear Power Plants*. Seattle, Washington: Battelle Human Affairs Research Centers.

Boyd, Francis.
1984. *Explosive Volcanism*. Washington, D.C.: National Academy of Sciences Press.

Brewer, James.
1903. Why St. Helens Quaked, *The Morning Oregonian* (Portland), p. 4, October 5.

Broom, Jack.
1980a. Major Eruption of St. Helens Predicted, *Seattle Times*, p. A1, April 3.
_____.
1980b. New Stronger Quakes Hit Volcano, *Seattle Times*, p. A1, April 1.

Bruner, M. T.
1974. *The Westmann Islanders Come Home to Heimaey.* Seattle: Department of Geography, University of Washington.

Bullard, Fred.
1962. *Volcanoes in History, in Theory, in Eruption.* Austin: University of Texas Press.

_____.
1976. *Volcanoes of the Earth.* Austin: University of Texas Press.

Bunnell, Clarence.
1933. *Legends of the Klickitats.* Portland, Oregon: Metropolitan Press.

Burnett, Peter.
1902. The Letters of Peter Burnett, *Oregon Historical Quarterly* 3 (December): 424-426.

Burton, Ian and Robert W. Kates.
1964. The Perception of Natural Hazards in Resource Management, *Natural Resources Journal* 3 (January): 412-441.

Burton, Ian, Robert Kates and Gilbert White.
1978. *The Environment as Hazard.* London: Oxford University Press.

Buzzetti, Bea.
1953. The Mt. St. Helens Area, *Cowlitz County Historical Quarterly* 4 (4): 13-15.

Christensen, Larry and Carlton Ruch.
1978. Assessment of Brochures and Radio and Television Presentations on Hurricane Awareness, *Mass Emergencies* 3 (4): 209-216.

Christiansen, Robert L.
1980. Eruption of Mt. St. Helens: Volcanology, *Nature* 285 (June): 531-533.

Clark, D. E. and H. Lee.
1965. *Ceniza Arena Cleanup in San Jose, Costa Rica.* Palo Alto, California: Stanford Research Institute.

Clark, Ella E.
1953. *Indian Legends of the Pacific Northwest.* Berkeley: University of California Press.

Colton, Harold.
1932. Sunset Crater: The Effect of a Volcanic Eruption on an Ancient Pueblo People, *The Geographical Review* 32 (4): 582-590.

The Columbian.
1980. *Mt. St. Helens Holocaust.* Vancouver, Washington: The Columbian, Inc.

Committee on Commerce, Science and Transportation.
1980. *Mt. St. Helens Impact.* Serial Number 96-108, Second Session, Ninety-Sixth Congress, United States Senate, Washington D.C.

Connelly, Joel.
1980. Sorting Through the Ashes of St. Helens Eruptions, *Seattle Post-Intelligencer*, p. A3, April 2.

_____.
1985. Life Amid the Ruins, *Seattle Post-Intelligencer*, pp. E1-3, May 12.

Costner, Herbert.
1971. Theory, Deduction and Rules of Correspondence. In Hubert Blalock, ed., *Causal Models in the Social Sciences*. Chicago: Aldine.

Council of State Government.
1979. *The States and Natural Hazards*. Lexington, Kentucky: The Council of State Governments.

Crandell, Dwight R.
1980. Personal communication to Marjorie R. Greene. U.S. Geological Survey, Denver, Colorado.

Crandell, Dwight R. and Donal Mullineaux.
1974. Appraising Volcanic Hazards of the Cascade Range of the Northwestern United States, *Earthquake Information Bulletin* 6 (5): 3-10.

_____.
1978. *Potential Hazards from Future Eruptions of Mt. St. Helens Volcano, Washington*. Geological Survey Bulletin 1383C. Washington, D.C.: United States Government Printing Office.

Crandell, Dwight, Donal Mullineaux and C. D. Miller.
1979. Volcanic Hazards Studies in the Cascade Range of the Western United States. In P. D. Sheets and D. Grayson, eds., *Volcanic Activity and Human Ecology*. New York: Academic Press.

Crandell, Dwight R., Donal R. Mullineaux and Mayer Rubin.
1975. Mt. St. Helens Volcano: Recent and Future Behavior, *Science* 187: 438-441.

Crespi, Irving.
1971. What Kind of Attitude Measures are Predictive of Behavior? *Public Opinion Quarterly* 35: 327-334.

Dacy, Douglas and Howard Kunreuther.
1969. *The Economics of Natural Disasters*. New York: Free Press.

Danzig, Elliott, Paul Thayer and Lila Galanter.
1958. *The Effects of a Threatening Rumor on a Disaster-Stricken Community*. Washington, D.C.: National Academy of Sciences Publication Number 517.

Dardarian, Suki.
1980. More Quakes Rock St. Helens: Evacuation Ordered, *Seattle Times*, p. C1, March 27.

Davenport, Sally S. and Penny Waterstone.
1979. *Hazard Awareness Guidebook: Planning for What Comes Naturally.* Austin: Texas Coastal and Marine Council.

Davidson, George.
1884. Notes on the Volcanic Eruption of Mt. St. Augustin, Alaska, October 6, 1883, *Science* 3 (54): 186-189.

Decker, Robert and Barbara Decker.
1981. The Eruptions of Mt. St. Helens, *Scientific American* 224 (March): 68-80.

Dierkes, Meinhof, Samuel Edwards and Robert Coppock.
1980. *Technological Risk.* Frankfurt, West Germany: Oelgeschlager, Gunn and Hain.

Diggory, James.
1956. Some Consequences of Proximity to a Disease Threat, *Sociometry* 19 (March): 47-53.

Douglas, Dorothy, Bruce Westley and Steve Chaffee.
1970. An Information Campaign that Changed Community Attitudes, *Journalism Quarterly* 47 (4): 479-487.

Douglas, Mary and Aaron Wildavsky.
1982. *Risk and Culture.* Berkeley: University of California Press.

Drabek, Thomas.
1968. *Disaster in Aisle 13.* Columbus: Disaster Research Center, Ohio State University.

_____.
1969. Social Processes in Disaster: Family Evacuation, *Social Problems* 16 (Winter): 336-347.

_____.
1986. *Human System Responses to Disaster.* New York: Springer-Verlag.

Drabek, Thomas and Keith Boggs.
1968. Families in Disaster: Reactions and Relatives, *Journal of Marriage and the Family* 30 (August): 443-451.

Drabek, Thomas and William Key.
1976. The Impact of Disaster on Primary Group Linkages, *Mass Emergencies* 1 (2): 187-203.

_____.
1985. *Conquering Disaster.* New York: Irvington Books.

Drabek, Thomas, William Key, Patricia Erickson and Juanita Crowe.
1975. The Impact of Disaster on Kin Relationships, *Journal of Marriage and the Family* 37 (August): 481-494.

Drabek, Thomas, Thomas Kilajanek and Chris Adams.
1980. *Search and Rescue Missions in Natural Disasters and Remote Settings.* Washington, D.C.: National Science Foundation, Division of Critical and Emerging Engineering Systems.

Drabek, Thomas and John Stephenson.
1971. When Disaster Strikes, *Journal of Applied Social Psychology* 1 (2): 187-203.

duBeth, Donna.
1980. Fireworks Are Just Beginning, *Daily News* (Longview, Washington), Volcano Reprint, p. 4, March 28.

Dynes, Russell and Enrico Quarantelli.
1972. Group Behavior Under Stress, *Sociology and Social Research* 52 (July): 416-429.

Dynes, Russell, Enrico Quarantelli and Gary Kreps.
1972. *A Perspective on Disaster Planning*. Newark: Disaster Research Center, University of Delaware.

Earle, Timothy and George Cvetkovich.
1983. *Risk Judgement and the Communication of Hazard Information*. Seattle, Washington: Battelle Human Affairs Research Centers.

Earney, Fillmore and Brian Knowles.
1974. Urban Snow Hazard. In Gilbert White, ed., *Natural Hazards*. New York: Oxford University Press.

Emmons, S. F.
1877. The Volcanoes of the Pacific Coast of the United States, *Journal of the American Geographical Society* 9 (1): 45-65.

Erickson, Kai.
1976. *Everything in Its Path*. New York: Simon and Schuster.

Findley, Rowe.
1981a. The Eruption of Mt. St. Helens, *National Geographic* 159 (January): 3-65.

_____.
1981b. Mt. St. Helens Aftermath, *National Geographic* 160 (December): 713-732.

Fischoff, Baruch, Sarah Lichtenstein, Paul Slovic, Stephen Derby and Ralph Keeney.
1981. *Acceptable Risk*. London: Cambridge University Press.

Fischoff, B. A., S. R. Watson and C. Hope.
1983. *Defining Risk*. Eugene, Oregon: Decision Research Corporation.

Fishbein, Martin.
1967. Attitude and the Prediction of Behavior. In Martin Fishbein, ed., *Attitude Theory and Measurement*. New York: John Wiley and Sons.

Flynn, Cynthia.
1979. *Three Mile Island Telephone Survey NUREG/CR-1093*. Washington, D.C.: Nuclear Regulatory Commission.

Fritz, Charles E.
1957. Disasters Compared in Six American Communities, *Human Organization* 16 (Summer): 6-9.

Fritz, Charles E.
1961a. *Disaster and Community Therapy*. Washington, D.C.: National Academy of Sciences, National Research Council.

_____.

1961b. Disasters. In R. Merton and R. Nisbet, eds., *Contemporary Social Problems*. New York: Harcourt, Brace and World.

_____.

1971. The Effects of U.S. Bombing on North Vietnam's Ability to Support Military Operations in South Vietnam (excerpt from Institute for Defense Analyses Report published as pp. 502-507). In *The Pentagon Papers*. New York: Bantam Books.

Fritz, Charles and Eli Marks.
1954. The NORC Studies of Human Behavior in Disaster, *Journal of Social Issues* 10: 26-41.

Fritz, Charles and J. H. Mathewson.
1957. *Convergence Behavior in Disasters: A Problem in Social Control*. Washington, D.C.: National Academy of Sciences, National Research Council.

Gairdner, Meredith.
1836. Letter, *The Edinburgh New Philosophical Journal* 20 (39): 206.

General Accounting Office.
1982. *Federal Involvement in the Mt. St. Helens Disaster*. Washington, D. C.: Document GAD/RCED-83-16, Comptroller General of the United States.

Geophysics Program.
1980. Eruption of Mt. St. Helens: Seismology, *Nature* 285 (June): 529-531.

Gillespie, David and Ronald W. Perry.
1976. An Integrated Systems and Emergent Norm Approach to Mass Emergencies, *Mass Emergencies* 1 (December): 303-312.

Gillins, Peter.
1985. Effects of Mt. St. Helens' 1980 Eruptions Still Felt, *Arizona Republic*, p. AA11, May 12.

Glass, Albert.
1970. The Psychological Aspects of Emergency Situations. In S. Abram, ed., *Psychological Aspects of Stress*. Springfield, Illinois: Charles C. Thomas.

Gough, William.
1985. Mt. St. Helens, *Seattle Times*, p. J1, May 12.

Green, F. H., V. Vallgathan, M. S. Mentnech, J. H. Tucker, J. A. Merchant, P. J. Kiessling, J. A. Antonius and P. Parshley.
1981. Is Volcanic Ash a Pneumoconiosis Risk? *Nature* 293: 216-217.

Greene, Marjorie, Ronald W. Perry and Michael Lindell.
1981. The March, 1980 Eruptions of Mt. St. Helens: Citizen Perceptions of Volcano Hazard, *Disasters* 5 (1): 49-66.

Griggs, Gary and John Gilchrist.
1983. *Geologic Hazards, Resources, and Environmental Planning*. Belmont, California: Wadsworth Publishing Company.

Grove, Noel.
1973. A Village Fights for Its Life, *National Geographic* 144 (July): 40-67.

Gruntfest, Eve, T. E. Downing and Gilbert White.
1978. Big Thompson Flood Exposes Need for Better Flood Reaction System to Save Lives, *Civil Engineering* 78 (February): 72-73.

Haas, Eugene, Harold Cochrane and Donald Eddy.
1976. *The Consequences of Large Scale Evacuation Following Disaster*. Boulder, Colorado: Institute for Behavioral Science.

Haas, Eugene, Robert Kates, and Martyn Bowden, eds.
1977. *Reconstruction Following Disaster*. Cambridge, Massachusetts: MIT Press.

Hague, Arnold and Joseph Iddings.
1883. Notes on the Volcanoes of Northern California, Oregon and Washington Territory, *American Journal of Science* 26 (153, 3rd series): 222-235.

Hamilton, R., R. M. Taylor and G. Rice.
1955. *A Social Psychological Interpretation of the Udall, Kansas Tornado*. Wichita, Kansas: University of Wichita Press.

Hanson, Susan, John Vitek and Perry Hanson.
1979. Natural Disaster: Long-Range Impact on Human Response to Future Disaster Threats, *Environment and Behavior* 2 (June): 268-284.

Harris, Stephen L.
1980. *Fire and Ice: The Cascade Volcanoes*. Seattle, Washington: The Mountaineers and Pacific Search Press.

Harvey, A. G.
1945. Meredith Gairdner: Doctor of Medicine, *British Columbia Historical Journal* 9 (April): 89-111.

Healy, Richard J.
1969. *Emergency and Disaster Planning*. New York: John Wiley and Sons.

Hedlund, Gerald.
1976. Mudflow Disaster, *Northwest Anthropological Research Notes* 10: 77-89.

Hill, Reuben and Donald Hansen.
1962. Families in Disaster. In G. Baker and D. Chapman, eds., *Man and Society in Disaster*. New York: Basic Books.

Hirose, Hirotada.
1979. Volcanic Eruption and Local Politics in Japan, *Mass Emergencies* 4 (1): 53-62.

Hodge, David, Virginia Sharp and Marion Marts.
1979. Contemporary Responses to Volcanism: Case Studies from the Cascades and Hawaii. In P. D. Sheets and D. Grayson, eds., *Volcanic Activity and Human Ecology*. New York: Academic Press.

Holmes, Kenneth L.
1955. Mt. St. Helens' Recent Eruptions, *Portland Oregon Historical Quarterly* 56: 196-210.

——————.
1980. *Mt. St. Helens: Lady with a Past*. Salem, Oregon: Salem Press.

Houts, Peter, Michael Lindell, Teh Hu, Paul Cleary, George Tokuhata and Cynthia Flynn.
1984. The Protective Action Decision Model Applied to Evacuation During the Three Mile Island Crisis, *International Journal of Mass Emergencies and Disasters* 2 (1): 27-39.

Hunt, Carl E. and J. Scott MacCready.
1980. *The Short-Term Economic Consequences of the Mt. St. Helens Volcanic Eruptions in May and June 1980*. Olympia: Washington State Department of Commerce and Economic Development, Research Division.

Interagency Flood Hazard Mitigation Team
Interagency Flood Hazard Mitigation Report in Response to the May 21, 1980 Disaster Declaration. FEMA-623-DR-WA . Bothell, Washington: Region X, Federal Emergency Management Agency.

Janis, Irving L.
1951. *Air War and Emotional Stress: Psychological Studies of Bombing and Civilian Defense*. New York: McGraw-Hill.

——————.
1962. Psychological Effects of Warnings. In Baker and Chapman, eds., *Man and Society in Disaster*. New York: Basic Books.

Janis, Irving and Leon Mann.
1977. Emergency Decision Making, *Journal of Human Stress* 3 (June): 35-45.

Jennings, P.
1969. *Disruptions of the Environmental Balance: The Eruptions of Mt. Agung and Mt. Kelvt*. Master's thesis, University of Hawaii, Honolulu.

Kahneman, Daniel and Amos Tversky.
1974. Judgment Under Uncertainty: Hueristics and Biases, *Science* 185 (September): 1124-1131.

Kane, Paul.
1925. *Wanderings of an Artist Among the Indians of North America*. Toronto: The Radisson Society.

Kartez, Jack.
1982. *Emergency Planning Implications of Local Governments' Responses to Mt. St. Helens.* Working Paper #46. Boulder: Institute of Behavioral Science, University of Colorado.

Kates, Robert W.
1962. *Hazard and Choice Perception in Flood Plain Management.* Department of Geography, Research Paper #78. Chicago: University of Chicago.

_____.
1971. Natural Hazard in Human Ecological Perspective: Hypotheses and Models, *Economic Geography* 47 (July): 438-451.

Katz, Arthur.
1982. *Life After Nuclear War.* Cambridge, Massachusetts: Ballinger Publishing Company.

Keesing, Felix.
1952. The Papuan Orokaiva Versus Mt. Lamington, *Human Organization* 2 (1): 16-22.

Kerr, Richard A.
1980. Research News: Mt. St. Helens: An Unpredictable Foe, *Science* 208 (June): 1446-1448.
Killian, Lewis.
1952. The Significance of Multiple Group Membership in Disaster, *American Journal of Sociology* 57 (January): 309-314.

_____.
1956. *An Introduction to Methodological Problems of Field Studies in Disasters.* Washington, D.C.: National Academy of Sciences, National Research Council.

Knott, Jack and Aaron Wildavsky.
1979. If Dissemination is the Solution, What is the Problem? *Knowledge* 1 (June): 537-578.

Korosec, Michael, James G. Rigby and Keith Stoffel.
1980. *The 1980 Eruption of Mt. St. Helens, Washington, Part I: March 20-May 19, 1980.* Information Circular Number 71. Olympia: Washington State Department of Natural Resources, Division of Geology and Earth Resources.

Kraus, Theodor and Leonard Von Matt.
1973. *Pompeii and Herculaneum.* New York: Harry Abrams.

Kreps, Gary.
1973. *Decision Making Under Conditions of Uncertainty.* Newark: Disaster Research Center, University of Delaware.

_____.
1984. Sociological Inquiry and Disaster Research, *Annual Review of Sociology* 10: 309-330.

Kunreuther, Howard, Ralph Ginsberg, Louis Miller, Philip Sagi, Paul Slovic, Bradley Borkan and Norman Katz.
1978. *Disaster Insurance Protection: Public Policy Lessons*. New York: John Wiley and Sons.

Lachman, Roy and William Bonk.
1960. Behavior and Beliefs During the Recent Volcanic Eruption at Kapoho, Hawaii, *Science* 131: 1095-1096.

Lachman, Roy, Maurice Tatsuoka and William Bonk.
1961. Human Behavior During the Tsunami of May 1960, *Science* 133 (May): 1405-1409.

LaCroix, A.
1906. The Eruption of Vesuvius in April, 1906, *Smithsonian Institution Annual Report (1906)*, 223-248.

Lang, Kurt and Gladys Lang.
1964. Collective Response to the Threat of Disaster. In G. Grosser, ed., *The Threat of Impending Disaster*. Cambridge, Massachusetts: MIT Press.

Lange, Larry.
1985. Eruption of Tourists Flows to St. Helens, *Seattle Post-Intelligencer*, p. A1, May 27.

Leonard, V. A.
1973. *Police Pre-Disaster Preparation*. Springfield, Illinois: Charles C. Thomas.

Leveson, David.
1980. *Geology and the Urban Environment*. New York: Oxford University Press.

Lewis, James, Philip O'Keefe and Kenneth Westgate.
1977. A Philosophy of Precautionary Planning, *Mass Emergencies* 2: 95-104.

Lindell, Michael and Timothy Earle.
1983. How Close is Close Enough, *Risk Analysis* 3 (December): 245-253.

Lindell, Michael and Ronald W. Perry.
1980. Evaluation Criteria for Emergency Response Plans, *Journal of Hazardous Materials* 3 (June): 349361.
_____.
1983. Nuclear Plant Emergency Warning: How Would the Public Respond? *Nuclear News* 26 (January): 49-53.

Lindell, Michael, Ronald Perry and Marjorie Greene.
1983. Individual Response to Emergency Preparedness Planning Near Mt. St. Helens, *Disaster Management* 3 (January): 5-11.

Lindell, Michael, Bill Rankin and Ronald W. Perry.
1980. *Warning Mechanisms in Emergency Response Systems*. Seattle, Washington: Battelle Human Affairs Research Centers.

Lipman, Peter and Donal Mullineaux.
1981. *The 1980 Eruptions of Mt. St. Helens*. Professional Paper 1250. Washington, D.C.:
    U.S. Geological Survey.

Lucas, Rex.
1966. The Influence of Kinship Upon Perception of an Ambiguous Stimulus, *American
    Sociological Review* 31 (April): 227-236.

Lyman, William.
1915. Indian Myths of the Northwest, *Proceedings of the American Antiquarian Society*
    25 (October): 375-395.

MacDonald, Gordon.
1972. *Volcanoes*. Englewood Cliffs, New Jersey: Prentice-Hall.

Martin, Roger and James Davis.
1982. *Status of Volcanic Prediction and Emergency Response Capabilities in Volcanic
    Hazard Zones of California*. Sacramento: California Department of Conservation.

Mayor's Disaster Review Task Force.
1977. *Disaster Response: The 1975 Omaha Tornado*. Omaha, Nebraska: City of Omaha.

McLuckie, Benjamin.
1970. *The Warning System in Natural Disaster Situations: A Selective Analysis*. Colum-
    bus: Disaster Research Center, Ohio State University.

_____.
1972. *Warning Systems in Disaster*. Columbus: Disaster Research Center, Ohio State
    University.

McLuckie, Benjamin and Robert Whitman.
1971. *A Study of Warning and Response in Ten Colorado Communities During the Floods
    of June 1965*. Columbus: Disaster Research Center, Ohio State University.

Meltsner, Arnold.
1979. The Communication of Scientific Information to the Wider Public, *Minerva* 17 (3):
    331-354.

Menninger, W. C.
1952. Psychological Reactions in an Emergency, *American Journal of Psychiatry* 109:
    128-130.

Midlarsky, Elizabeth.
1968. Aiding Responses: An Analysis and Review, *MerrillPalmer Quarterly* 14: 229-
    260.

Mileti, Dennis.
1974. *A Normative Causal Model Analysis of Disaster Warning Response*. Ph.D.
    Boulder: Department of Sociology, University of Colorado.

_____.
1975. *Natural Hazard Warning Systems in the United States: A Research Assessment*.
    Boulder: Institute for Behavioral Science, University of Colorado.

Mileti, Dennis and E. M. Beck.
1975. Communication in Crisis, *Communication Research* 2 (January): 24-29.

Mileti, Dennis, Thomas Drabek and Eugene Haas.
1975. *Human Behavior in Extreme Environments: A Sociological Perspective*. Monograph #21. Boulder: Institute of Behavioral Science, The University of Colorado.

Mileti, Dennis and Patricia Harvey.
1977. Correcting for the Human Factor in Tornado Warnings. Paper read at the 10th Conference on Severe Local Storms, Omaha, Nebraska.

Mogil, Michael and Herbert Groper.
1977. The NWS's Severe Local Storm Warning and Disaster Preparedness Programs, *Bulletin of the American Meteorological Society* 58: 318-329.

Montz, Burrell.
1982. The Effect of Location on the Adoption of Hazard Mitigation Measures, *Professional Geographer* 34 (4): 416-423.

Moore, Harry E.
1958. *Tornadoes Over Texas*. Austin, Texas: University of Texas Press.

Moore, Harry E., Fred Bates, M. Layman and V. R. Parenton.
1963. *Before the Wind: A Study of the Response to Hurricane Carla*. Washington, D.C.: National Academy of Sciences, National Research Council.

Murton, Brian and Shimzo Shimabukuro.
1974. Human Adjustment to Volcanic Hazard in Puna District, Hawaii. In Gilbert White, ed., *Natural Hazards*. New York: Oxford University Press.

National Academy of Sciences.
1975. *Earthquake Prediction and Public Policy: Report of the Panel on Public Policy Implications of Earthquake Prediction of the Advisory Committee on Emergency Planning*. Washington, D.C.: National Academy of Sciences, National Research Council.

National Academy of Sciences.
1980. *Disasters and the Mass Media*. Washington, D.C.: National Academy of Sciences, National Research Council.

National Governors' Association.
1979a. *Comprehensive Emergency Management: A Governor's Guide*. Washington, D.C.: National Governors' Association, Center for Policy Research for Defense Civil Preparedness Agency.

_____.
1979b. *Nineteen Seventy-Eight Emergency Preparedness Project: Final Report*. Washington, D.C.: National Governors' Association, Center for Policy Research for Defense Civil Preparedness Agency.

Nigg, Joanne.
1982. Awareness and Behavior. In Thomas Saarinen, ed., *Perspectives on Increasing Hazard Awareness*. Boulder: Institute of Behavioral Science, University of Colorado.

Ollier, Cliff.
1969. *Volcanoes*. Cambridge, Massachusetts: The MIT Press.

Olson, Robert A.
1973. Individual and Organizational Dimensions of the San Fernando Earthquake. In L. Murphy, ed., *San Fernando Earthquake of February 9, 1971*. Washington, D.C.: U.S. Government Printing Office.

Padang, Neumann Van.
1960. Measures Taken by the Authorities of the Volcanological Survey to Safeguard the Population from the Consequences of Volcanic Outbursts, *Bulletin Volcanologique* 23: 181-192.

Parker, D. J. and D. M Harding.
1979. Natural Hazard Evaluation, Perception and Adjustment, *Geography* 64 (285): 307-316.

Pennsylvania Emergency Management Agency
n.d. *Flash Flood Handbook*. Harrisburg: Pennsylvania Emergency Management Agency.

Perkins, Carol.
1980a. Fiddling While Volcano Burns, *Seattle Post-Intelligencer*, p. A1, May 10.
_____.
1980b. Volcano Napping and Locals Flapping, *Seattle Post-Intelligencer*, p. A1, April 7.

Perri, Karla.
1980. *Mt. St. Helens: An Assessment: Issue Brief Number IB80066*. Washington, D.C.: Congressional Research Service, Library of Congress.

Perry, Ronald W.
1976. Attitude Scales as Behavior Estimation Devices, *Journal of Social Psychology* 100: 137-142.
_____.
1979. Incentives for Evacuation in Natural Disaster: Research Based Emergency Planning, *Journal of the American Planning Association* 45 (October): 440-447.
_____.
1982. *The Social Psychology of Civil Defense*. Lexington, Massachusetts: Heath-Lexington Books.
_____.
1983. Warning Source Credibility in Natural and Nuclear Disasters, *Disaster Management* 3 (July): 138-148.
_____.
1985. *Comprehensive Emergency Management*. Greenwich, Connecticut: JAI Press.

Perry, Ronald W., David Gillespie and Roy Lotz.
1976. Attitudinal Variables as Estimates of Behavior, *European Journal of Social Psychology* 6 (2): 227-243.

Perry, Ronald W., David Gillespie and Dennis Mileti.
1974. System Stress and the Persistence of Emergent Organizations, *Sociological Inquiry* 42 (December): 113-121.

Perry, Ronald W. and Marjorie Greene.
1982. Emergency Management in Volcano Hazards, *The Environmental Professional* 4 (3): 340-350.

_____.
1983. *Citizen Response to Volcanic Eruptions.* New York: Irvington Publishers.

Perry, Ronald W., Marjorie Greene and Michael Lindell.
1980. *Human Response to Volcanic Eruptions: Mt. St. Helens, May 18, 1980.* Seattle, Washington: Battelle Human Affairs Research Centers.

Perry, Ronald W., Marjorie Greene and Alvin Mushkatel.
1983. *American Minority Citizens in Disaster.* Seattle, Washington: Battelle Human Affairs Research Centers.

Perry, Ronald W. and Michael Lindell.
1978. The Psychological Consequences of Natural Disaster, *Mass Emergencies* 3 (2): 105-115.

_____.
1980. Pre-Disaster Planning to Promote Compliance with Evacuations. In E. J. Baker, ed., *Hurricanes and Coastal Storms.* Report Number 33. Tallahassee: Sea Grant College, Florida State University.

_____.
1986. *Twentieth Century Volcanicity at Mt. St. Helens.* Tempe: School of Public Affairs, Arizona State University.

Perry, Ronald W., Michael Lindell and Marjorie Greene.
1979. *Evacuation Decision-Making and Emergency Planning in Four Communities.* Seattle, Washington: Battelle Human Affairs Research Centers.

_____.
1980. Mt. St. Helens: Washingtonians View Their Volcano, *Hazard Monthly* 1 (2): 1-3.

_____.
1981. *Evacuation Planning in Emergency Management.* Lexington, Massachusetts: Heath-Lexington.

_____.
1982. Threat Perception and Public Response to Volcano Hazard, *Journal of Social Psychology* 116 (2): 199-204.

Perry, Ronald W. and Alvin Mushkatel.
1986. *Minority Citizens in Disasters.* Athens: University of Georgia Press.

Perry, Ronald W. and Joane Nigg.
1985. Emergency Management Strategies for Communicating Hazard Information, *Public Administration Review* 45 (January): 72-77.

Pipes, Nellie.
1934. The Journal of John H. Frost, *Oregon Historical Quarterly* 35 (December): 373-374.

Plummer, Fred.
1893. The Flying Rocks of Mt. St. Helens, *Scientific American* 69 (December): 355.

Poppleton, Phillip and George Pilkington.
1964. A Comparison of Four Methods of Scoring an Attitude Scale in Relation to Its Validity and Reliability, *British Journal of Social and Clinical Psychology* 3: 36-39.

Preusser, Hubertus.
1973. Der Vulkanausbruch auf Heimaey/Vestmannaeyjar und Seine Auswirkungen, *Geographische Rundschau* 25 (9): 337-350.

Quarantelli, Enrico L.
1960. A Note on the Protective Function of the Family in Disasters, *Marriage and Family Living* 22 (August): 263-264.

_____.
1970. Emergent Accommodation Groups: Beyond Current Collective Behavior Typologies. In Tomatsu Shihutani ed., *Human Nature and Collective Behavior*. Englewood Cliffs, New Jersey: Prentice-Hall.

_____.
1977. Social Aspects of Disasters, *Disasters* 1 (1): 98-107.

_____.
1980. *Evacuation Behavior and Problems: Findings and Implications from the Research Literature*. Miscellaneous Report No. 27. Columbus: Disaster Research Center, Ohio State University.

_____.
1982a. *The Study of Disaster Movies*. Newark: Disaster Research Center, University of Delaware.

_____.
1982b. *Inventory of Disaster Field Studies in the Social and Behavioral Sciences*. Newark: Disaster Research Center, University of Delaware.

Quarantelli, Enrico L. and Russell Dynes.
1970. Property Norms and Looting: Their Patterns in Community Crisis, *Phylon* 31 (Summer): 168182.

_____.
1972. When Disaster Strikes, *Psychology Today* 5 (February): 67-70.

_____.
1976. Community Conflict: Its Absence and Its Presence in Natural Disasters, *Mass Emergencies* 1: 139-152.

_____.
1977. Response to Social Crisis and Disaster, *Annual Review of Sociology* 3: 23-49.

Quarantelli, Enrico L. and Verta Taylor.
1977. Some Views on the Warning Problem in Disasters as Suggested by Sociological Research. Paper read at the American Meteorological Society Conference on Severe Local Storms.

Rees, John D.
1970. Paricutin Revisited: A Review of Man's Attempts to Adapt to Ecological Changes Resulting from Volcanic Catastrophe, *Geoforum* 4: 7-25.

_____.
1980. Effects of the Eruption of Paricutin Volcano on Landforms, Vegetation and Human Occupancy. In P. D. Sheets and D. Grayson, eds., *Volcanic Activity and Human Ecology*. New York: Academic Press.

Regulska, Joanna.
1979. Public Awareness Programs for Natural Hazards. Paper prepared for Hazard Awareness Workshop, March 22-23, 1979, Corpus Christi, Texas.

Reynolds, Cheryl A. and Margaret Reynolds.
1980. Letter to the Editor. *The Daily News* (Longview, Washington), p. A8, May 6.

Rosenfeld, Charles L.
1980. Observations on the Mt. St. Helens Eruption, *American Scientist* 68 (September-October): 494-509.

Rowe, William.
1977. *An Anatomy of Risk*. New York: John Wiley and Sons.

Rubin, Claire B.
1979. Disaster Mitigation: Challenge to Managers, *Public Administration Times* 2: 1-2.

_____.
1979. *Natural Disaster Recovery Planning for Local Public Officials*. Columbus, Ohio: Academy for Contemporary Problems.

Saarinen, Thomas.
1976. *Environmental Planning: Perception and Behavior*. Boston, Massachusetts: Houghton Mifflin Company.

_____.
1979. The Relation of Hazard Awareness to Adoption of Approved Mitigation Measures. Paper prepared for Hazard Awareness Workshop, March 22-23, 1979, Corpus Christi, Texas.

_____.
1980. *Public Response to Mt. St. Helens Volcano Hazard Warnings*. Washington, D.C.: National Science Foundation, Division of Engineering Systems.

_____.
1982. *Perspectives on Increasing Hazard Awareness*. Boulder: University of Colorado, Institute of Behavioral Science.

Sarason, Seymour.
1974. *The Psychological Sense of Community*. San Francisco: Jossey-Bass Publishers.

Schiff, Myra.
1977. Hazard Adjustment, Locus of Control and Sensation Seeking, *Environment and Behavior* 9: 233-254.

Semple, Eugene.
1888. The Olympic Mountains, *The West Shore* 18 (August): 428-429.

Shearer, Clement.
1980. Personal communication to Marjorie R. Greene. U.S. Geological Survey, Reston, Virginia.

Sillar, William.
1975. Planning for Disasters, *Long Range Planning* 8 (October): 2-7.

Sims, J. and Duane Bauman.
1972. The Tornado Threat: Coping Styles of North and South, *Science* 176: 1386-1392.

Slovic, Paul.
1964. Assessment of Risk Taking Behavior, *Psychological Bulletin* 61 (3): 220-233.

_____.
1978. The Psychology of Protective Behavior, *Journal of Safety Research* 10 (Summer): 58-68.

Slovic, Paul, Baruch Fischoff and Sarah Lichtenstein.
1979. Rating the Risks, *Environment* 21 (3): 14-20, 36-39.

_____.
1980. Facts and Fears: Understanding Perceived Risk. In Schwing, Richard Schwing and Walter Albers, eds., *Societal Risk Assessment*. New York: Plenum.

Slovic, Paul, Howard Kunreuther and Gilbert White.
1974. Decision Processes, Rationality and Adjustment to Natural Hazards. In G. F. White, ed., *Natural Hazards: Local, National and Global*. New York: Oxford University Press.

Slovic, Paul, Sarah Lichtenstein and Baruch Fischoff.
1980. *Images of Disaster: Perception and Acceptance of Risks from Nuclear Power*. Eugene, Oregon: Decision Research Corporation.

Smart, G. M.
1981. Volcanic Debris Control, Hunung Kelvt, East Java, *International Association of Hydrological Sciences Publications* 132: 604-623.

Sorenson, John.
1982. Emergency Planning for Rare Events: Some Behavioral Science Lessons for Volcano Science Management. In R. E. Martin and J.F. Davis, eds., *Status of Volcano Prediction and Emergency Response Capabilities in Volcanic Hazard Zones of California*. Sacramento: California Department of Conservation.

_____.
1983. Knowing How to Behave Under the Threat of Disaster, *Environment and Behavior* 15 (July): 438-457.

Sorenson, John and Philip Gersmehl.
1980. Volcanic Hazard Warning System, *Environmental Management* 4 (2): 125-136.

Sorkin, Alan.
1982. *Economic Aspects of Natural Disasters*. Lexington, Massachusetts: Heath-Lexington.

Stallings, Robert.
1971. *Communications in Natural Disaster*. Columbus: Disaster Research Center, Ohio State University.

Stothers, Richard.
1984. The Great Tambora Eruption in 1815 and Its Aftermath, *Science* 224 (June): 1191-1198.

Strong, Emory.
1969. Early Accounts of the Eruptions of Mt. St. Helens, *Geological News Letter* 35 (January): 3-5.

Surjo, I.
1965. Casualties of the Latest Activity of the Agung Volcano, *Bulletin of the Geological Society of Indonesia* 2 (1): 22-26.

Sweeney, Michael.
1980. Hundreds Flee: St. Helens Erupts; Explosion Could Come 'In Minutes,' *Seattle Post-Intelligencer*, p. A1, March 28.

Sweeney, Michael and Carol Perkins.
1980. Crater Belches Giant Rocks, *Seattle PostIntelligencer*, p. A1, April 3.

Swift, Charles and David Kresch.
1983. *Mudflow Hazards Along the Toutle and Cowlitz Rivers from a Hypothetical Failure of Spirit Lake Blockage*. Tacoma, Washington: Office of the District Chief, U.S. Geological Survey.

Taylor, Jon A.
1980. Personal communication to Marjorie R. Greene. Cowlitz County Sheriff's Office, Kelso, Washington.

Titmuss, Richard.
1950. *Problems of Social Policy*. London: HM Stationary Office.

Todd, Daniel J.
1980. Personal communication to Marjorie R. Greene. Toutle Fire Department, Toutle, Washington.

Travis, Richard and William Riebsame.
1979. Communicating Environmental Uncertainty, *Journal of Geography* 78 (5): 168-172.

Turner, Ralph.
1964. Collective Behavior. In Faris, Robert, ed., *Handbook of Modern Sociology*. Chicago: Rand McNally.

U.S. Forest Service.
1981. *Mt. St. Helens Interpretation and Recreation Plan*. Vancouver, Washington: Gifford Pinchot National Forest.

U.S. Forest Service.
1984. *Mt. St. Helens National Volcanic Monument.* Vancouver, Washington: Gifford Pinchot National Forest.

U.S. Senate Hearings.
1980. *Disaster Assistance Pacific Northwest: Mt. St. Helens Eruption.* Washington, D.C.: Committee on Appropriations.

Van Arsdol, Maurice, Georges Sabagh and Francesca Alexander.
1964. Reality and the Perception of Environmental Hazards, *Journal of Health and Social Behavior* 5 (Winter): 144-153.

Vlek, C. and P. J. Stallen.
1980. Rational and Personal Aspects of Risk, *Acta Psychologica* 45: 273300.

Waesche, Hugh and Dallas Peck.
1966. Volcanoes Tell Secrets in Hawaii, *Natural History* 75 (March): 2029.

Wallace, Anthony F. C.
1956. *Human Behavior in Extreme Situations.* Washington, D.C.: National Academy of Sciences, National Research Council.

Warren, Gordon, David Kaufman and Kenneth Hammond.
1982. *Come Hell and High Water: Mt. St. Helens and the Federal Response on the Lower Cowlitz River.* Ellensburg: Department of History, Central Washington University.

Warrick, Richard.
1975. *Volcano Hazard in the United States.* NSFRA-E75012. Boulder: University of Colorado Institute of Behavioral Science.

_____.
1979. Volcanoes as Hazard. In P. D. Sheets and D. Grayson, eds., *Volcanic Activity and Human Ecology.* New York: Academic Press.

_____.
1981. *Four Communities Under Ash.* Boulder, Colorado: Institute of Behavioral Science, University of Colorado.

Washington State Department of Emergency Services.
1980. *Restricted Access-News Release (June 3).* Olympia, Washington: Department of Emergency Services.

_____.
1981a. *Hazard Mitigation Report for the J1980! Eruptions of Mt. St. Helens.* Olympia, Washington: Department of Emergency Services.

_____.
1981b. *Mt. St. Helens Closure: Rules for Permitted Entry and/or Occupation.* Olympia, Washington: Department of Emergency Services.

Waterstone, Marvin.
1978. *Hazard Mitigation Behavior of Urban Flood Plain Residents.* Natural Hazards Research Working Paper 35. Boulder: University of Colorado.

Weller, Jack and Dennis Wenger.
1972. Disaster Subcultures: The Cultural Residues of Community Disasters. Paper presented at the annual meeting of the North Central Sociological Society, Cincinnati, Ohio.

Wenger, Dennis, Thomas James and Charles Faupel.
1980. *Disaster Beliefs and Emergency Planning.* Newark: Disaster Research Center, University of Delaware.

White, Gilbert.
1974. *Natural Hazards: Local, National and Global.* New York: Oxford University Press.

White, Gilbert and Eugene Haas.
1975. *Assessment of Research on Natural Hazards.* Cambridge, Massachusetts: MIT Press.

Wicker, Alan.
1969. Attitudes Versus Action, *Journal of Social Issues* 25: 41-78.

Wilkes, Charles.
1845. *Narrative of the United States Explorations During the Years 1838-1842 (Volume 4).* Philadelphia: Peterson and Company.

Williams, Harry.
1957. Some Functions of Communications in Crisis Behavior, *Human Organization* 16 (Summer): 15-19.

_____.
1964. Human Factors in Warning and Response Systems. In G. Grosser, ed., *The Threat of Impending Disaster.* Cambridge, Massachusetts: MIT Press.

Williams, Harry and Charles Fritz.
1957. The Human Being in Disaster: A Research Perspective, *The Annals* 309 (January): 42-51.

Wilmer, Harry.
1958. Toward a Definition of the Therapeutic Community, *American Journal of Psychiatry* 114: 824-834.

Windham, G. O., E. Posey, P. Ross and B. Spencer.
1977. *Reactions to Storm Threat During Hurricane Eloise.* State College: Mississippi State University.

Withey, Stephen.
1962. Reaction to Uncertain Threat. In G. Baker and D. Chapman, eds., *Man and Society in Disaster.* New York: Basic Books.

_____.
1964. Sequential Accommodations to Threat. In G. Grosser, ed., *The Threat of Impending Disaster.* Cambridge, Massachusetts: MIT Press.

Yin, Robert.
1984. *Case Study Research*. Beverly Hills: Sage Publications.

Young, Michael.
1954. The Role of the Extended Family in a Disaster, *Human Relations* 7: 383-391.

Zahler, Richard.
1980. Red Cross Getting Ready for Evacuees, *Seattle Times*, p. D3, March 28.

Zen, M. T. and D. Hadikusumo.
1965. The Future Behavior of Mt. Kelut, *Bulletin Volcanologique* 28: 275-282.

Zoretich, Frank.
1980. If St. Helens Really Clears Its Throat, Watch Out ..., *Seattle Post-Intelligencer*, p. A1, March 28.

I N D E X